PUBLIC POLICY
AND POLITICS IN INDIA

PUBLIC POLICY
AND POLITICS IN INDIA

KULDEEP MATHUR

OXFORD
UNIVERSITY PRESS

Oxford University Press is a department of the University of Oxford.
It furthers the University's objective of excellence in research, scholarship,
and education by publishing worldwide. Oxford is a registered trademark of
Oxford University Press in the UK and in certain other countries

Published in India by
Oxford University Press
YMCA Library Building, 1 Jai Singh Road, New Delhi 110 001, India

First Edition published in 2013
Oxford India Paperbacks 2016

ISBN-13: 978-0-19-946605-4
ISBN-10: 0-19-946605-X

Typeset in 10.5/13 Dante MT Std
by Excellent Laser Typesetters, Pitampura, Delhi 110 034
Printed in India by Rakmo Press, New Delhi 110 020

For
Rekha

Contents

Tables

Preface

Public policymaking, in the context of the emerging style of governance in India, is becoming increasingly complex. In addition to state institutions, the corporate sector and civil society organizations have begun to play an interactive role in producing public policy. These interactions are not merely informal. They are being institutionalized and formalized through the creation of new kinds of agencies and partnerships. A multi-layered governance structure is replacing the all-familiar single focal point of government. What is the nature of this new style of governance? How does it affect the role of the state in framing public policy? Questions like these and many more need to be answered, and this book is a plea to explore, in greater depth, the nature and role of these networks in determining public policy. It is not only an illustration of how policies are determined in India, but also an effort to spark interest in investing greater research in this area.

In the present volume, I have attempted to put together some of my research essays that focus on an analysis of India's public policies. These studies have been carried out through the last decade or so, and published as articles in journals, as monographs, or included as chapters in volumes edited by others. They are not an inclusive account of how public policies are crafted in India, but reflect some concerns regarding the way they are formulated. The collection, therefore, represents diverse subjects but a common theme. That theme is concerned with exploring the processes of policymaking.

These essays have been written at various times and in some cases there may be repetition in parts. Each of them can be read independently and is self-sufficient by itself.

I would like to thank the team at Oxford University Press for initiating the idea for the publication of this collection and carrying it through.

KULDEEP MATHUR
Gurgaon

Public Policy Analysis

An Introduction

The contributions in this volume stem from a concern about the neglect of studies of policy processes in India. This is an area that has largely slipped from the concerns of scholars and practitioners. Even though some formal programmes of study in public policy have been initiated in a few institutes of management and universities in India, empirical research, which explores the way public policies are formulated and the dynamics of interaction of government institutions and others in the policy formulating process has not received adequate consideration. The disciplines of political science and public administration in India have not given the attention that policy analysis deserves. Apart from the USA and UK, there are many countries around the world where policy studies are an expanding area of research and study.[1] This is not to suggest that substantive issues in policy have not attracted research attention. During the planning era, economic policies were indeed analysed and were also part of public debate. But the discipline of economics remained more interested in designing choices and considerably less so in focusing its attention on the way these choices were arrived at, how policy conflicts were settled, and what factors shaped

[1] See R. Kent Weaver and Paul B. Stares (eds), 2001, *Guidance for Governance: Comparing Alternative Sources of Public Policy Advice*, Tokyo and Washington, D.C.: Japan Centre for International Exchange and Brookings Institution Press.

final choices. Other social scientists came on the scene once the planning strategy became less centralized to understand and analyse the political as well as the socio-cultural impact of many macro-decisions. The result is that we have little understanding of how state institutions actually function and the kind of values and assumptions that underlie their public policy perspectives.

Several scholarly contributions in the past decade or so mark a shift in focus in the framework of policy analysis from what was known as the top-down approach. These contributions are critical of this approach which was closely associated with the idea of scientific decision-making or what Stone terms as a 'rationality project'.[2] In this traditional, top-down perspective, policy process is based on a rational choice of the alternatives available to the decision-maker. The process of a rational choice consists of: *a.* identifying the problem, *b.* defining and ranking goals, *c.* identifying all policy alternatives for achieving these goals, *d.* identifying the costs and benefits of each alternative and ranking them according to trade-offs and then, *e.* choosing the best alternative. It is assumed that goals can be identified in advance and all information is available to identify trade-offs of each alternative from which the best choice can be made.

In turn, this approach helped demarcate various stages in the process of policymaking, beginning from the stage of agenda setting to that of evaluation and feedback. Each stage was perceived as independent of the other and led to the growth of technically-oriented analysis. The introduction of the computer encouraged and deepened the use of quantitative techniques and modelling. This approach is more often than not, associated with planners and professional policy analysts who see the possibility of best technical solutions to social and economic problems. When these solutions are not implemented, or cannot be implemented, they blame politics and its irrational manifestations, in both administrative structures as well as in society. Much of the field of policy analysis has been dominated by the literature emanating from such a techno-rational perspective. As a matter of fact, a distinctive area of research as implementation analysis emerged particularly after the publication of

[2] Diane Stone, 1988, *Policy Paradox and Political Reason*, Glenview, Illinois: Scott Foreman & Co., pp. 232–57.

the volume by Pressman and Wildawsky.[3] Implementation researchers divided the policy process into policy formation and policy implementation, and raised questions on how policies were formulated and, once made into law, implemented. More attention was focused on how the intentions and goals of policymakers were translated into action and achievement. The approach forced the researchers to accept the goals of policy as given which in principle had to be followed because the legitimacy of the decision at the top could not be questioned.[4]

Apart from the fact that the top-down approach precluded understanding of policy as a process of negotiation,[5] it reduced political and social issues to technical considerations for achieving goals through administrative means. Vexing social and economic problems were interpreted as issues that needed to be managed better with improved programme design; their solutions were to be found in the objective collection of data and the application of technical decision-making approaches. This rational-technocratic approach in large part defined the policy sciences since the 1960s.[6] It found resonance in the value of efficiency embedded in all economic and managerial thinking and therefore dominated the way governments defined their problems and found solutions for them.

What was lost sight of in this dominant theme pursued by most scholars was that policy was an arena of contestation—of bargaining and compromises—of politics. Reducing conflict ridden questions to the bureaucratic imperative of impersonality and neutrality inhibited an understanding of how policies were formulated and implemented. It viewed social and political issues as questions of efficiency, performance, and productivity amenable to bureaucratic methods of decision-making. Fischer has further argued that these positivist methods of policy analysis have served intentionally or unintentionally to facilitate and bolster bureaucratic governance.[7] He goes on to suggest that the

[3] Jeffrey L. Pressman and Aaron Wildavsky, 1973, *Implementation*, Berkeley: University of California Press.

[4] P. Bogason, 2000, *Public Policy and Local Governance Institutions in Post-Modern Society*, Cheltenham, UK: Edward Elgar, p. 100.

[5] Ibid., p. 103.

[6] Frank Fischer, 2003, *Reframing Public Policy: Discursive Politics and Deliberative Practices*, Oxford: Oxford University Press, p. 5.

[7] Ibid., p. 14.

post-empiricist call for the use of interpretative (hermeneutic) and discursive (deconstructionist) techniques are an effort to demonstrate that politics and policy are grounded in subjective factors. The attempt is to demonstrate that what is identified as 'objective' truth by rational techniques is as often as not the product of deeper, less visible, political pre-suppositions. Their analysis starts with the recognition that different discourses, definitions, and questions lead to different policy outcomes. What are known as 'facts' are social constructions and framed through the discourses of the actors themselves. It is important, therefore, to explore and investigate the pre-suppositions, values and beliefs on which empirical assertions rest, and uncover the many dimensions inherent to many deliberations and debates relevant to most policy issues.

In what has come to be known as *The Argumentative Turn in Public Policy Analysis and Planning*,[8] many scholars have turned to an analysis of the nature of debates and exploration of politics which define problems and provide them with meaning. These scholars focus attention on the social and political ideas that define the problems that governments face. The ideas however, do not emerge in an institutional vacuum. Policymaking practices are grounded in institutions which not only facilitate, but also constrain the process through which debates and interactions take place. There are rules, procedural routines, roles, organizational structures and strategies which constitute an 'institutional construction of meaning' that shape actors' preferences, expectations, experiences, and interpretations of actions. As a dominant force determining meaning, they shape the ways people communicate and argue with one another.[9] Institutions play a major role in shaping the choices of politicians and administrators.

Perhaps the most seminal contribution to the re-emergence of institutions in the political science policy literature is the work of March and Olsen.[10] They understand institutions not as formal structures, but rather as a collection of norms, rules, understandings, and, more

---

[8] Frank Fischer and John Forrester (eds), 1993, *The Argumentative Turn in Policy Analysis and Planning*, Durham: Duke University Press.

[9] Fischer, *Reframing Public Policy: Discursive Politics and Deliberative Practices*, p. 29.

[10] James G. March and John P. Olsen, 1989, *Rediscovering Institutions: The Organizational Basis of Politics*, New York: The Free Press.

importantly, routines.[11] They go on to say that institutions possess an almost inherent legitimacy that commits their members to behave in ways that may even violate their self-interest.[12] An important feature of their characterization is that institutions tend to have a 'logic of appropriateness' that influences behaviour. They suggest that what is appropriate for a particular person in a particular situation is defined by political and social institutions and transmitted through socialization. Political actors associate specific actions with specific situations by rules of appropriateness. Appropriate behaviour is contrasted with the logic of consequentiality wherein individuals have to evaluate the consequences of their behaviour in making choices.

March and Olsen argue that individual behaviours will be motivated by the values of their institutions.[13] That is, individuals will make conscious choices, but those choices will remain within the parameters established by the dominant institutional values. Those choices will also require each individual to interpret just what the dominant institutional values are.[14] Thus, the emerging perspective recognizes that institutional values also set limits to individual choices or in turn shape them. Institutions provide the 'logic of appropriateness' that influences behaviour. The worldviews of actors find echoes in the institutional constraints and values, and these need to be considered when examining the dimensions of the policy discourse.

This alternative perspective in policy studies then seeks to provide an improved reflection of the world of practice as far as policy process is concerned. Instead of attempting to insulate decision-making from everyday politics, it attempts to show that policy problems are defined in a subjective fashion and are dependent on the worldview of the actors involved. The worldviews are open to debate and contestation and a policy is an outcome of the one that prevails over a period of time. Changes occur because relationships among actors change and a new constellation of social forces may emerge. Thus policymaking is a dynamic process occurring in a 'networking' society, rather than within one with hierarchies.

[11] Ibid., pp. 21–6.
[12] Ibid., pp. 21–3.
[13] Ibid., p. 161.
[14] B. Guy Peters, 1999, *Institutional Theory in Political Science: The 'New Institutionalism'*, London and New York: Pinter, p. 29.

Policy changes may also occur as knowledge brings about shifts in the beliefs and perceptions of the actors. Hajer and Wagenaar point out during the 1990s that the critics of traditional policy analysis have shown that epistemological beliefs, wittingly or unwittingly, have normative consequences for one's own political preferences.[15] What counts as justified belief and valid knowledge sets limits to the kind of questions and information that are acceptable in the political debate.

The networks and the questions acceptable in a political debate mutually influence each other and are marked by a fluid not stable social context and interaction of actors not limited to national boundaries or governments. The emergence of the concept of governance has brought into focus a new range of relationships among various governmental institutions and between these institutions and social organizations. International organizations have come to play an increasing role in setting limits to what national governments should or can do. Social movements and NGOs have also entered the public domain with greater assertion of their point of view, which is usually critical of what the government wants to do. If the governments get linked with supranational bodies, the civil society organizations also have a global reach.

For many scholars, however, public policies are deduced from the properties and propensities of the state. Their lack of adequate attention on the processes of public policy stems from the kind of explanations that are offered for the reasons why a state pursues some activities and not others. These explanations have much to do with what the state is perceived to be and what it is supposed to do. Within traditional Marxist analysis, the basic proposition is that politics is the manifestation of class conflict based on the economic conflicts in society. This basic proposition leads to the argument that the primary function of the state is to ensure the legal, institutional, and ideological hegemony of the dominant class or class alliance over the subordinate classes.[16] This primary function means that the purpose of policy is to advance the interest of the dominant class(es). Only in later interpretations based

[15] Maarten A. Hajer and Hendrik Wagenaar (eds), 2003, *Deliberative Policy Analysis: Understanding Governance in the Network Society*, Cambridge: Cambridge University Press, p. 13.

[16] Merilee Serrill Grindle and John W. Thomas, 1991, *Public Choices and Policy Change: The Political Economy of Reform in Developing Countries*, Baltimore: The Johns Hopkins University Press, pp. 20–2.

on the reading of Engels has it been postulated that, under certain circumstances like those in which there may be conflict among the dominant classes, the state can exercise some degree of autonomy to pursue policies to maintain capitalist development.[17]

Two important consequences flow from this theorizing. One is that policy change occurs because of the shifting relationships among social classes, and research analysis should concentrate on when and why these shifts occur. More importantly, it also follows that 'men and women, organized in classes, are the collective actors of history [but] that the play itself is very largely shaped by forces which are not greatly affected by a single will or the will of small groups of people'.[18] The role of policymakers is not considered central to the understanding of the processes of policy change because their influence is not decisive in any way.

If individual policymakers are inconsequential in the Marxist tradition, the pluralist approach perceives them as neutral arbitrators in negotiating compromises among diverse conflicting groups. The groups in conflict are competing for state resources or attempting to advance the interests of their own members. The shared concerns of the members may be economic, but can also be ethnic, religious, linguistic or regional. The state is the political arena where battles are fought among these groups and a chosen policy only reflects the compromise or the bargain that has been struck. State institutions and procedural rules do little more than channel the competition into appropriate conflict resolution systems. The role of the state is to act as arbitrator among competing interests and the principal role of public officials is to respond to pressures placed on them by organized groups in society.[19] The research analyses in this pluralist perspective tend to emphasize the rise of interest groups, their access to policymakers, and their strength in the bargaining processes. These studies do not accord much importance to individual policymakers who are perceived as instruments facilitating the process of bargaining and compromise.

[17] N. Poulantzas, 1973, *Political Power and Social Classes*, London: New Left Books.

[18] Ralph Miliband, 1983, *Class Power and State Power: Political Essays*, London: Verso, p. 134.

[19] Grindle and Thomas, *Public Choices and Policy Change: The Political Economy of Reform in Developing Countries*, p. 23.

The currently popular public choice theory among neo-classical economists provides a variation on both perspectives and studies within the pluralist approach. It shows how public officials themselves compete to extract benefits and can form alliances with other self-seeking groups to distort the goals of a policy. Treating politics as a market place, public choice theorists argue that the rational way is to allow groups to compete freely without encumbrances and the role of the state is to facilitate the interplay of the social forces by diminishing its own role as well as those of its officials in this political market. However, public choice theory assumes that the policymakers are part of a group seeking its own interest and thus influence policy outcomes.[20] Significantly, the focus shifts from state institutions per se to societal institutions which provide the arena wherein diverse political interests can compete with each other. It is assumed that the public interest is best served by a public policy that emerges from such competitions.[21]

Thus, the field of policy studies has received different kinds of attention from different scholarly persuasions. Some have chosen to concentrate on the nature of the state and the outcomes of class struggles in society to explain the kind of policies that emerge. These studies have not considered institutions, particularly of the state, and the choices of policymakers as important determinants of policy outcomes. For them, the outcomes are a result of the interplay of forces outside their control. Within this understanding, the technocratic approach was a non-starter. The liberal-democratic framework provided a momentum to policy studies. In this framework, the state represents the only legitimate form of exercise of power because it is a necessary condition for the development of a nation. In this view, the legitimacy of the state does not come merely from elections or its democratic character; rather it comes from its rational character to direct a programme of development for the nation.[22] Public policies emerge as instruments of state action. It

[20] Vincent Ostrom, 1991, *The Intellectual Crisis in American Public Administration*, Tuscaloosa: University of Alabama Press, pp. 42–64.

[21] Anne Krueger, 1974, 'The Political Economy of the Rent-Seeking Society', *American Economic Review*, vol. 64, no. 3, pp. 291–303.

[22] See Partha Chatterjee, 1994, 'Development Planning and the Indian State', in T.J. Byres (ed.), *The State, Development Planning and Liberalization in India*, New Delhi: Oxford University Press, pp. 202–5.

is in this perspective that the rational scientific approach has been the dominant methodology in the search for policy alternatives.

For post-empiricists, the emphasis on discourse analysis recognizes the political and social contestation in policy concerns, and accepts the need to explicate multitude dimensions inherent to deliberation and debate and relevant to most policy issues. In this way, it moves away from the pretence of objective and neutral policy analysis assumed in the scientific approach.[23] Within this perspective, policy analysts stress the need for a participatory democracy where citizens can take part in meaningful debates and contest policy issues that deeply affect them. Unlike the technocratic approach, post-empiricists argue that such analysis will empower the citizens to participate in decision-making rather than merely augment the skills of the politician and the bureaucrat.

The policy studies in India reflect the rich diversity of approaches to policy analysis briefly surveyed above. The following section highlights some of the major trends and underlines the gaps that need attention.

POLICY STUDIES IN INDIA[24]
While Indian scholars have focused on policy goals and consequences, less attention has been paid to policy processes. This is due to various reasons. During the period when centralized planning was the dominant strategy of development and the state determined development outcomes, policies framed within the state agencies were rarely disputed. Research institutes that emerged during this period supplemented the work of the government by filling gaps in analysis and providing alternative sources of data. Within social sciences, economic decision-making held primary attention. The Planning Commission was the pivotal agency for this activity, with scholarly interests and scholars gravitating around the interests of this agency. Little critique of the policy as such was undertaken, for the policy failures were seen as failures of implementation, and consequently, India witnessed a burgeoning of the field of public administration. The questioning of policies began to take place primarily after the consensus on centralized

---

[23] Fischer, *Reframing Public Policy: Discursive Politics and Deliberative Practices*, p. 15.

[24] This is does not purport to be an exhaustive review of literature, but an effort to point to some major trends.

planning as a strategy floundered with poor economic performance and the declaration of Emergency in 1975. Strong criticism of state-centric economic policies followed and the second coming of Mrs Gandhi in 1980 saw a measure of liberalization and loosening of economic controls. This marked the beginning of a period when new research institutes with different perspectives emerged and a large number of studies on policy consequences followed. Policy debates became more open and flourished as India began on a path of a liberal economy highlighted in 1991 when major economic reforms took place.[25]

An exploration of the reasons and context of the introduction of economic reforms emerged as a major area of scholarly interest in the 1990s. Scholars and practitioners from various academic persuasions and disciplines joined in this exploration. One full-length study has been that of Jenkins which looked at the interpretation of political mechanisms that made the reform processes possible in India.[26] He examined the interplay of the role of elites by categorizing his study into a discussion on incentives, institutions, and skills. Variations in this theme where research attention is focused on the role of various groups in the polity and examination of the beneficial outcomes for groups or individuals has been the more popular mode of analysis in the literature on policy processes in India.[27] Some scholars have addressed the same issue from the perspective of class analysis and questioned why 'Indian capital, which was obviously a beneficiary of the protection offered under the earlier regime of intervention went along with and in fact celebrated liberalization of the kind introduced in 1980s and

[25] See J. Mooij and V. de Vos, 2003, 'Policy Processes: An Annotated Bibliography on Policy Processes, with Particular Emphasis on India', mimeo, London: Overseas Development Institute. This draft was prepared under the project on 'Comparative Studies of Public Policy Processes' funded by the Ford Foundation and conducted at the Centre for Economic and Social Studies, Hyderabad, India.

[26] Rob Jenkins, 1999, *Democratic Politics and Economic Reform in India*, Cambridge: Cambridge University Press.

[27] See for example, Atul Kohli, 1989, 'Politics of Economic Liberalization in India', *World Development*, vol. 17, no. 3, pp. 305–28; and Ashutosh Varshney, 1995, *Democracy, Development, and the Countryside: Urban-Rural Struggles in India*, Cambridge: Cambridge University Press.

1990s.'[28] The answers lie in the kind of linkages and support that domestic capital, international financial capital, and the middle class forged to work for liberalization.

Still other scholars have propounded that economic reforms were a response to the economic crisis that the country faced in 1991 and was an instrument of crisis management by the government. 'It is plausible to argue, but difficult to prove, that any other government in office in mid-1991 would have done roughly the same in terms of fire-fighting and crisis management simply because there was little choice.'[29] The argument is that while there was a balance of payments crisis in the early 1990s that needed to be addressed, there was no reason to treat this relatively minor and temporary crisis of liquidity as an indication of (alleged) fundamental flaws in India's post-independence development strategy.[30] The government, however, did just that. It asked the IMF for assistance and was forced to accept a reform package that was not based on India's 'experience and learning' but on 'outside thinking'.[31]

Nayar concludes that opening up India's economy has not compromised its autonomy, but has only augmented it.[32] According to him, pressures from the international financial institutions were not that much; they were towards an already open door; and they were disregarded when they were thought to be inappropriate.[33]

Some of the studies cited above also focused on the role international agencies played in influencing the policies for economic reform. Patnaik, for example, has been in the forefront of those economists who have argued that the kind of economic reforms that were introduced served the interests of the international finance capital which gained most

---

[28] Jayati Ghosh and C.P. Chandrashekhar, 2002, 'The Political Economy of the Indian Reform Process', Paper presented at a Seminar on The Politics of Economic Reform in India, Centre for Economic and Social Studies 2002.

[29] Amit Bhaduri and Deepak Nayyar, 1996, *The Intelligent Person's Guide to Liberalization*, New Delhi: Penguin Books, p. 49.

[30] Ibid.

[31] Ibid., pp. 51–2. See also Jos Mooij (ed.), 2005, 'Introduction' in *The Politics of Economic Reforms in India*, New Delhi: Sage Publications, p. 25.

[32] Baldev Raj Nayar, 2003, 'Globalization and India's National Autonomy,' *Commonwealth and Comparitive Politics*, vol. 41, no. 2, pp. 1–34.

[33] Ibid., p. 25.

from the removal of restrictions on capital flows and currency unifica-
tion and convertibility.[34] This is the reason why the multinationals as
well as the Bretton Woods institutions played a significant role in influencing the changes in economic policy. Bhaduri and Nayyar have also
gone on to suggest that while there was a crisis of balance of payments,
the remedy did not lie in condemning all the policies that had been
pursued since the beginning of the plan period.[35] The reform package
adopted was not based on India's 'experience and learning', but on the
'outsider's thinking.'[36] Mooij, on the other hand, contends that it would
be going too far to argue that these international pressures explain
the whole content and scope of India's reforms.[37] There was a certain
amount of willingness, if not eagerness, among India's policymakers
as well.[38]

The theme of external influence on India's domestic policymaking
appears in some earlier studies too. These studies have been concerned
with the examination of changes in agricultural and rural development
policies in the 1960s and 1970s. A study by Lewis supplements the
broader understanding of how the new agricultural strategy was adopted
in the late 1960s.[39] On the basis of personal experience, documents, and
interviews of the main actors, he has been able to unfold the story of
the way American aid-giving agencies (personally President Johnson)
and technical experts located in them were able to influence the policy
of intensive agriculture by giving greater attention to the pricing
and marketing of agricultural products. In another effort, Mathur
demonstrated the influence of various international aid-giving agencies
in designing and implementing poverty alleviation programmes, and
argued that the complementarities led to an increase in aid and greater

---

[34] Prabhat Patnaik, 2000, 'Economic Policy and Its Political Management
in the Concurrent Conjuncture', in Francine Frankel, Zoya Hasan, Rajeev
Bhargava, and Balveer Arora (eds), *Transforming India: Social and Political
Dynamics of Democracy*, New Delhi: Oxford University Press, p. 235.

[35] Bhaduri and Nayyar, *The Intelligent Person's Guide to Liberalization*, pp. 51–2.

[36] Ibid.

[37] Mooij, *The Politics of Economic Reforms in India*, p. 25.

[38] Ibid.

[39] John P. Lewis, 1995, *India's Political Economy: Governance and Reform*, New
Delhi: Oxford University Press.

recognition in the West of the effort made by Indian policymakers to alleviate poverty.[40]

One can discern elements of institutional analysis in a study of the agricultural policy by Varshney.[41] Three Ministries are directly involved in formulating agricultural policy—Agriculture, Planning, and Finance. These bureaucracies are driven partly by their institutional concerns, if also by political considerations. The Agriculture Ministry is normally driven by a micro-view of agriculture. Its task is to increase agricultural production, and if price incentive and input subsidies are necessary to achieve that, as is likely to be true in the short-run, a case for higher prices and subsidies will be made. The Food Department, concerned with feeding people, would plead for the lowering of prices. The Planning Commission, though concerned with raising agricultural production, would also resist high food prices because of the impact on the larger economy. The Finance Ministry holds the purse and is wary of subsidies and price rises because they upset the budget. Varshney shows how individuals played their roles within these institutional parameters and the battle for policy was fought within state institutions by political leaders and bureaucrats with different visions for the agrarian economy when the new agricultural strategy was adopted.

The behaviour of individuals within an institutional framework is the focus of a study by Mathur and Bjorkman.[42] In this study, an attempt is made to explore the role of cabinet ministers and civil servants in policymaking. The authors suggest that the institutional framework within which they work, the nature of their career and recruitment, and the characteristics of their professional experience determine their contribution to policymaking. These factors have meant that the characteristic feature of policymaking is the predominance of political over administrative inputs. Concerns of efficiency and technical

[40] Kuldeep Mathur, 1994, 'Designing Poverty Alleviation Programmes: International Agencies and Indian Politics', in G.K. Chadha (ed.), *Policy Perspectives in Indian Economic Development*, New Delhi: Har-Anand Publications, pp. 179–99.

[41] Varshney, *Democracy, Development, and the Countryside: Urban-Rural Struggles in India*.

[42] Kuldeep Mathur and J.W. Bjorkman, 1994, *Top Policy Makers in India: Cabinet Ministers and their Civil Service Advisors*, New Delhi: Concept Publishers.

optimality do not have the significance that an image of rational decision-making evokes.[43]

In a well-known contribution, Bardhan used a neo-Marxist perspective to analyse the reasons for poor public investment in agriculture and industrial infrastructure in India.[44] He argued that the nature of balance among the proprietary classes in the country determined the pattern and volume of public investment. He identified three classes—large industrial bourgeoisie, the rich farmer, and the professional classes, and shows how conflict management of these classes slowed down public investment.

Another significant stream in the general area of policy studies which has attracted considerable scholarly attention is that of policy evaluation. Critical evaluations of various policies and programmes have sought to identify the factors responsible for policy failures and to suggest what the government should have done to improve their chances of success. The general framework of these studies was that of acceptance of the goals of the policy, and then looking for reasons of its failure. In the initial years of India's experience with planned development, problems of implementation took precedence and it was assumed that policies failed and/or could not achieve their objectives because the bureaucracy and administration were not adequate.[45] Little attention was paid to the policies themselves and their appropriateness. The situation changed in the late 1960s when the country was confronted with a food crisis, industrial stagnation, a resource crunch, and the ensuing plan holiday. Policies began to be assessed in relation to plan models, sectoral relationships, and the global economic context. Studies of economic policies particularly expressed these concerns.

[43] With the proliferation of state institutions—regulatory and standard setting—there is a growing interest in the design of institutions and their role in the system of governance. (See, for instance, Devesh Kapoor and Pratap Bhanu Mehta (eds), 2005, *Public Institutions in India: Performance and Design*, New Delhi: Oxford University Press.)

[44] Pranab Bardhan 1984, *The Political Economy of Development in India*, New Delhi: Oxford University Press.

[45] The literature concerning implementation is very large, but the arguments cited in the reports of the Administrative Reforms Commission (1969) set up by the Government of India summarize the reasons for failures in achieving the plan goals and targets.

As mentioned earlier, traditionally, evaluations of public policies have primarily focused on the dimensions of efficiency and effectiveness. These assessments are important, but they make one very significant assumption. They accept the officially stated goals or objectives of the policy and do not question their validity. Such assessments are useful and provide a wealth of data and analysis to the policymakers, but are unable to provide alternatives to the policies being pursued. Efficiency criteria may only promote particular types of programmes or policies. The evaluations of the Integrated Rural Development Programme (IRDP) at the end of the Sixth Plan (1976–81) are an illustration of how the focus on the efficiency/effectiveness dimension circumscribed the discussion on finding ways to improve the implementation of a given policy and marked a departure from the kind of studies that were being conducted. It is only when the issue of appropriateness was raised— would India be a society of wage earners or entrepreneurs—that the policy alternatives came into sharper focus.[46] While administrative factors were important, the goals of the policy began to be disputed.

It is also in this perspective that a study by Mathur and Jayal attempts to examine the policy process regarding drought in India.[47] It interrogates the assumptions on which the drought policy was formulated, and shows how by defining drought as a crisis, only short-term concerns for alleviating the immediate hardship of the people affected, dominated the policy discourse. Thus, the policy contributed to exacerbating the social consequences of the drought, even as political mileage was derived from drought management. A crisis was met, but little preparation was made to face another drought.

Environmental policy has attracted a rich critical contribution. The appropriateness of the policy and its consequences on the social and cultural life of the people has been examined together with an assessment of economic benefits. The environmental policy debate has hinged on the issues of livelihood and ecological security with the paradigm of modernization and development pursued in India.

[46] See Neelkanth Rath, 1985, 'Garibi Hatao: Can IRDP Do It?', *Economic and Political Weekly*, vol. 20, no. 6, pp. 238–46; and M.L. Dantwala, 1985, 'Garibi Hatao: Strategy Options?', *Economic and Political Weekly*, vol. 20, no. 11, pp. 475–6.

[47] Kuldeep Mathur and Niraja Gopal Jayal, 1993, *Drought Policy and Politics: The Need for a Long-Term Perspective*, New Delhi: Sage Publications.

There have been series of struggles and conflicts for water and forest rights which have raised issues regarding community rights in forests, rehabilitation and displacement through large projects, and the utility of large dams. Only recently, environmental degradation in the urban areas has entered the public agenda. Among the early studies that were crucial in foregrounding the debate was that of Guha.[48] In studying the Chipko movement in the Garhwal area, where deforestation was occurring at a rapid rate, Guha highlighted the concerns of the local community—their loss of livelihood by gradual erosion of their control of local resources like forests. The movement questioned the forest policy of India and was a precursor to major changes that followed in the 1980s.

There was perhaps no project more volatile and contentious in recent times than the construction of the Sardar Sarovar dam on the Narmada River. It evoked sharp reactions from both its critics and supporters and led to a large number of studies and research. The justification for the dam was questioned in terms of its technical and engineering attributes. For the dams in this project were not isolated water harvesting and power generation projects, but part of a larger project that would harness the entire Narmada River in a comprehensive manner. Narmada was also seen not only as a river for the people, but a symbol of their life, culture, and eternal heritage. 'Damming of the river is like rape of the virgin goddess because of the people's eternal reverence of rivers.'[49] These perceptions were the propelling force for people's struggles in the Narmada Valley that attracted world attention.

The policy discourse emanating from the construction of the Sardar Sarovar project encompassed a large number of issues and attracted considerable scholarly attention. The movement against the dam projected appeals to a participatory ideal of democracy in which people have a right to information as also the right to be consulted about development plans likely to affect their lives. It also asserted, on behalf

[48] Ramachandra Guha, 1989, *The Unquiet Woods: Ecological Change and Peasant Resistance in the Himalaya*, New Delhi: Oxford University Press.

[49] Quoted from S. Santhi, 1994, *The Sardar Sarovar Project: The Issue of Developing a River*, INTACH, in Archana Prasad, 2004, *Environmentalism and the Left: Contemporary Debates and Future Agendas in Tribal Areas*, New Delhi: Leftword Books, p. 79.

of the tribal oustees, a set of cultural rights to a way of life and the associated material rights to natural resources, in and by which they have lived.[50]

Another recent example of discursive analysis of public policy has been a contribution by Chakraborty on the debate on economic reforms introduced in India in 1991.[51] Based on the writings of a select group of economists, he attempts to examine the rhetorical strategies that the participants in reforms' debates have followed to persuade their audiences.[52] He begins by arguing that there is a definitional cleavage which then leads the participants to use different metaphors to persuade their audiences. What is simply reform to the pro-reform economists, is liberalization to the others. Reform tends to evoke images of progress. Liberalization, on the other hand, points to the unfettered operation of market forces, and connotes negative perceptions. The use of these definitions has considerably shaped the kind of debates that have taken place. Chakraborty argues that practicing good rhetoric, the essence of which lies in sensitivity towards ones' audience, is important in democracy.[53]

This brief review has cited some studies that illustrate the scope and extent of policy literature in India. Policy discourse in India has been characterized by pervasive technocratic influence since the country embarked upon its strategy of planned economic development. This was also the period when economic analysis occupied a prominent space in the social sciences. Policy practitioners and analysts alike agreed that objective policy research—based on the rational actor 'economic man' and substantiated by sufficient evidence statistically manipulated and displayed—was the only basis by which the policy sciences could aspire to predictive models and thereby gain credibility

---

[50] As pointed out, there is a large amount of literature that has responded to the issues raised by the construction of the Sardar Sarovar Dam. A useful guide is Niraja Gopal Jayal, 1999, *Democracy and the State: Welfare, Secularism, and Development in Contemporary India*, New Delhi: Oxford University Press, p. 254. See also Amita Baviskar, 1995, *In the Belly of the River: Tribal Conflicts Over Development in the Tribal Areas*, New Delhi: Oxford University Press.

[51] Achin Chakraborty, 2005, 'The Rhetoric of Disagreement in Reform Debates', in Jos Mooij (ed.), *The Politics of Economic Reforms in India*, pp. 46–68.

[52] Ibid., p. 49.

[53] Ibid., p. 66.

within policymaking circles.[54] This approach regarded itself as providing the best solutions to economic and social problems. When these solutions were not implemented or could not be implemented, the analysts blamed politics and its irrational manifestations. During the twentieth century, the field of policy analysis was dominated by literature emanating from this rational-scientific perspective. Even its critics accepted its basic assumptions.

The leaders who took the reins of government at independence identified the country's future with the development performance of the West. Of particular significance in this view was a perception about the role that science and technology play in transforming society. Nehru was impressed by the strides Soviet Russia had made through judicious planning and the rational use of resources. He envisioned that India would rapidly attain the levels of economic development achieved by Western nations through industrialization and modernization.[55]

To pursue such goals, the services and advice of experts and technocrats were necessary. Nehru sought to establish the superior rationality of scientists and economists in policymaking and the Planning Commission became the exclusive theatre where economic policy was formulated.[56] The public and its representatives had little say in wider deliberations about India's future. This lack of participation was justified by the argument that the economic strategy demanded 'technical evaluation of alternative policies and determination of choices on scientific grounds'.[57] Participation in policy deliberations would have opened up the whole debate about the directions that India should take—a debate symbolized by the widely known different views of Gandhi and Nehru. Committees of experts became an important instrument for resolving the political debate and, even though Planning Commission did not have a long life in this powerful role, the idea of

[54] Peter de Leon, 1988, *Advice and Consent: The Development of the Policy Sciences*, New York: Russell Sage Foundation, p. 147.

[55] B.R. Nayar, 1972, *The Modernization Imperative and Indian Planning*, Delhi: Vikas Publications, pp. 113–28.

[56] Sunil Khilnani, 1997, *The Idea of India*, London: Hamish Hamilton, p. 81.

[57] Chatterjee, 'Development Planning and the Indian State', p. 274.

technical conceptualization and resolution of problems of social conflict had come to stay.[58]

At the end of Nehruvian era, the consensus began to break down and the years between 1966 and 1980 were a period of turmoil. Economic difficulties threatened the persistence of democracy itself when it was suspended during 1975–8. With the return to power of Indira Gandhi in 1980, a process of liberalization began. This process gained momentum during the regime of Rajiv Gandhi and the period of economic reform was set in motion in 1991. Policy processes reflected these political and economic changes and began to open up. A market for alternative policies and forums to articulate competing public choices emerged. It is also at this time that other social scientists, apart from economists, entered policy debates. The demands for equality, justice, and development now dominated politics. Public discourse became concerned with 'what went wrong' and a space was created for the articulation of alternatives.

There was also some disappointment with the role that technocrats and professionals had come to play in decision-making. Sukhamoy Chakravarty, an eminent economist, involved in economic policy-making and who had served as a member of the Planning Commission expressed himself thus in 1987: 'Issues that bear upon India's development prospects are inevitably very complex. Moreover, they cannot be devised merely by technocratically inclined civil servants. While technocrats can obviously suggest more efficient means for pre-assigned goals, the problem of goal setting is inherently a socio-historical process.'[59]

The frustration felt by technical and professional people about the failure of the government system was a catalyst to the idealism of youth in promoting NGOs. Many young people forsook lucrative careers to pursue idealistic goals in the fields of health, education, and the environment. The result was that research-based institutions emerged together with those that worked at the grassroots level. Both kinds of institutions have gained acceptance in government policymaking

---

[58] J.W. Bjorkman and Kuldeep Mathur, 2002, *Policy Technocracy and Development: Human Capital Policies in India and the Netherlands*, New Delhi: Manohar Publications.

[59] Sukhamoy Chakravarty, 1987, *Development Planning: The India Experience*, Oxford: Clarendon Press, p. 89.

although the incorporation of their advice in formal government policy formulation has been slow. Government institutions have not responded at the pace with which non-governmental institutions have multiplied. The old notion of reliable in-house expertise dominated by bureaucrats has not been completely eroded but, as alternative sources of policy struggle to find space in decision-making processes, things have begun to change.

Another running theme in Indian policy literature has been analyses of policy implementation. During the period when centralized planning was the dominant strategy of development, policies framed within state agencies were rarely disputed. Policies were accepted and, if they did not achieve their stated goals, it was assumed that the implementation had been faulty. Policy evoked an image of rational decision-making based on efficiency and technical optimality. Little criticism of the policy as such was undertaken, for the policy failures were seen as failures of implementation and therefore administration became the reason for poor performance. The focus of research was more concentrated on the failures of implementation structures and their functioning. Consequently, government focused its attention on reforming the administrative system and immense energy was spent on suggesting changes through government committees and commissions. These reform measures had varied success. This also meant that an analysis of interaction between government institutions, politics, and key policy influencing individuals received much less attention.

As can be seen from some of the illustrations cited earlier, studies exploring policy process are few and far between in India. Most scholarly attention has been devoted to critical evaluation of policy goals, policy consequences, and policy implementation. Even practitioners who were critical participants in policymaking and chose to write their biographies have not shared information about who advised what and why, and the kind of role that institutions played. There are frequent newspaper reports about institutional conflicts that take place within the government.[60] Scholars have shied away from providing empirical

---

[60] An *Indian Express* report titled 'Is Someone Listening? PMO Reminder to Ministries', 23 June 2005, p. 3, states that the PMO has asked all ministries to consult it before finalizing a Cabinet note in case there are conflicts among them. Inter-ministerial squabbles have been reported between Commerce and Finance on trade policy, Finance and Petroleum on petrol price hike, Heavy

data on such institutional relationships and may also have kept away due to the denial of data on the grounds of secrecy, as well as gatekeepers within the government. The result is that there are few openings that have increased our understanding of how policies are shaped and designed. Social scientists need to fill this gap in our understanding of how state institutions function particularly when we understand that policy is a political statement and not a techno-rational output of state action.

Industries and Finance on disinvestment, and Civil Aviation and Finance on Air India's Boeing deal.

1

Guidance for Governance in India

*Alternative Sources of Policy Advice**

That the character of a political system is key to the way public policy is deliberated, formulated, and implemented is a widely accepted notion. The two extremes of an open and a closed political system are associated with distinctive and opposite policy processes. Theoretically speaking, a closed political system is more likely to have a policy process that is centralized, secretive, and unresponsive, whereas an open political system is likely to be allied with a policy process that is decentralized, consultative, and responsive. The characteristics associated with a closed political system, however, are not limited to authoritarian regimes and may persist in new democracies in the developing world.[1] There may also be variations of policy processes as a political system evolves from a formal democratic system to a more meaningful, participatory democracy.

India is an example of a political system undergoing such an evolution. In 1950, democracy was introduced to India with the formal

---

* Kuldeep Mathur, 2001, 'Guidance for Governance in India: Alternative Sources of Policy Advice', in R. Kent Weaver and Paul B. Stares (eds), *Guidance for Governance: Comparing Alternative Sources of Public Policy Advice*, Tokyo: Japan Centre for International Exchange, pp. 207–30.

[1] Mark Robinson, 1998, 'Democracy, Participation, and Public Policy: The Politics of Institutional Design', in Mark Robinson and Gordon White (eds), *The Democratic Developmental State: Political and Institutional Design*, Oxford: Oxford University Press, pp. 150–86.

institutions of elections, political parties, and a Parliament. The parliamentary system of government was, however, created in the image of its colonial ruler, the United Kingdom. Through the years, India's democratic institutions have grown to give fuller representation to the country's people, providing them with a greater voice in determining public policy. But India's particular politics and national aspirations have contributed to its forging its own democratic identity, making it a little different from the UK model.

This chapter attempts to delineate the way that India's public policy processes have evolved. In the early years of democracy, consensus over development policies was widespread, and formulation of these policies was based on rational economic and technocratic criteria. Specialists and experts, who were incorporated into government institutions, played a major role in the deliberative process. This consensus began to break down with the end of the Nehruvian years, and the period from 1966 to 1980 was marked by turmoil. Economic difficulties beset the country, and democratic institutions were suspended in 1975. With the return to power of Indira Gandhi in the 1980s, the government started on the path of liberalization, which gained momentum under the regime of Rajiv Gandhi, and subsequently with a series of economic reforms put in place in 1991. Policy processes at the time were a reflection of these political and economic changes.

From around the period of 1980s, a market for alternative policies and forums to articulate competing public choices has emerged. The development strategy espoused during the administrations of Jawaharlal Nehru and Indira Gandhi had neither alleviated poverty nor strengthened the country industrially. Disparities in wealth had grown further, and politics grew to be dominated by demands for equality, justice, and development. Public discourse began to focus on what had gone wrong and what instead should be done. Research institutes that had operated within familiar paradigms began to suggest different formulations. Even government committees, which had relied exclusively on in-house advice, sought policy advice from elsewhere. Non-governmental organizations (NGOs) that advocated new options and means of implementation caught the imagination of the people.

The frustration that technicians and professionals had known was transformed into an idealism centered on NGOs. Many young people forsook lucrative careers to pursue work in the fields of education, health, and environment. The result was the emergence of research-based institutions and grassroots organizations, both of which have gained but slow acceptance in the government's policymaking process. Why slow? NGOs have grown at a speed that governmental institutions have not been able to keep up with. The major hurdle has been the structure and role of bureaucracy, which now includes at least a few more individuals interested in constructive social change.

Even so, political leadership has not adequately responded to the demands of long-term policymaking. One reason is that political parties and members of Parliament have little professional or research support that could help them articulate alternative choices. Another is, after the decline of the Congress Party, coalition politics has led to the rise of regional parties and sectional interests. Emergence of a national perspective was difficult with several coalition governments coming into power during mid-1990s and policy became secondary consideration to a politics of survival.

DEMOCRACY AND GOVERNANCE

With its size and heterogeneity, India is not an easy country to govern. In areas as well as population, many Indian states are larger than sovereign nations. India has a federal system of government, but in contrast to the United States, which has a population of 311 million divided among fifty states, India has a population of 1.22 billion in twenty-nine states and six union territories. The border areas in the northeast and northwest have continued to be trouble spots since independence in 1947. As a result, 'national unity' has always dominated the policy concerns of the government, but a consequence of such thinking has been hesitant decentralization and a reluctant opening up of the decision-making process.

India's adoption of a democratic parliamentary system of government with universal adult enfranchisement occurred at a time when its literacy rate was 35 per cent and more than half its population was living below the poverty line. Much of the government's effort since then has been to equip its people to exercise their franchise effectively—by raising the literacy rate and reducing the level of poverty. The discourse on democracy also centred on the core Western liberal concepts of individual rights, freedom, and equal opportunity, and it is in this context that claims of the failure of Indian democracy are often heard.

The wanting quality of public life and the state's incapacity to meet the demands of the people are attributed to the pathology of India's political system.

Indeed, India faces a paradox. On the one hand, the incidence of social conflict has risen, the economy has undergone difficulty, and democratic institutions are continuously under pressure by the tide of protest and violence. On the other hand, Indian democracy seems to have deepened and widened its reach. The proportion of the socially and economically deprived who exercise their right to vote has risen. If there is turbulence at the electoral level, one reason is that the participatory base of the electorate has expanded since the 1990s.[2]

This kind of democratic experience has severely strained the system of governance. Difficulties are compounded by the pattern of economic development in the country, wherein some regions have done well, while others with large populations have lagged behind considerably. While economic growth and the removal of poverty have been the twin goals of public policy, with population growth hovering at 2–2.5 per cent per year and the rate of per capita income growth a little less than this, poverty levels have remained largely untouched. Illiteracy rates have reduced, but less than half the population is still unable to read or write. The dilemma of increased political participation within a system of limited economic benefits is the major challenge for policymakers as India enters the second millennium.

STATE AND BUREAUCRACY

India's development experience is embedded in a highly expanded role of the state. In Nehru's vision of planned development, the state occupied a preeminent position. It was the agency that would be instrumental in providing to society the public goods from which everyone would benefit. The state would occupy commanding heights in the economy, producing goods and services when the private sector could not or where the private sector created inequities. Accordingly, India became a highly interventionist state that pursued welfare and socialist objectives by itself becoming an entrepreneur and by controlling and

[2] Yogendra Yadav, 1999, 'Electoral Politics in the Time of Change: India's Third Electoral System 1989–99', *Economic and Political Weekly*, vol. 34, nos 34–5, pp. 2393–9.

regulating the private sector. This resulted in a public sector with a huge army of employees whose interest lay in its self-perpetuation and in the acquisition of as much benefit as possible from the economy. As L.I. Rudolph and S.H. Rudolph argue:

The state sector that burgeoned and flourished on the way to socialism began to acquire and vest interests. Means began to become ends. Those in the pay of state firms became the beneficiaries of monopoly profits and administered prices; petty bureaucrats and senior officials became the beneficiaries of rents, the petty and grand larceny made possible by administrative discretion in the application of rules.[3]

Thus, the feeble development record of the Indian state could be explained in terms of the pulls and pressures of various groups that had subordinated the state to their interests.[4]

The policymakers' faith in the ability of the state to undertake the enormous task of development had stemmed from the perceived strength and efficiency of the bureaucracy that the British had left behind. At a time when other developing countries were struggling to establish a professional and career-based civil service, the standing of the Indian Civil Service (ICS) was exceptional. It had served the colonial masters well, and in the initial years of independence, it had provided tremendous support to the integration of the country, quelling riots that surrounded the 1947 Partition of British India. It had quickly assumed the role of upholding the law of the new sovereign state. These civil servants together with their successors, the Indian Administrative Service (IAS), also became great supporters of the Nehruvian policy of state-led development. As a result, the legacy of British administrative structure has remained untouched, even when questions about its suitability have been raised.

A powerful metaphor for the ICS was 'the steel frame,' which signi-fied the service's endurance in the maintenance of law and order in the face of local pressures to the contrary. Another was that of 'guardian-ship,' which suggested how the ICS worked in the public interest. In

---

[3] L.I.Rudolph and S.H. Rudolph, 1987, *In Pursuit of Lakshmi: The Political Economy of the Indian State*, Hyderabad: Orient Longman, pp. 62–3.

[4] Pranab Bardhan, 1984, *The Political Economy of Development in India*, New Delhi: Oxford University Press.

everyday life, it imparted a sense of superiority to the civil servants who believed in their heaven-born status to rule over the common man. Significantly, the ICS tradition also resulted in the celebration of the generalist and the amateur, who were placed in positions of authority to filter and process specialist and technical advice. This role came naturally to them because of their perceived monopoly on understanding and working for public interest, and it is this legacy that has shaped and circumscribed the Indian administrative system in the independence era.[5] Little in the way of administrative reform has since occurred.

In actual practice, the economic strategy that relied on the state for development translated into an unprecedented expansion of the public sector. Public enterprises were initially limited to manufacturing in the basic industries and the defence sector, but gradually, starting with the administration of Indira Gandhi, their role expanded. Banks were nationalized, and hotels and services that interacted directly with citizens were subsumed by the state. At the same time, the traditional functions of government, including regulation of the private sector, were also expanding, making the role of the bureaucracy in Indian society all-pervasive. Bureaucrats became arbiters of public interest, refusing the advice and consent of citizens—so much so that one aspect of the democratic struggle in India has been to make government more responsive to the needs of citizens.

It would not be entirely correct, however, to depict the bureaucracy with a single stroke of the brush. There are some members of the Indian bureaucracy who stand today as a progressive force working for greater decentralization, democratization, and the widening of the consultative process.

In the past decade, whether by emulation or innovation, country after country has embarked on reform in the administration of government. Reform is stylish today. On the one hand, changes in technology, particularly information technology, have necessitated changes in the management. But on the other, under the terms of globalization and liberalization, international financial agencies have called for internal structural reform. While administrative changes may be profoundly domestic concerns, the fact that they are part of a new,

[5] David C. Potter, 1986, *India's Political Administrators, 1919–1983*, Oxford: Clarendon Press.

more comprehensive, package opens them up to external pressure and influence. For example, the International Monetary Fund (IMF) and the World Bank, which funded NGOs for the implementation of development programmes, have pushed strongly for reducing fiscal deficits by downsizing the government and cutting down on subsidies.

In contrast to earlier decades, when government leadership initiated change, now it is the society and victims of ham-handed administration who are demanding administrative reform. As decentralization is effected, democracy in the country has deepened, even as local institutions such as the panchayats (village-level government created through constitutional amendments) have articulated frustration and anger with the functioning of the state.

In the give and take, the government itself expressed concern about the need to be more open and responsive. In 1997, it established a working group to examine the feasibility of a full-fledged Right-to-Information Act.[6] The President of Common Cause, an NGO active in consumer issues, was named Chairman of the group. Other members included lawyers and heads of government agencies, including railways and telecommunications. When the group had done its work, it issued a public report recommending enactment of a freedom-of-information bill.

This experience seems to have established a precedent, leading to organized pressure from below for government reform. NGOs have acted as catalysts in this movement. *Jan sunwais* (public hearings) are now held regularly. These hearings were initiated by *Mazdoor Kisan Shakti Sangathan* (Labour Peasant Unity Organization), an organization of rural labourers and farmers, giving people an opportunity to demand accountability from the government, to expose corruption, to focus on specific issues concerning decentralization, and to build grassroots democracy.[7]

---

[6] The Right to Information Act was enacted in 2005. It has evoked considerable interest among citizens for unravelling the way government decisions are taken and their impact on them. The Act has fuelled citizens' movements for bringing about honesty and transparency in the government, and since 2011 a movement led by social activist, Anna Hazare, has caught the imagination of the whole country.

[7] *The Hindu*, 1999, New Delhi, 12 December.

HISTORY OF THE PLANNING PROCESS

The leadership of the national movement for government reform spearheading the independence struggle was by and large urban professionals and intellectuals who identified the future of India with the developments in the West. Of particular significance was their perception of the role that science and technology played in transforming society. Nehru was further impressed by the strides Soviet Russia had made through judicious planning and the rational use of resources, and he envisioned that India should quickly attain the levels of economic development achieved by Western nations through industrialization and modernization. Rational allocation of resources, industrialization, and modernization became key words in the vocabulary of development during this period. A corollary element in this thinking was the principal role the state would play: It would initiate development and the market would function under its overall direction. The private sector was willing to accept these terms, for which there was broad national consensus based on agreement among the leaders of the Congress Party, industrialists, technocrats, and bureaucrats. Because the discussion required knowledge not only of economics but also of science and technology, expert advice was needed. In 1950, the Planning Commission was created for this purpose.

The Commission, as a body of technical experts, was granted a certain degree of autonomy in decision-making. Its power and prestige flowed from Nehru's own patronage and the fact that he assumed chairmanship of the group. Over the next decade, the economic development of India was thus placed in the hands of about twenty men, most of whom were civil servants, with some representing private interests as well.[8]

In quick succession, professional economists and technocrats came to dominate all public discussion on economic development, and the Planning Commission became the exclusive theatre for formulation of economic policy. The Cabinet and Parliament were merely informed of the decisions made by these experts. By the time of the Second Five-Year Plan (1956–61), political decisions made by the Commission were camouflaged in technical terms to insulate them from public scrutiny.[9]

[8] Sunil Khilnani, 1997, *The Idea of India*, London: Hamish Hamilton, p. 81.
[9] Ibid., p. 86.

Another way of ensuring its influence in executive decisions was to create a link between the Planning Commission and the bureaucracy. The Cabinet Secretary, who is the top bureaucrat in the country and to whom the Secretaries of all Ministries are accountable, was named the Secretary to the Planning Commission in the 1950s. This practice was discontinued in 1964 when a separate Secretary to the Planning Commission was appointed. This interlocking of offices had the effect of making the advice of the Planning Commission tantamount to a command.

As a result, experts and technocrats who worked within the government rose in power and influence. If an expert chose not to join the government, the government was pleased to support his research, if it was policy-oriented. In the period prior to 1964, the government established and funded several institutes involved in such research. Examples included the National Council of Applied Economic Research, the Institute of Applied Manpower Research, the National Council of Education Research and Training, the National Institute of Education Planning and Administration, the National Institute of Family Planning and Health (now Welfare and Health), and the Indian Institute of Public Administration. These institutes—which maintained close links with the government and the Planning Commission—brought in academics to monitor and evaluate development programmes. The data of their research provided direct input in the government's formulation of public policy.

Research organizations that generated alternative points of view were few. Therefore, there was neither a need for the government to seek advice elsewhere, or for it to consult its citizenry. For the government knew best! Whatever dissent there may have been came from the Gandhians, but their voice did little in countering the prevailing influence of the modernizers.

In the post-Nehruvian period, beginning in 1964, by which time the Planning Commission had lost its glamour, the link between the Planning Commission and the bureaucracy was cut. Lal Bahadur Shastri, the new Prime Minister, established his own secretariat and created a group of experts who could serve as alternative sources of advice. During his administration, as well as that of Indira Gandhi's, the Prime Minister's office was staffed by career economists, and thus the government's dependence on the Planning Commission diminished.

Shastri's arrangement continues till date with trained economists being replaced by civil servants.

GROWTH OF RESEARCH INSTITUTIONS

The Planning Commission's support for extra-governmental research was funded through its Research Planning Committee (RPC). However, the Commission's work came under a cloud when a plan holiday was declared during the year 1966–8 and formulation of the Fourth Five-Year Plan was postponed. During this period, the funds administered by the RPC were transferred to an autonomous body that was enjoined to fund research institutes and sponsor independent research. This body was the Indian Council of Social Science Research (ICSSR).

Promotion of research in social sciences was the major objective of the Council. It did this mainly by (a) keeping track of literature, research, and trends in social science research in the country; (b) inviting new research proposals from scholars; and (c) among other functions, conducting seminars, trainings, and workshops for India's young social scientists. A major function of the Council has been to sponsor institutes outside the university system with the purpose to encourage multidisciplinary and policy-oriented research.

Today, there are twenty-seven research institutes spread throughout the country supported by the ICSSR. Each institute decides its own direction of research, which spans a wide spectrum of subjects related to agriculture and rural development, industrial structure and growth, income distribution and poverty, employment and wages, interregional differences in development, education, health, nutrition, women, energy, technology, the environment, and social, cultural, and institutional aspects of development.

The ICSSR supported only nine institutes until 1974, after which the number increased gradually. The reason for this was the need for regional orientation that could be brought to bear in policy. Through a funding programme that required institutes located outside Delhi to secure matching funding from state governments, regional involvement in the policy process was assured. And conversely, state governments found these research institutes to be a source of advice and expertise for their own programs.

Usually, the initiative for the establishment of a research institute was taken by individual scholars or public figures who enjoyed the support of the state or central government. The prestige of the institute and the access it had in governmental circles depended largely on the influence of the founder. In addition, it was the academic standing of the founder that attracted other university scholars to the institutes. Part of the appeal of these institutes was the research facilities, which universities could ill-afford. The drawback was that while many scholars joined these institutes, universities suffered. Recently, however, with the ICSSR unable to maintain good research facilities and high salaries, the situation has begun to change.

The ICSSR gave block grants as well as project funds (see Table 1.1). Over the years, block grants have dwindled, even as state governments have matched them and shared in the capital cost of land and buildings. The institutes that have endured are those that have been successful in securing additional funding.

Another purpose that these institutes provided was the inclusion of non-economic social sciences in the formulation of policy. Most institutes carried names underlining the multidisciplinary nature of their interest. Thus, if there was the Centre of Development Studies at Trivandrum and the Madras Institute of Development Studies, there was also the Institute for Social and Economic Change at Bangalore and the Sardar Patel Institute of Social and Economic Research at Ahmedabad. Yet, it was eminent economists like V.K.R.V. Rao, K.N. Raj, Malcolm Adiseshiah, and D.T. Lakdawala who led most of these institutes, and despite expectations to the contrary, the major research projects were dominated by economists. As studies focused on the evaluation and impact of government programmes, input from other social scientists was necessary, and the character of the institute faculty changed.

How the government responded to the findings of these research institutes depended on the influence of the leadership of the relevant bureaucracy. If the leadership comprised members of important government committees, they could act as policy brokers, promoting the research findings of the institutes and mobilizing funds for further research. As the cast of leaders changed, however, the connections between the institutes and government became tenuous. Today, for the most part, these institutes do not command the status they once did. Those established after 1989 are struggling.

TABLE 1.1: Research Institutes Supported by ICSSR, 1997–8

| Research Institute | Research Projects | | Staff Strength | | ICSSR Grants |
	Completed	Ongoing	Faculty	Others	(Rs Million)
A.N. Sinha Institute of Social Studies, Patna	5	4	36	33	2.34
Centre for Economic and Social Studies, Hyderabad	12	13	14	21	1.42
Centre for Policy Research, New Delhi	17	16	41	38	1.55
Centre for Research in Rural and Industrial Development, Chandigarh	4	19	–	–	1.73
Centre for Study of Developing Societies, New Delhi	8	27	17	24	5.27
Centre of Social Studies, Surat	9	6	–	–	1.53
Centre for Study in Social Sciences, Calcutta	3	27	15	42	4.01
Council for Social Development, Hyderabad	10	14	10	11	1.02
Centre for Women's Development Studies, New Delhi	4	10	10	30	1.84
Gandhian Institute of Studies, Varanasi	8	11	–	–	2.46
Giri Institute of Development Studies, Lucknow	7	11	22	27	2.57
G.B. Pant Social Science Institute, Allahabad	5	9	15	42	2.68
Gujarat Institute of Development Research, Ahmedabad	5	4	–	–	1.12
Indian Institute of Education, Pune	2	5	4	19	1.46
Centre for Multi-Disciplinary Development Research, Dharwad	2	9	–	–	0.77

(contd.)

Table 1.1 (*contd.*)

Research Institute	Research Projects		Staff Strength		ICSSR Grants
	Completed	Ongoing	Faculty	Others	(Rs Million)
Dr. Baba Saheb Ambedkar National Institute of Social Science, Mhow	3	7	8	–	0.64
Institute of Development Studies, Jaipur	2	13	–	–	2.55
Institute of Economic Growth, New Delhi	22	–	36	67	2.93
Institute of Public Enterprises, Hyderabad	3	4	–	–	1.51
Institute for Social and Economic Change, Bangalore	29	36	45	90	3.48
Institute for Studies in Industrial Development, New Delhi	–	2	3	10	2.45
M.P. Institute for Social Science Research, Ujjain	3	7	5	5	5.08
Madras Institute of Development Studies, Chennai	7	4	17	27	2.45
N. Choudhary Centre for Development Studies, Bhubaneswar	9	9	13	21	3.41
O.K. Das Institute of Social Change and Development, Guwahati	2	4	3	10	0.86
Sardar Patel Institute of Economic and Social Research, Ahmedabad	5	4	13	57	2.90

Source: Based on data collected through various annual reports of ICSSR.

In a study of research conducted under the sponsorship of the ICSSR, Myron Weiner acknowledged the wide variation in quality. But he stressed that 'though these institutes have not yet made a conspicuous impact on public debates over policies, several have made state governments—at least some officials, if not politicians—aware of the value of research for policy and programme development and for assessing the consequences of governmental interventions'.[10]

It is difficult to assess the actual role that these research institutes play in the policy process. Perhaps, as the director of one institute pointed out, the main function of these institutes has been in the generation of ideas. A politician or a bureaucrat will sometimes act upon ideas proffered, he recounted, but ideas required constant repetition, like the chanting of a mantra, in order to make an impact. Politicians, in his view, were more receptive to change than bureaucrats.

Bureaucrats, as noted by a member of another institute, need a lot of convincing, which is time-consuming. Once a bureaucrat is convinced, he is transferred. With his replacement, a new round of convincing begins. Bureaucrats alone do the processing of the research; the researcher is not involved. What is or is not accepted for policy formulation—and why—is not to be known. As ideas have diverse and multiple sources, it is difficult to identify a specific study that has made a difference to policy. This has had a disheartening effect on staff at these institutes. A long-time ICSSR administrator laments that 'today neither policy relevance nor excellence in research are the identifying features of these institutes.'

It is due to this increased awareness that a number of institutes outside the gambit of the ICSSR have emerged. Some have partial central government support; others have raised funds through endowments from state governments. Still others have received support through international sources. Most do not depend on a single source of funding. Institutes that have caught the public eye as promoters of alternative policies include the National Institute of Public Finance and Policy, the Centre for Science and Environment, the Tata Energy

---

[10] Myron Weiner, 1982, 'Social Science Research and Public Policy in India', in James D. Stifel, Ralph K. Davidson, and James S. Colemen (eds), *Social Sciences and Public Policy in the Developing World*, Lexington, Massachusetts: Lexington Books, p. 315.

Research Institute (now The Energy and Resources Institute), and the Institute of Social Sciences. Common among these institutes is the fact that, apart from conducting research, they play an important advocacy role by publicizing their studies in the media and holding seminars for policymakers. The Director of the then Tata Energy Research Institute defined his role by asserting that the institute 'has generated a wealth of information and data and it is our job to bombard policymakers through letters, workshops, and individual meetings. I think the challenge starts from here'.[11]

The National Institute of Public Finance and Policy was established by a leading advocate of liberalization, who had been a member of the Planning Commission after a stint on the research staff of the IMF. The Institute has a close relationship with the government, its faculty members serving on special committees as they conduct the relevant research. Under the leadership of its founder, R.J. Chelliah, the Institute played a prominent role in shaping the economic reforms of 1991.

The Centre for Science and Environment has had a critical influence on environmental policy. It publishes a journal of state-of-the-art studies and crusades against policies that will lead to environmental degradation. Its influence in reducing air pollution in Delhi has been clear.

TEMPORARY BLUE-RIBBON COMMISSIONS

Dominated by a generalist civil service, the Indian government has little space for experts or technocrats. Wherever there is, the circumstances adhere to the philosophy of experts on tap, not on top. As such, within Ministries there are no specialized units that keep a long-term perspective in mind.

To meet this need, the Administrative Reforms Commission in 1969 recommended the establishment of policy units within each Ministry. Little came of this. The result is, when there is a need, the government appoints a blue-ribbon commission, which is responsible for generating new ideas for framing policy. These commissions usually consist of well-known experts, technicians, economists, and social scientists; they might also include retired civil servants. But apart from preparing a report, these commissions have no role in the formulation or

---

[11] *Express Newsline*, 2000, New Delhi, 24 February.

implementation of policy. The government decides whether to make the commission's report public, or to confine it to the archives or, to actually use it for policy purposes.

The Education Commission of 1964–6 offers a case study of how the government sought policy advice. The 1948–9 University Education Commission and the 1952 Secondary Education Commission had each looked at the state of education within their specific purview, but never had a governmental committee or commission considered education on a more basic level, despite the country's low literacy rate. Thus, the Education Commission of 1964–6 became the first comprehensive effort after independence to assess the country's educational system. It was also charged with responsibility to propose a national education system for the country.

Membership of the Education Commission was large, drawing upon educational expertise both in India and abroad. In the course of its work, the Commission traveled the length and breadth of the country, holding discussions and seminars, visiting schools, colleges, and universities. There were two conferences with student representatives. All told, more than nine hundred people were interviewed, and notes and memoranda sent to the Commission numbered about 2,450. In addition, the Commission met international consultants, including Edward Shils and Lord Lionel Robbins.

After two years, the Education Commission completed its labours and submitted its report in June 1966. In January of that year, following the death of Shastri, in whose tenure the Commission had been appointed, Indira Gandhi had become the Prime Minister. Even so, there was continuity as M.C. Chagla was retained as the Education Minister in the new Cabinet. When the report was submitted, he held a press conference and made its recommendations public for debate and discussion. Copies of the report were distributed to state governments, the Vice-Chancellors' Conference, the Central Advisory Board of Education, and members of both houses of Parliament, which represented different political parties. The expectation was that, after comments were received, the government would issue a statement on the education policy.

Even though elections were announced in early 1967, the process of consultation continued until a new government under Indira Gandhi was installed in March. Triguna Sen, who had been a member of the

Education Commission, was appointed Education Minister. Although Sen was committed to implementation of the report, he lacked a political base.[12] When he lost the political support of the Prime Minister, he found it difficult to carry the state governments, among other constituencies. Undaunted, Sen proceeded to appoint a committee comprised of members of Parliament representing all hues of political opinion. His hope was that, based on the report of this parliamentary committee, a draft for the national education policy could be formulated and put before Parliament.

Discussions in this parliamentary committee were contentious; the wide differences in opinion could be gauged from the fact that no fewer than nine of the thirty members wrote minutes of dissent amounting to twenty-three pages of a report twenty-six pages long. Discussions in the committee had centered on but a few issues such as selectivism in admissions, special funding for universities, and the medium of instruction. Larger issues were ignored.[13] Still, Sen made the report of this parliamentary committee available for wider public debate. The education policy document that finally emerged was a considerably watered down version of the recommendations made by the Education Commission in its original 1966 report.

Through subsequent Education Ministers, the recommendations of this report were kept alive, but even the pretense of future implementation was dropped as the country moved on to more immediate concerns, such as the war in Bangladesh and national elections, during the 1970s. The report, however, has become the standard by which all education policy is now measured. Even after the New Education Policy was adopted in 1986, it continues as a source of ideas for policy-makers.

The recommendations of the Education Commission were dealt a blow by politics. Nonetheless, the report contributed a wide range of ideas that raised the level of discussion, and this contribution refused to go away even though the government did not accept many of its significant recommendations. It may be said that, after all, the report

---

[12] J.P. Naik, 1982, *The Education Commission and After*, New Delhi: Allied Publishers, p. 31.
[13] Ibid.

has been quite influential—its effect on policy has been a slow, ongoing trickle.

The Administrative Reforms Commission, which was appointed during the same time, underwent a similar political experience and met a similar fate. This reinforces the notion that such blue-ribbon commissions serve as storehouses of ideas whose influence on government is imperceptible. Usually, bureaucrats will pick up an idea here or there in a piecemeal manner, and then incorporate it into policy. In the example of the two Commissions here, the entrenched educational and administrative systems proved to be too strong, and at the time, most recommendations and ideas for change battled unsuccessfully with the politics of survival of the government and the status-quo self-interest of the bureaucracy.

STATUTORY COMMISSIONS

The Indian Constitution has provision for several statutory commissions. One such, the National Commission for Scheduled Castes and Scheduled Tribes (NCSC&ST), was established by the 65th Constitutional Amendment of 1990 as a national advisory body on all policy matters related to the development of historically disadvantaged sections of society. The function of this Commission is to monitor the implementation of government policies, to inquire into complaints with respect to the deprivation of rights, to safeguard these deprived communities, and to recommend measures to make policies more effective.[14]

All members of the NCSC&ST, who serve a three-year term, come from a political background, even though the government in its notification stipulated that experts in the fields of social anthropology, social work, and other social sciences might be included. No experts have been appointed. The Commission does, however, employ an academic, who heads a unit of professional staff that conducts studies, surveys, and evaluations.

Reports of the NCSC&ST are submitted to the President, who in turn sends them to Parliament for discussion and debate. To date, Parliament has not found time to discuss any recommendations made

---

[14] National Commission for Scheduled Castes and Scheduled Tribes (NCSC&ST), 1997, *A Handbook*, http://india.gov.in/govt/documents/amendment/amend65.htm, New Delhi: Government of India.

by the NCSC&ST, let alone implement them. This experience is not unique to the NCSC&ST. It is the case with most statutory commissions, even when political leaders sit on them.

Due to heightened national and international interest, one particular statutory commission seems to have been successful in getting its recommendations not only heard but actually implemented. This is the National Human Rights Commission (NHRC), established in 1993 to advise the government and to respond to complaints of human rights violations. The NHRC was created as the result of the campaign for human rights waged by NGOs, both national and international. While the Indian Constitution reflects all articles included in the Universal Declaration of Human Rights, the provisions could be enforced only through a long drawn-out judicial process, complicated by the fact that evidence was to be gathered by the very agencies accused of violations. It was in this context that the NHRC was established as an autonomous body. It was given proactive powers of inquiry, investigation, and review. It was also empowered to recommend punitive action against any public servant or agency and, if necessary, appeal to the Supreme Court.

The NHRC has its own staff, headed by a senior police officer, and has the authority to utilize the services of any person or investigative agency of the central or state government. Elaborate processes have been devised to ensure its autonomy. A retired Chief Justice of the Supreme Court chairs the Commission, which is comprised of two other retired justices and two persons of eminence in public life with interest in human rights. The President appoints NHRC members on the advice of a committee headed by the Prime Minister which also includes the leader of the opposition in Parliament. A fixed tenure of five years helps to ensure the independence of the Commission.

Obviously, in contrast to the NCSC&ST, the NHRC has been able to meet its goals to a considerable degree. The reason lies not only in the broad significance of its work but also in the monitoring of its progress by NGOs and activist groups.

PARLIAMENTARY COMMITTEES
In recent years, the role of Parliament in providing input to policy through discussion on financial proposals of the government has seriously eroded. First, members of Parliament do not have research

assistance. Second, their primary focus is on the political considerations of their constituency. During the period 1985–95, Parliament held discussions on the financial proposals of only a few ministries—seven, to be specific. The demands for grants for as many as eleven ministries received no detailed discussion; often in this period, more than 85 per cent of the budget was passed without discussion.[15]

In view of this state of affairs, Parliament, in 1993, set up standing committees for most of the Ministries. These committees consist of members from both houses of Parliament, and the chair is chosen by proportional party representation. Usually, highly regarded parliamentarians are chosen to lead the committees, even if they belong to the opposition. Every committee has a maximum of forty-five members, and each Member of Parliament serves a two-year term on at least one committee.

The hope was that standing committees would provide a forum for discussion on financial proposals and for more thoughtful opinion on the policy issues involved. Here, legislators could consider technical matters that Parliament, as a whole, had not the time to discuss. Ostensibly, legislative oversight would be ongoing in a setting where members could avail themselves of expert testimony, initiate studies, issue reports, and examine draft legislation as a prelude to legislative action or postponement.[16]

Despite the establishment of these committees, legislators have expressed continuing dissatisfaction with the limitations imposed on their roles in governance. In interviews,[17] parliamentarians complain of inadequate resources at their disposal as compared with those available to the executive branch. Not surprisingly, the committees' in-depth studies have yielded perfunctory reports that the government and the media give no weight to.

Another issue is that ministers have no incentive to take these standing committees seriously as long as they do not have to testify before them. With sessions closed to the public and only secretaries—

[15] Sandeep Shastri, 1998, 'Department-Related Standing Committees in the Indian Parliament: An Assessment', *The Indian Journal of Public Administration*, vol. 44, no. 2, pp. 185–6.
[16] Arthur G. Rubinoff, 1996, 'India's New Subject-Based Parliamentary Committee', *Asian Survey*, vol. 36, July, p. 727.
[17] Ibid.

that is, civil servants heading the Ministries—required to appear, busy cabinet ministers can easily choose not to participate in a committee's activities. Further, since secretaries are not confirmed by Parliament and enjoy permanency of tenure through Constitutional provision, they are not accountable to the parliamentary system. Their arguments have often overwhelmed legislators lacking alternative sources of ideas. All of this does not bode well for the role of these committees in effective policymaking.[18]

The work of the legislature does not stop at approving the financial outlays at the start of the year. It includes the examination, at the conclusion of the year, of audit reports of the Comptroller and Auditor General, to determine if public money was spent appropriately. The Public Accounts Committee and the Committee on Public Undertakings, both of which are viewed as watchdogs of democracy, have oversight of these fiscal matters. Unfortunately, this responsibility is not taken seriously, often, fiscal examination is delayed by several years. 'As far as it has been possible to find out, the central Public Accounts Committee has not yet given its report about even the Bofors audit which is sometimes credited with bringing down the government of Rajiv Gandhi'.[19] It seems that financial irregularities uncovered by the Comptroller and Auditor General are of little interest to either parliamentarians or to the media.[20]

Parliamentarians also face a bottleneck of information. That is, because they lack research staff, policy ideas coming from diverse sources sometimes go by the board. Only politically volatile and visible issues will catch their attention. This lack of expertise, it goes without saying, has hurt the workings of the standing committee system.

In India, there is little tradition of research cells that provide support to legislative activities. Parliament has a rudimentary staff that can collect relevant data or refer to important sources, and there is a well-equipped library. The actual research, however, or the study or policy

---

[18] Ibid.

[19] K.P. Joseph, 2000, 'Budget Deficits Are Forever', *Economic and Political Weekly*, vol. 35, no. 34, p. 2999.

[20] However, the findings of CAG are now being increasingly noticed by people even though the Parliament may not generally give them importance. Several scams in 2011–12 have caught public attention due to the publicity given to the findings highlighted in the CAG Reports.

implications from available data is left to the legislators themselves. Not many are inclined to do this, and even if they did, most do not have the capability. The tendency instead is to stick to politically visible issues. The result is that these committees fall short of the role that congressional committees play in the United States, even if that is their model.[21]

In general, one might dare say that Parliament has lost its sheen. There is general apathy among its members, absenteeism has assumed alarming proportions, and defections for money and office have been a common phenomenon.[22] Frequently, debates turn into unruly fighting matches, and pandemonium prevails on the floor of the House. The result is that, as regards, the formulation of public policy, Parliament as the voice of the people has been ineffectual.

Nor do representatives come to office prepared for their role in policy. Political parties have no research organization that can frame alternative policy ideas. It is left to the individual legislators to seek out such opinions from professionals and academics whom they may know. It bears repeating that most of this is of an ad-hoc nature, generated only through personal volition and personal contacts.

One reason parliamentarians do not demand research support is that they may not consider their role as lawmakers very important. In contrast, their constituency demands are so strong that they ignore them only at the peril of losing the next election. For a constituency, a member of Parliament is an intermediary it has installed to sort out difficulties or roadblocks. Concerns run the full gamut—from municipal problems, to securing employment, to getting the gas and telephone connections, even to jumping the queue for air and rail tickets. 'The MP [Member of Parliament] may be an acknowledged authority on constitutional law, foreign relations or defence. But this will hardly

---

[21] For a discussion on the drought policy in Parliament, see Kuldeep Mathur and Niraja Gopal Jayal, 1993, *Drought Policy and Politics: The Need for a Long Term Perspective*, New Delhi: Sage Publications, pp. 117–26. For a similar discussion on the electronics policy, see R.B. Jain, 1985, 'Electronics Policy and Indian Parliament', *Indian Journal of Public Administration*, vol. 31, no. 2, pp. 239–74.

[22] Subhash Kashyap, 2000, 'Institutions of Governance: The Parliament, the Government and the Judiciary', in V.A. Pai Panandikar (ed.), *Problems of Governance in South Asia*, New Delhi: Centre for Policy Research and Konark Publishers, p. 138.

please his constituents. The clogged drains and bad roads will in all probability seal his fate'.[23]

EMERGENCE OF NGOs

With the adoption of economic reform policies in 1991, there came explicit recognition of the role of markets and NGOs in the life of India. The Eighth Five-Year Plan (1992–7) reexamined the role of the government and stressed the importance of a participatory democracy. Development had to be made a people's movement. If people's institutions could be created and held accountable to the community, then, the Plan suggested, a great deal could be achieved in such areas as education (especially literacy), health, family planning, land improvement, land use, minor irrigation, watershed management, recovery of wastelands, afforestation, animal husbandry, dairy farming, fisheries, and sericulture. This was in contrast to the Second Five-Year Plan of 1956–61, which stipulated that 'the state had to take on heavy responsibilities as the principal agency speaking for and acting on behalf of the community as whole.' The Eighth Plan made a strong plea for an increased role for the voluntary sector.[24]

Organized voluntary action in India has a long history. In the first half of the twentieth century, the struggle for independence was a galvanizing factor in the growth of voluntary agencies. Mass mobilizations and political campaigns were undertaken during this period, and Gandhi's 'constructive work,' which began in the 1920s, spoke to dimensions of economic and social reform. This would be a model for voluntary agencies to go by. In the post-independence period, many of these Gandhian organizations were led by public figures who did not, or could not, join the ruling Congress government. These organizations worked closely with government for the development of handicrafts and cottage industries, credit and other cooperatives, and educational institutions. Official institutions such as the Central Social Welfare Board, the Khadi and Village Industries Commission, and the People's Action Development India were established in the

[23] A. Surya Prakash, 1995, *What Ails Indian Parliament: An Exhaustive Diagnosis*, New Delhi: Harper Collins, p. 50.

[24] Kuldeep Mathur (ed.), 1996, *Development Policy and Administration*, New Delhi: Sage Publications, pp. 24–40.

1950s and 1960s to promote and fund similar voluntary social work organizations.[25]

Since that time, voluntary organizations have grown further as educated and professional people joined the ranks of voluntary agencies in large numbers. The NGOs that came into being kept close links with professional research institutions like the Tata Institute of Social Sciences, the Institute of Rural Management, the Indian Social Institute, and the Centre for Women's Studies. The accomplishments of several NGOs brought recognition to their principals, and government began to incorporate these NGOs into official agencies. Sanjit (Bunker) Roy of the Social Work and Research Centre (SERC), Tilonia, became adviser to the Planning Commission during Rajiv Gandhi's tenure as Prime Minister, and Ela Bhatt of the Self Employed Women's Association (SEWA), Ahmedabad, was nominated as a member of the upper house of Parliament and appointed Chairperson of the National Commission on Self-employed Women.

There is no complete inventory of development NGOs in India. As Ghanshyam Shah notes, 'Our guess, based on available directories of NGOs, our own studies on NGO's in Gujarat and West Bengal, and discussion with NGO activists, is that there are around 15,000 development NGOs in the country'.[26] Niraja Jayal estimates that NGOs active in rural development alone can range from ten thousand upwards and are probably between fifteen thousand and twenty thousand.[27] Most are registered under the Societies Registration Act, which gives them legal entitlement to raise funds from government and non-government sources, and binds them to rules of financial scrutiny by the government as well as their own membership. Any NGO group of five or more people can present its memorandum of association, which is a statement of activities, to the local authority. Once registered, the association is a legal entity. It has been estimated that NGOs currently

[25] Azeez Mehdi Khan, 1997, *Shaping Policy: Do NGOs Matter? Lessons from India*, New Delhi: Society for Participatory Research in Asia, p. 5.

[26] Ghanshyam Shah, 1991, Non-Governmental Organizations in India', mimeo, Surat and Amsterdam: Centre for Social Studies and Centre for Asian Studies, p. 6.

[27] Niraja Gopal Jayal, 2001, 'India', in Yamamoto Tadashi and Kim Gould Ashizawa (eds), *Governance and Civil Society in Global Age*, Tokyo: Japan Centre for International Exchange, pp. 116–53.

receive around Rs 9–10 billion in foreign funding; and according to the Seventh Plan, government funded NGOs with Rs 1.5 billion.

Traditionally, NGOs have worked with local groups, providing services, supplementing efforts of the government in delivering services, and enabling communities to organize to procure services and access entitlements. Their scope is limited, and whatever engagement they have with state or other groups is to facilitate their primary task of working for their constituency. An assessment of their performance or role in development, however, is of less interest here than their means of influence on policy.

NGOs, by their nature, wish to make an impact on society. If their projects are replicated by the state, this impact can be felt nationwide. Thus, NGOs often seek to establish feasibility for wider application by replicable models. But,they also attempt to influence policies and practices directly rather than through example. For instance, in the concerns of poverty, participation, democratization, and equity, Indian NGOs have organized advocacy in fields as diverse as informal, unor-ganized sector and child labour; affirmative action and protection for the disabled; women's issues; environment, forests, and issues such as displacement and rehabilitation; health; judicial reform; participatory management and governance; consumer rights; technology; shelter and the urban poor; and work space.[28] Successful policy changes, like the adoption of joint forest management and the representation of women in local institutions, have come about through advocacy as well as social action promoted by NGOs. There is bound to be some overlapping in the process of influence.

Grassroots NGOs engage in policy advocacy by protesting and organizing campaigns or by joining networks or issue-based coalitions. Azeez Khan, in a volume published by the society for Participatory Research in Asia (PRIA), documents the activities of five such NGOs.[29] One, which campaigned for a comprehensive law for construction labour, had a national perspective. Others were concerned with changes at the state or local level.

In influencing national policies, the role of research institutes that have become nodal institutions for creating networks or coalitions

---

[28] Khan, *Shaping Policy: Do NGOs Matter? Lessons from India*, p. 13.
[29] Ibid.

is very important. The role of Walter Fernandes of the Indian Social Institute, for example, was critical to formulation of the alternative draft of the national rehabilitation policy.[30] Initially, a research paper addressing the problems of displaced persons was circulated among activist NGOs working in the field. The NGOs responded by organizing meetings to discuss the paper and to identify principles on which the rehabilitation policy should be based. A database was created, and alternatives to displacement projects were proposed.

Pushing the process further, a national workshop in Delhi was convened to bring together the field experience of the activists, professional thinking, and issues raised at state-level meetings. What emerged from this workshop was a programme that included (a) mobilization of affected people, members of Parliament, and members of the Legislative Assembly; (b) involvement of NGOs and other support groups; (c) a press campaign; (d) work on amendments to the draft policy and dialogue with ministers; and (e) suggestion of alternatives to projects.

Fernandes notes that the role of NGOs has evolved over the years.[31] As NGOs involve themselves more in the policy process, they should re-evaluate their situation and foster alliances that can produce a broader impact.

The rights of women represent another area where alliances among NGOs have made their voices more powerful. The National Commission of Women and the Centre for Women's Development Studies (CWDS) have stated their support of NGOs as umbrella organizations that can provide a forum for influencing public policy as regards women's issues. In her introduction to the CWDS *Annual Report* (1996–7), the Director of the Centre emphasizes that CWDS 'is committed to creating integral links between women's studies and the women's movement and has continued to blend research, action and advocacy in its work while confronting the process of marginalization of women.... It does not view a positive value-based social intervention as being detriment to social science research.'[32]

[30] Walter Fernandes, 1995, 'An Activist Process around the Draft National Rehabilitation Policy', *Social Action*, vol. 45, July–September, pp. 277–98.

[31] Ibid., p. 291.

[32] Centre for Women's Development Studies, 1996–7, *Annual Report*, New Delhi: Centre for Women Development Studies.

From 1990 onwards, support given in turn by various umbrella organizations to activists groups has enlarged the scope of the public debate on policy. Awareness has been raised considerably. While the government has not been impervious to new kinds of policy input, it has not been entirely receptive either. In 1999, the Voluntary Health Association of India (VHAI) submitted to the central government the voluminous report of the Independent Commission on Health in India. Based on extensive discussion and the experiences of NGOs working in the field, the report made over 350 recommendations. The government response was not, to say the least, encouraging. In a letter to the VHAI, the Joint Secretary of Health in the Ministry of Health and Family Welfare made reference to the tremendous government effort already in progress and then went on to defend government policy. The letter, absolving the government of its shortcomings, suggested that 'a responsive and a conscious user will be able to revitalize the sector and make it more accountable than structural changes might be able to achieve'.[33]

POLITICAL AND ADMINISTRATIVE CONSTRAINTS TO ALTERNATIVE POLICY ADVICE

While the last fifty years has seen the government opening up to alternative policy advice, the general perception continues to be that of a closed system. The political leadership within the government has neither the inclination nor institutional support to do otherwise. Crises of one kind or the other have dominated the political scene from 1970 onwards: India went to war over the creation of Bangladesh in 1971, and then in 1975, Emergency was declared. The return of democracy in 1978 was marked by a less than stable coalition, and another election was called in 1980. In 1984, the Prime Minister was assassinated, and another assassination took place a couple of years later.

The post-1970 period also saw the disintegration of the Congress Party, which had until then dominated the national and state governments. The major task of the leadership was to hold the party together. Thus, even though the Congress Party came back to power in 1990 upon the collapse of a coalition government, it was a minority administration, voted to power by smaller parties in Parliament. Since 1996, several

[33] Government of India Letter, 18 January 1999, p. 3.

coalition governments have come and gone in quick succession. With such apparent instability, politics and short-term issues have dominated the national agenda. Fire fighting has been the characteristic mode of the government, and little concern for long-term policy has been expressed. Politicians have not been able to think beyond the next election.

With the political leadership lacking research support or professional staff, as noted earlier, basic policy choices are left to committees or commissions appointed within specific sectors or for special purposes. In recent years, the government has relied on this mechanism for internal debate as well. Increasingly now, NGOs and representatives of influential groups have been invited to serve on these committees. Since economic liberalization in 1991, for example, the government has turned to business organizations for advice, and the Finance Minister meets frequently with the Federation of Indian Chambers of Commerce and Industry and the Confederation of Indian Industry (CII).

To this extent, the government has opened up. Yet, the structure of the government is such that an all-powerful civil service vets all new advice. The civil service's preferred method for seeking advice is the appointment of a committee. The committee encourages wide public participation and, when necessary, authorizes a special study on specific areas of policy. Persons connected to the government in some way dominate these committees. Time has gradually seen the nomination of experts and NGO leaders to these committees, but there is less likelihood of the inclusion of persons holding opinions in opposition to the government's. This was truer during the planning era of Nehru and the liberal era of various governments after liberalization in 1991.

Usually, then, the next step in the process is that the committee makes recommendations that have been based on consensus, although dissenting notes are appended as well. The task, however, of sifting through the recommendations and deciding what will be kept and what will not, is solely that of the civil service. There will be no consultation with—or explanation to—the committee or responsible individuals.

This makes the role of the civil service quite critical. A civil servant may be named secretary or adjunct to the committee to help determine the feasibility of suggestions. But in this administrative and political capacity, the civil servant is not a neutral figure. Often, s/he will guide the committee in a particular direction. It is unclear what takes place at this stage, but the general sentiment among committee members is that the government does not have an open mind. As noted earlier, the director of an institute was constrained to remark that politicians were more open to alternative policy advice than were civil servants.

Transfers from one position to another make the processing of recommendations/suggestions even more problematic. As a member of an NGO remarked, 'Just as we were hoping that some of our suggestions will get a positive response from the government, the concerned civil servant was transferred and we had to begin the process of advocacy again.'

In the political circumstances India finds itself, strong, alternative policy advice struggles to be heard. The political system grapples with the challenges of democracy, the civil service system is firmly entrenched in its own interest, and the structure of the government bears vestiges of a colonial post. As research institutions or NGOs produce policy ideas, they have the effect of lending support to the opposition groups and threatening current orthodoxy. In reaction, a precarious coalition in power responds by closing up the process rather than opening it up. As Diane Stone argues in her paper analyzing a comparable situation in Britain:

By elaborating on policy options, increasing the number of alternatives and outlining possible problems, [these] policy research bodies potentially overload the collective decision making processes, disrupt established programmes, undermine consensus and question the legitimacy of a government's chosen policy.... Identifying flaws in policies or promoting superior policy design does not endear these organizations to politicians and bureaucrats.[34]

PROSPECTS AND CHALLENGES

In today's India, with changes occurring on many levels, it will be most difficult to respond adequately to the increasingly complex issues of society unless there are far-reaching changes in India's political institutions. The issue of technology offers a clear case in point. While the state of knowledge in government demands the input of experts

[34] Diane Stone, 2000, 'Guidance for Governance in Great Britain', Paper presented at the Global Think Net Conference, Japan Center for International Exchange, Tokyo, 28–30 May.

and specialists in the field, policymakers have been loath to call upon them. The shibboleths that policy should be left to generalists and that civil servants should be coordinative and not creative have continued to prevail, and the result has been a contraction in policy ideas. Institutions are bent on keeping alternative policy advice out of the final decision-making process. While some advice does manage to enter the deliberative process, usually it is because the ideas have been filtered through concerns of political and administrative feasibility.[35]

Ministers need to create new channels through which alternative advice can be solicited and advanced. Unless this is done, the powerful bureaucracy will dominate as always and choke off much needed fresh policy ideas. During the last several decades, ministers have been able to install secretaries of their choosing, but these choices have been determined more by patronage than by policy. There are exceptions to the rule, but in the current climate of coalition governments and regional parties, patronage has had the upper hand.

The time-tested practice of secrecy in the operations of government has not helped. There is no way to learn the nature or the source of policy advice. The files are closed to the public, and the bureaucracy itself upholds this principle even when a government minister may wish otherwise. In a recent case, an order by the Urban Development Minister, who is an eminent lawyer, to release such information to the public was squashed by the Cabinet Secretary on grounds of public interest. NGOs have now taken up the struggle for the right to information, with proposed legislation still pending as of May 2001. It is hoped that enactment of law will create a situation of greater accountability for advice givers and takers and will expand the market for alternative policy advice.

In a system of government inherited from the British, civil servants were the protectors and promoters of public interests. This was followed by a centrally planned economy in which the planners, bureaucrats, and technocrats again knew best. The point is that, under these terms, the tradition of civil society in India has been weak. Among people, there is a syndrome of dependence.

---

[35] Kuldeep Mathur and J.W. Bjorkman, 1994, *Top Policy Makers in India— Cabinet Ministers and their Civil Service Advisors*, Delhi: Concept Publishers, p. 76.

This is changing with the emergence of NGOs. Their role is still limited, however, and it is only in the last decade that NGOs have achieved such prominence that the alternative policy advice they offer has been taken seriously. Yet, the rationalist, technocratic view has not been easy to displace, its intransigence aided by well-publicized irregularities in some NGOs. The credibility of policymakers and the confidence of people must be earned continuously—an uphill task for NGOs as well as the government's own commissions.

2

Policy Analysis in India

*Research Bases and Discursive Practices**

This chapter examines the patterns in policy analysis and its research bases in India. Due to India's post-colonial developing country orientation, policymaking and policy research have been framed through the terms of 'development' and 'planning.' As a consequence, the conversation about policy research and analysis is inevitably about development policy as applied to various sectors such as poverty, industrialization, education, and employment, seen through an economistic framework. Moreover, Soviet-style central planning was the only broad methodological strategy that was considered to move India along that path of economic development. In this chapter, we identify the dominant paradigm of policy analysis (economic planning) and show how it evolved from factors rooted in the specific context of India's political development. More specifically, we discuss how the hegemony of economics as a discipline was central to the framing of political issues and the consequent establishment of a particular pattern of policy analysis. We find that, while a well-developed field of policy analysis has yet to be clearly identified, public administration as a subject of study and an applied field has received considerable attention in India. Currently, there

* © 2007. From 'Policy Analysis in India: Research Bases and Discursive Practices', by Navdeep Mathur and Kuldeep Mathur in F. Fischer, G.J. Miller, and M.S. Sidney (eds), *Handbook of Public Policy Analysis: Theory, Politics, and Methods*, pp. 603–15. Boca Raton, FL: CRC Press, Taylor and Francis Group. Reproduced by permission of Taylor and Francis Group, LLC, a division of Informa plc.

is a strong trend in the growth of the activity of documentation of the institutional bases of policy analysis and research capacity. However, a reflection on tools and methodologies of analyses has yet to emerge as an important theme in mainstream academia. We argue that the field of policy analysis, as it evolved in India, has developed in the interaction space between the state and the sphere of civil society organizations rooted in a participatory politics, and show how policy debates and research broke the economistic mould to take on a life of their own.

In order to provide an account of the dominant form of policy analysis in India, we direct attention towards the relationship between the political order and the practice of policy analysis,[1] where the initially dominant developmental paradigm termed 'the Nehruvian Consensus'[2] created and maintained reliance upon economic-expert institutions as the primary tools of developmental policy research.[3] From the 1950s onwards, this paradigmatic political programme, framed through a technical rationality of economic development, was supported by a mainly generalist bureaucracy, whose key role was to manage the implementation of development policy in India. More recently, the growth of independent research institutions that variously play roles of advocacy and political campaigners has created a process of redefining of public problems. In terms of policy analysis, greater attention is paid to policy impacts at the level of target populations, and problems are increasingly reframed through a diversity of lenses, especially accounting for the protest movements against inappropriate or inadequate state action. As a challenge, social analyses and methodologies began to poke holes in the rigid economistic system. Government institutions, experts and technocrats, in this current context, have been far from successful in setting such debates, faced with alternative experts and alternative

---

[1] Frank Fischer, 1993, 'Policy Discourse and the Politics of Washington Think Tanks' in F. Fischer and J. Forrester (eds), *The Argumentative Turn in Policy Analysis and Planning*, Durham and London: Duke University Press, p. 21.

[2] This was named after India's first Prime Minister, Jawahar Lal Nehru, who took the lead in articulating the strategy of India's developmental framework.

[3] Kuldeep Mathur, 2001, 'Governance and Alternative Sources of Policy Advice: The Case of India', in R.K. Weaver and P.B. Stares (eds), *Guidance for Governance: Comparing Alternative Sources of Public Policy Advice*, Tokyo and Washington, D.C.: Japan Centre for International Exchange and Brookings Institution Press, pp. 207–30.

sources of evidence that bring the experience of policy-community interaction to the table. The space for debate about alternatives has expanded and a new generation of policy professionals, both within and outside the bound of state institutions has helped facilitate deliberation on issues that were previously in the domain of state control. Now, technocratic claims from the establishment elites are tested through alternative empirical evidence that incorporates the lived experience and counter-factual claims of those academic experts-turned-activists who represent disadvantaged communities.[4] Environmentalists have particularly highlighted governmental policy failures, and brought up critical perspectives on community-based governance and the need for expert institutions to pay attention to local knowledge.[5] The move from 'Government to Governance'[6] rather than the consequence of the 'hollowing out of the state' apeared in India as a political struggle to redefine the nature of Indian democracy, from an elite one to more participatory polity. These set of factors, in our assessment, have contributed to the emergence of policy analysis as a more diverse field in its own right, weakening the hegemonic economism to some extent.

POLICY ANALYSIS: FROM ECONOMIC PLANNING TO IMPLEMENTATION FAILURE

Policy analysis has not been a mainstream Indian research or academic tradition. The major goals emerged through a consensus between the Indian political leadership, the industrial elite, and civil service intellectuals[7] that comprised the first democratic regime in India (from

[4] For example, Dr Medha Patkar in the Narmada Dam controversy.

[5] Guha, 1989, *Unquiet Woods: Ecological Change and Peasant Resistance in the Himalaya*; Baviskar, *In the Belly of the River: Tribal Conflicts over Development in the Narmada Valley*; J. Dreze, M. Samson, and S. Singh (eds), 1997, *The Dam and the Nation: Displacement and Resettlement in the Narmada Valley*, New Delhi: Oxford University Press; Neeru Nanda, 1999, *Forests for Whom? Destination & Restoration in the U.P. Himalayas* New Delhi: Har-Anand Publications.

[6] R.A.W. Rhodes, 2000, 'Governance and Public Administration', in Jon Pierre (ed.), *Debating Governance*, Oxford: Oxford University Press, pp. 54–91.

[7] This consensus or convergence between these groups is illustrated by the overlaps and dialogue between the Congress Party that led the national movement for independence, the Bombay industrialists, and the writings of well-known civil service intellectuals.

1950 onward). Apart from a basic democratic imperative, the overthrow of colonial rule was framed as a response to the growing impoverization of the vast mass of India's population. As a consequence, major policy goals were framed as how can India achieve the standards of development, and as a corollary, the quality of life that exists in Western developed nations in a shorter span of time. At a micro-level this translated into questions about how to end widespread hunger and illiteracy were seen as the main obstacles on the path to Western developmental standards and for Indian population to become productive in a modern sense. Within government, therefore, policymaking was chiefly conceptualized as, and began with, the acceptance of centralized economic planning as the overarching strategy of social and economic development. The Planning Commission, established as a core policy institution that would manage sectoral coordination of different planning themes for achievement of socio-economic goals set by the political leadership. Planning synonymous with policymaking, and the value consensus over goals was not up for disccussion. Goals were treated as fixed with only a process to technically design plans for their achievement. Such designing was based on theoretical exercises conducted by technical policy experts in the Planning Commission. In addition, the primary activity in policy analysis, besides economic modeling, was the intense search and collation of more quantitative data, mainly as an effort to make models reflect reality more closely. Toward this end, the later establishment of public policy institutes by the Planning Commission— often in conjunction with foreign funds from organizations such as the United Nations, Ford Foundation, or USAID (United States Agency for International Development)—was geared towards developing external capacity and outsourcing the collection, collation, and supply of data.

Over time, the base of expertise expanded to include national and internationally recognized economists. During the preparation of the Second (1956–61) and Third (1961–6) Five-Year Plans, the Planning Commission became an experimental school for those policy-oriented economists who contested and debated models of social and economic development for developing countries. Economists from both the Western Bloc (such as J.K. Galbraith from Harvard University, Jan Tinbergen from The Netherlands) as well as the Eastern Bloc (Oskar Lange from Hungary) came to India and were part of this expert community that deliberated the models that should be followed in India to achieve its development objectives. However, the first three Five-Year Plans were not able to achieve their expected targets. The rate of economic growth was lower than anticipated in the Plan while population growth was much higher, resulting in an acute food crisis. The production and release of the Fourth Five-Year Plan was postponed in order to buy time to correct the perceived weaknesses of earlier planning models and micro-level strategic interventions. Postponement of the introduction of the Fourth Five-Year Plan in 1966 marked the end of a 15-year period of dominance of the technocratic paradigm for policy analysis and research in India. The Planning Commission lost its hegemonic position of policy research and decision-making, and policy decisions shifted to political and civil service leadership in the executive departments of the Government of India. This shift, therefore, implied some loss of credibility for the Planning Commission's expertise, and policy became more open to the public, particularly once government ministers began to initiate discussions about specific policies. Ministers and other legislators further brought policy issues into public focus by raising discussions in Parliament, an institution that provided relatively higher public access and transparency. The era of insulation of policy analysis from politics had come to an end. Planning-related crises continued to worsen and public assessments helped policy analysis become more and more democratic over time. This became apparent in varying forms in public debate as well as in outputs from research institutions.

In the period from the late 1960s onwards, failure of plan objectives was blamed on poor implementation and projected in the public sphere as a crisis of implementation. Yet, there was no critical reflection on the econometric modeling or on the formulation of methodologies of the Plans themselves. As a direct consequence, Plan failures did not entail a critical thinking about policy analysis. Rather, the focus turned towards reform of administrative structures and process, and ended up as an issue concerning the administration of Plan objectives. For example, one of the major moves was to invite public administration experts from the United States and the United Kingdom to advise on the improvement and reform of administrative structures and process, the idea being that Western bureaucracies' attributes of efficiency and effectiveness need to be employed in the Indian situation to achieve success in plan implementation.

This closed policy analysis paradigm, as we have outlined above, had consequences for the development of policy research institutions as well as the development of the discipline and practice of public administration. Early policy research institutes were established to supply data because the failure of policies/plans was framed as the lack of adequate or accurate data interlinked with (and also a consequence of) poor implementation. Independent institutes as well as departments of public administration were also established in a large number of universities to develop a more professionalized practice. As a consequence, attention shifted to public administration and not towards policy analysis. Given that the policy process was understood as consisting of two successive stages—formulation, then implementation—the key problems were framed as gaps in implementation, lack of coordination, and poorly developed roles of policymaking. Studies conducted in these public administration departments concerned relationships between bureaucrats and politicians, local administrators and politicians, which mainly demonstrated divergences in policy outlooks of these pairings. Following these studies, decision-making units and processes within ministries and departments were established to standardize and simplify rules and administrative processes of decision-making behaviour and conduct. There was a strong influence of Zero-Base Budgeting (ZBB) and Performance-Based Budgeting (PPBM) from the United States. The entry-point for this influence came from the Ford Foundation and USAID, with both playing a major role in providing technical expertise and funds for adaptation of Indian institutions and bureaucratic processes.[8] The thrust of the US influence was shaped by the recommendations of Paul Appleby of the Maxwell School at Syracuse University who had been invited by the Government of India in 1953 to study Indian administration and make suggestions for reform. Appleby's suggestions emanated from his belief that an administration, which served imperial rulers could not fulfill the aspirations of an independent India. The idea that there was a dichotomy between bureaucratic dispositions and

---

[8] The Ford Foundation alone spent $360,400 in grants to institutions and $76,000 in providing consultants and specialists to improve public administration in India during the period 1951–62. See Ralph Braibanti, 1966, 'Transnational Inducement of Administrative Reform: A Survey of Scope and Critique of Issues', in J.D. Montgomery and W.J. Siffin (eds), *Approaches to Development: Politics, Administration and Change*, New York: McGraw Hill, p. 148.

development needs was widely accepted and the whole enterprise of implementation reform began to take shape under the American experience and influence. Professionalization of the administrative system through improved technical processes of decision-making and imbibing a professional outlook among the administrators became the dominant themes of reform. Considerable American scholarly writing during this period emphasized these themes.[9] Most of the American scholars and consultants stressed the need to convert to a more flexible, freewheeling, administrative system where a clear responsibility of tasks was laid down. Indian public administration scholars began to move away from the legal framework of administering rules and regulations to behavioural orientations of commitment, dedication, and discretion. Led by the Indian Institute of Public Administration (IIPA), the graduate study of public administration in universities began to stress the role of individual behaviour in attaining development goals and the relationships that bureaucrats forged with politicians.

There were only small voices of dissent against the dominance of the implementation failure framework. These came from within the field of economics too, mainly from B.R. Shenoy—the first major critic of the approach to planning and policymaking—who argued in favour of a more open economy and much less government control. Rather than argue for alternative methods of policy analysis and planning, Shenoy's critique was substantive and he appeared to be committed to laissez faire methods in so doctrinaire a manner that no one outside business circles took much notice of his criticisms.[10] He was among those economists who challenged the core strategy of investment in heavy industries that produced machinery to carry forward the process of industrialization and industrial production. The process of transfer of agricultural labour to the industrial sector to reduce rural unemployment and poverty and increase savings for investment by postponing

[9] See for example, R. Braibanti and J. Spengler (eds), 1963, *Administration and Economic Development in India*, Durham, NC: Duke University Press; and C.C. Taylor, D. Ensminger, H.W.U. Johnson, and J. Joyce (eds), 1966, *India's Roots of Democracy: A Sociological Analysis of Rural India's Experience in Planned Development Since Independence*, Bombay: Orient Longman.

[10] A.H. Hanson, 1966, *The Process of Planning: A Study of India's Five Year Plans 1950–6*, Oxford: Oxford University Press, p. 128.

consumption was seen as skewed in their view. Essentially, the argument of these economists was that centralized planning would stultify
India's economic development rather than stimulate it, while accepting that economic growth has been achieved in some countries with
this strategy. These economists argued that the implicit economic and
political costs of such growth were disproportionately high in comparison to any long-term benefits. However, these writings failed to provide clear alternatives and consequently did not engender widespread
debates to seriously challenge India's dominant development paradigm.

To summarize, policy analysis emerged from the technical imperative of designing Five-Year Plans and was supported by overseas economic development experts. Lacking a historical indigenous tradition
and a failure to look at the enterprise of policy analysis in favour of
implementation (a consequence of the classical economics tradition),
the dominant paradigm in Indian policy analysis remained a technocratic and economics-led field of research and practice. This emphasis
in government led to the establishment and further development of
public administration, influenced primarily by trends in the United
States. In turn, this influence was reflected in the focus of the curricula of university departments and institutes, to the neglect of policy
analysis as an independent field of study. Due to the multi-disciplinary
character of the development of social science research in the 1970s
(and beyond) and the participatory imperatives in the policy sphere,
policy analysis began to emerge as a critique of the dominant paradigm.
These developments are illustrated below through an examination of
the trends in social research and policy studies.

SOCIAL RESEARCH AND POLICY STUDIES

Apart from economics and history, other social science disciplines were
slow to develop as major fields of study. Until the 1970s, political science
was in its infancy, and its attention focused on the legal and constitutional
structures/institutions of government in the colonial period. Sociology
was oriented to and carried out by Western sociologists and was limited
to describing and interpreting the 'Indian social group, structure and
interaction' to a primarily Western audience. There was little direct
analysis of public policy from sociological perspectives. The debate
among Western analysts was concerned with the problem of 'tribes' or
traditional societies within developing countries—whether they would

benefit from being incorporated in the mainstream of modernization or left untouched to pursue their own cultural norms.[11]

Empirical political science emerged from a focus on the impact of social groups on electoral behaviour. Developed mainly as psephology, questions were restricted to electoral behaviour, the social basis of elections, and participation of socially deprived groups.[12] It then, turned its attention to implementation studies. With the acceptance of core planning objectives and goals, political science went on to do research about the implementation of *panchayati raj* (local self-governance at the village level). It neither attempted to theorize the appropriateness of decentralization in the face of diverse sets of local contexts nor sought to examine the unintended consequences of *panchayati raj* institutions, such as fragmentation of decision-making and accountability. Political scientists rarely questioned the underlying norms of policy or planning objectives, rather analysis placed importance on their performance with respect to the procedural aspects of the establishment and operation of *panchayats*.

Economics was the most well-established discipline in Indian universities. Research institutes were also staffed by economists. Hence, policy debates were chiefly initiated and conducted by economists, and therefore they were able to set the terms of the debate, restricting it to this field. As economic planning was accepted as the dominant paradigm, voices of dissent were either suppressed or ignored, but dissent also came from economists. For example, the classical economist, A.D. Shroff established the Forum of Free Enterprise that attempted to offer free-market alternatives to centralized planning. The Forum was unable to make much impact given the dominant paradigm, yet it floated a political party based on the free enterprise philosophy and offered candidates for election in 1961.

Institutionally, universities had traditionally been organized as faculty of arts (that included political science, history, sociology, and mostly English-language literature) and technical faculties of medicine, engineering, and pure sciences. There were changes in the 1970s with

[11] Ramachandra Guha, 1999, *Savaging the Civilized: Verrier Elwin, His Tribals, and India*, New Delhi: Oxford University Press.

[12] Rajni Kothari, 1970, *Politics in India*, Boston: Little and Brown. This was an early study that employed the structural-functional approach to analyse Indian politics and was published in the series edited by Gabriel Almond.

Jawaharlal Nehru University, New Delhi, adopting a more multi-disciplinary mode of study in organizing its departments. Currently, policy analysis has been adopted as a full fledged topic of study at the University's Centre for the Study of Law and Governance. Many other institutions have followed this course.

More recently, policy studies in India have gained considerable ground. These have mainly drawn upon theoretical approaches developed in the West.[13] Here, we briefly examine some exemplars for illustration and their theoretical approach to policy analysis in India. Broadly, recent mainstream policy literature has drawn upon cost-benefit evaluation studies, neo-institutionalism,[14] neo-Marxist analysis, and a mix of pluralist approaches. Through a programme evaluation approach, evaluation studies of various policies and programmes have been carried out, which sought to identify the factors responsible for policy failures and suggest changes in programme management and design to succeed in future iterations. Embedded within the centrally-planned developmental framework, problems of implementation took precedence in these studies under the guiding assumption that policies failed and/or could not achieve their objectives because of inadequacies in bureaucracy and administration, related to the values of efficiency and effectiveness.[15] There was therefore an uncritical acceptance of the legitimacy of the goals of the policy, and sources of failure were seen to be located in the bureaucratic/managerial process rather than in programme design and formulation of objectives. Little attention was paid to the appropriateness of particular policy goals or the means for their achievement.

The situation changed in the late 1960s when the country was con-fronted with a food crisis, industrial stagnation, a resource crunch, and suspension of the Central plan. Policies began to be assessed in relation

[13] While this section is illustrative and summative rather than comprehen-sive and substantive, our selection of the literature is representative of wide-ranging policy analysis scholarship.

[14] James G. March and John P. Olsen, 1989, *Rediscovering Institutions: The Organisational Basis of Politics*, New York: The Free Press.

[15] The literature concerning implementation is very large but the arguments cited in the reports of the Administrative Reforms Commission (1969) set up by the Government of India summarize the reasons for failures in achieving plan goals and targets.

to plan models, cross-sectoral relationships, and the global economic context. While evaluation studies primarily focused on the efficiency and effectiveness dimensions of the bureaucratic structures and process, they failed to even explore the assumptions implicit in the officially-stated policy goals and strategies. While this orientation was useful in collecting and collating basic data, the methodology failed to provide a conceptual framework for seeking policy alternatives. Consequently, economic evaluation studies began to take on a normative assessment element as well, where questions of appropriateness became more salient. It was acknowledged that efficiency criteria may only promote particular types of programmes or policies, and preclude others. The focus began to shift from narrow managerial bureaucratic consider-ations to challenging the very goals that a policy was seen to promote.

As a result, the theoretical focus shifted from state institutions per se to societal institutions that provide the arena for political contestation between groups. Derived from pluralist democratic theory,[16] the assumption was made that the public interest is best served by a public policy that emerges from such competitions.[17] Policy scholarship, more recently, began exploring the reasons and the context of the introduction of economic reforms. Scholars and practitioners from various academic persuasions joined in this exploration. Jenkins[18] utilized an institutionalized approach to interpret the political mechanisms that facilitated reform processes in India. Through a discussion of incentives, institutional frameworks, and skills, he highlighted the interaction between elite groups to explain the policy shifts that were labeled as 'liberalization.' Other influential studies have used a mix of pluralist-institutional approaches to model individual and group behaviour through institutional incentives to achieve beneficial outcomes.[19]

Neo-Marxist analysis has also grappled with this major recent move for economic reform, posing the question of 'why Indian capital, which

[16] Robert Dahl, 1961, *Who Governs?* New Haven, CT: Yale University Press.

[17] Krueger, 'The Political Economy of the Rent-Seeking Society'.

[18] Rob Jenkins, *Democratic Politics and Economic Reform in India*.

[19] Atul Kohli, 1989, 'Politics of Economic Liberalization in India', *World Development*, vol. 17, no. 3, pp. 305–28; and Ashutosh Varshney, 1999, 'Mass Politics or Elite Politics: India's Economic Reforms in Comparative Perspective', in J.D. Sachs, A. Varshney, and N. Bajpai (eds), *India in the Era of Economic Reforms*, New Delhi: Oxford University Press, pp. 222–60.

was obviously a beneficiary of the protection offered under the earlier regime of intervention went along with and in fact celebrated liberalization of the kind introduced in 1980s and 1990s'.[20] Their analysis identifies macro-level social and economic factors as explanatory variables to suggest that class linkages forged between domestic capital, international financial capital, and the Indian middle class contributed to such a reform process. Other scholars suggest that such economic reforms were a normal/fire-fighting response to the economic crisis that the country faced in 1991 and was an instrument of crisis management by the government, given a neo-liberal international framework.[21]

Elements of March and Olsen's neo-institutional analysis[22] are salient in Varshney's study[23] of the design of India's 'new' agricultural policy (1966–8). Using a neo-institutionalist view of institutions as a complex of routines, norms, rules, and understandings, he identified institutional incentives in the three Ministries of Agriculture, Planning, and Finance that were directly involved in formulating agricultural policy. Such incentives are mediated through the logic of appropriateness as well as the logic of consequentiality of the political context within which institutional actors operate. Varshney points out that institutional actors involved in the micro-process of production sought growth through increasing production, while at the same time making a political case for raising prices as well as subsidies. However, actors in the food department, concerned with feeding people, would make a case for lowering prices, acting on a different set of incentives. In his analysis, the Planning Commission was driven by dual and competing incentives, attempting to balance on the one hand raising agricultural production and on the other resisting raising food prices and subsidies. The Finance Ministry actors controlled spending and displayed resistance to subsidies

[20] Ghosh and Chandrashekhar, 'The Political Economy of the Indian Reform Process'.

[21] 'It is plausible to argue, but difficult to prove, that any other government in office in mid-1991 would have done roughly the same in terms of firefighting and crisis management simply because there was little choice.' (Bhaduri and Nayyar, *The Intelligent Person's Guide to Liberalization*, p. 49).

[22] March and Olsen, *Rediscovering Institutions: The Organizational Basis of Politics*.

[23] Ashutosh Varshney, 1995, *Democracy, Development, and the Countryside: Urban-Rural Struggles in India*, Cambridge: Cambridge University Press.

and price rises to prevent imbalances in their budget. Varshney shows how the logic of consequentiality shaped individuals' roles within institutional parameters, and sketched out the state-institutional space for straggle over policy outcomes by political leaders and bureaucrats who held distinct visions of the agrarian economy.

Mathur and Bjorkman utilized an institutionalist perspective to explore the role of key individuals by focusing on cabinet ministers and civil servants in policymaking.[24] Their analysis identifies determinants such as actors' situational institutional framework, nature of career and recruitment, and characteristics of professional experience that mediate the contribution of India's elite decision-makers to policymaking. Highlighting the predominance of political over administrative inputs into the policy process, their research suggests that the dominant image of rational decision-making articulated through the values of efficiency and technical optimality is undermined by a more dynamic interaction of values and beliefs of key actors and the framework of institutional constraints they impose on policy issues.

In a critical analysis of state action, Mathur and Jayal examined the policy process regarding drought in India.[25] By examining the assumptions on which drought policy is formulated, they showed how the powerful definition of 'drought as crisis' led to the dominance of solutions that covered a short-time horizon, leading to the institution of measures to alleviate the immediate hardship of the affected people. Blaming drought on unpredictable vagaries of nature, erratic monsoon, and, in some instances, on 'the changing mood of the gods,' this dominant view of drought then precluded the formulation of a long-term strategy that would include the provision of better infrastructural farming facilities in drought prone areas. Due to the assumptions about the causes of drought, long-term concerns simply did not enter the definition of the crisis. Thus policy contributed to exacerbating the social consequences of drought even as political mileage was derived from drought management. Government performance evaluations were conducted at a technical level, only accounting for responses to

---

[24] Mathur and Bjorkman, *Top Policy Makers in India—Cabinet Ministers and Civil Service Advisors.*

[25] Kuldeep Mathur and Niraja Gopal Jayal, 1993, *Drought Policy and Politics: The Need for a Long-Term Perspective*, New Delhi: Sage Publications, p. 93.

immediate needs, which, unsurprisingly, produced positive evaluations. An example of discursive policy analysis, this study identified the frames through which the drought as crises discourse was formulated upon which, in turn, solutions were constructed. In addition to showing the substantive weakness of government response, the analysis carried a critique of the narrow technical focus of evaluations which are embedded within the dominant empiricist epistemological position. The authors suggested that the failure to consider policy alternatives was a direct consequence of the dominance of the crisis discourse and the consequent inability of other discourses (where radically different strategies emerge from alternative problem definitions) to arise and enter the deliberative space.

The field of environmental policy has attracted a rich contribution through a critical-analysis approach. Scholarship has examined the appropriateness of environmental policy and compared its social and cultural consequences with economic benefits. There have been a series of struggles and conflicts for water and forest rights which have raised issues regarding community rights in forests, rehabilitation, and displacement through large projects and the utility of large dams. Guha's study[26] was among the early critiques that played a crucial role in opening up the debate on environmental issues. In studying the Chipko (Tree-Hugging/Conservation) movement in the North Indian Himalayan region of Garhwal, Guha highlighted the concerns and responses of the indigenous community to its loss of livelihood and control of local forest resources, in a context of commercial, state-sanctioned deforestation. His analysis portrayed this movement as a challenge to India's national forest policy, which influenced both future public debate and policy reflection.

A more recent issue, and a highly controversial and contested one, is the case of the construction of the Sardar Sarovar dam on the Narmada River. It evoked sharp reactions from both its critics and supporters and led to a large number of research studies. With government-oriented and international economists justifying construction of another big dam on technical and engineering attributes and its 'contribution' to an abstract ideal of universal social progress, this technocratic growth narrative was challenged on grounded factors that drew attention to

---

[26] Guha, *Unquiet Woods*.

the displacement of inhabitants and the loss of their livelihoods based around the affected river systems. Not only has the popular struggle against the construction of the Narmada Dam attracted global attention, it has engendered policy argumentation that encompasses enormous amounts of technical concerns as well as challenges the basic meanings of development.[27] The movement against the dam project appeals to a participatory ideal of democracy where people not only have the right to information and be consulted about development plans likely to affect their lives, but where people have a right to play a role in the design and outcomes of such plans. As a consequence, the movement articulates a set of cultural rights to a way of life and the associated material rights in natural resources, in and by which they have lived.[28] Other studies in the postmodern tradition are too numerous to list here but have contributed immensely in opening the door to a more grounded social science outlook and enriched policy research while facing tremendous resistance from the mainstream. However, this change in policy analysis has occurred simultaneously and partly due to the growth of a participatory politics in India, spearheaded through NGOs, as illustrated in the following section.

NGOS AND THE DEMOCRATIZATION OF POLICY ANALYSIS

Over the past 21 years, India has undergone a process of market-oriented economic reforms that have gone hand-in-hand with a 'modernization' programme for government. Governmental reform, though slow, has helped expand the democratic space for dominant social and political values to be contested. For example, greater decentralization and capacity building in village councils (panchayats) were brought about through constitutional amendment, and have consequently provided

[27] Dilip D'Souza, 2002, *The Narmada Dammed: An Inquiry into the Politics of Development*, New Delhi: Penguin Books; Dreze, Samson, and Singh (eds), *The Dam and the Nation: Displacement and Resettlement in the Narmada Valley*; Baviskar, *In the Belly of the River: Tribal Conflicts over Development in the Narmada Valley*.

[28] As pointed out, there is a large amount of literature that has responded to the issues raised by the construction of the Sardar Sarovar project. For a source of this literature see Jayal, *Democracy and the State: Welfare, Secularism, and Development in Contemporary India*, p. 254, Baviskar, *In the Belly of the River: Tribal Conflicts over Development in the Narmada Valley*.

a wider space for the expression of frustration and anger with the failure of state policies and action.[29] The state's overall response to such demands for 'deeper democracy' from civil society has been varied, ranging between greater cooperation and dialogue in some instances and ignoring them in others. Representing civil society in this democratic expansion and transformed relationship with the state have been NGOs—the civil sphere institutions of policy research and advice. Building on a more general call for reform from the grassroots upwards, NGOs are becoming catalytic agents in facilitating a movement for deeper democracy in India. Several directories provide lists of NGOs that straddle the functions of research, advocacy, mobilization, and empowerment through campaigns and education.[30] Estimates indicate that tens of thousands of NGOs operate in the sector broadly labeled 'development' and receive USD 9–10 billion from international sources and USD 35 million from domestic sources.[31]

NGOs operate at several levels, ranging from service provision at the local level, working to offset the impact of the failure of state provision, to alternative programme formulation to organizing protests. In time, they have grown to co-produce and co-deliver government services and have helped communities to organize themselves to procure services or access entitlements. At the delivery level, their impact is limited to the demands of their target population, and statutory constraints. However, their micro-level experience and practice influences wider patterns of debate about policymaking and delivery. NGOs have attempted to apply their success models to other situations and areas in the country. As alternative democratic mechanisms that consider development as a bottom-up approach, NGOs have argued for a nationwide transformation in the developmental planning process in order to expand the positive outcomes for a greater number of people at the local level.

[29] A. Roy, N. Dey, and S. Singh, 2001, 'Demanding Accountability', *Seminar*, vol. 500, no. 2, pp. 91–7.

[30] Ghanshyam Shah, 'Non-Governmental Organizations in India', mimeo.

[31] The figure on the amount of foreign funding that NGOs receive has been revised. In the context of the recent Kudankulam nuclear power plant protests, the government said that in 2009–10, NGOs received Rs 10,340.25 crore. (Source: 'NGOs' Foreign Aid: Rs. 31,000 Crore in Four Years', *Times of India*, 15 March 2012).

NGOs attempt to directly shape public policy through advocacy rather than the above-described approach of replication of best-practice models. 'They may enter policy advocacy directly by organizing campaigns and protest themselves or joining policy networks or issue-based coalitions.'[32] In the context of poverty, participation, democratization, and equity concerns, Indian NGOs have engaged in organized advocacy in fields as diverse as the informal, unorganized sector and child labour; affirmative action and protection for the disabled; a wide range of women's issues; environment, forests, and related issues such as displacement and rehabilitation; health; judicial reform; participatory management and governance; consumer rights; appropriate technology; shelter and other issues affecting the urban poor; and issues relating to their own working space.[33] The advocacy role of NGOs and their role in popular mobilization has contributed to successful policy changes such as the adoption of a joint forest management model,[34] as well as enabling improvement in top-down policy changes such as the mandated representation of women in local government institutions.[35]

In the space between service delivery and direct advocacy for policy change, NGOs have developed alliances with other non-state entities to further an alternative and participatory discourse of development. In concrete terms, NGOs have developed relationships with research institutions that tended towards a more progressive policy outlook. In turn, these institutes have played a key role as nodal institutions in the formation of policy networks and coalitions. For example, take the case of the alternative draft of the national rehabilitation policy that

[32] Khan, *Shaping Policy: Do NGOs Matter? Lessons from India*, p. 13. Khan has provided several case studies of how grassroots NGOs have pursued their advocacy activity. Of the five cases documented, the campaign for a comprehensive law for construction labour had a national perspective. Others were concerned with changes at the state or local level.

[33] Ibid.

[34] A. Joshi, 1999, 'Progressive Bureaucracy: An Oxymoron? The Case of Joint Forest Management in India', Paper 24a, London: Overseas Development Institute; Society for Promotion of Wastelands Development (SPWD), 1993, *Joint Forest Management: Regulations Update*, New Delhi: SPWD.

[35] P. Vyasalu and V. Vyasalu, 2000, 'Women in the Panchayati Raj: Grassroots Democracy in India', Proceedings of *Women's Political Participation and Good Governance: 21st Century Challenges*, New Delhi: UNDP, pp. 41–8; and A.K. Jha (ed.), 2004, *Women in Panchayati Raj Institutions*, New Delhi: Anmol Publications.

was spearheaded by Walter Fernandes, Director of the Indian Social Institute.[36] Using this institutionalized research base, a process of information-sharing and deliberation among nationwide NGOs was facilitated. This network of actors, comprising NGOs, activists, and researchers through extensive deliberations, produced not only a set of abstract principles to underpin rehabilitation policy for internally displaced persons or refugees, but also concrete alternative policy objectives and strategies to achieve them. In another example, an independent statutory commission and research institute facilitated the formation of networks in the area of the rights of women. The National Commission of Women (NCW) and the Centre for Women's Development Studies (CWDS) have supported NGOs as umbrella organizations providing a research base and form for influencing public policy, going beyond their remit of 'pure academic research' to an advocacy role.[37]

In the past few years, the support given by research institutes and NGOs that function as umbrella organizations to activists groups, including other NGOs, has enlarged the scope of public debate in searching for policy alternatives. However, government in its own right has been only half-receptive to this alternative source of policy research and action. A case in point is the report of an Independent Commission on Health submitted by the Voluntary Health Association of India (VHAI) to the central government. Formulated through participatory research and deliberative processes organized by several NGOs, it contained more than 350 recommendations in pursuit of an overhauled national health policy. To say the least, the government response was not encouraging. In a letter to VHAI, the Joint Secretary of Health in the Ministry of Health and Family Welfare referred to the tremendous effort that the government was already making by initiating

[36] Fernandes, 'An Activist Process around the Draft National Rehabilitation Policy'.

[37] The Director of CWDS in her introduction to the Centre's Annual Report emphasizes that the CWDS 'is committed to creating integral links between women's studies and the women's movement and has continued to blend research, action, and advocacy in its work while confronting the process of marginalization of women.' She adds that 'it does not view a positive value-based social intervention as being detrimental to social science research.' CWDS, 1996–7, *Annual Report*, New Delhi: CWDS, p. 1.

new programmes, and then went on to defend government policy. The letter sought to absolve the government of its failures by suggesting that 'a responsive and a conscious user will be able to revitalize the sector and make it more accountable than structural changes might be able to achieve'.[38]

However, the government has been more responsive in other instances. A demand by a network of women's groups for a more gender-just budget in 2005 was met with a surprisingly constructive response. The Joint Action Group for Women, a forum of 50-odd NGOs working on gender issues, had written to the Finance Minister pointing out the inherent failures in the bureaucratic approach and the need for greater participation of organized women's groups in the formulation of the national budget.[39] The Finance Minister responded by making relevant budget performance data reports from 18 ministries and departments available to this network as a first step towards a gender-just budgeting process. Further, alternative policy movements have used budget-setting as a key focus for transformation. The relevance of budget analysis lies in the fact that it has provided civil society with a tool through which it can effectively bring the perspectives and the concerns of the poor and marginalized into the process of policy formulation. More importantly, through budget analysis, civil society organizations have successfully demonstrated the importance of strategic engagement with the state for promoting a people-centric discourse.[40]

NGOs have also developed an independent character to mobilize challenges to the dominance of governmental policy prescriptions, envisioning an alternative kind of democratic order in India. For instance, a peoples' grassroots organization in the western state of Rajasthan, known as Mazdoor Kisan Shakti Sangathan (or Labourers and Farmers Solidarity Association), has led a struggle to fight corruption and demand government accountability, genuine decentralization, and

---

[38] Government of India, 8 January 1999, *Letter to VHAI*, New Delhi, p. 3.

[39] See Priya Sehgal, 2005, 'Budget 2005: Chidambram Promises Gender-sensitive Budget, Women Groups Compile Wish List', *India Today*, February 28, available at http://indiatoday.in/story/budget-2005-chidambram-promises-gender-sensitive-budget-women-groups-compile-wish-list/1/194181.html.

[40] Y. Aiyar and A. Behar, 2005, 'Budget Work in India: Civil Society Experiments in Democratic Engagement', *Economic and Political Weekly*, vol. 40, no. 2, pp. 108–12.

build real participatory democracy. This struggle snowballed into a countrywide movement, which ultimately led to the enactment of the Right to Information Act in 2005.[41]

The evolution of NGOs thus reflects a multi-layered transformation not only in filling gaps of state failure, but in articulating and acting through an alternative democratic discourse and providing alternative policy analyses. While early policy research institutes primarily acted as sources of data for fitting into government policy (and subsequent institutes only partly succeeded in becoming more independent, influential and inter-disciplinary), NGO-type policy institutions marked a wholesale shift in the means of policy research, analysis, and contestation. The cross-fertilization of ideas and strategies between NGOs and research institutes has developed into a vibrant dynamic of providing a clear set of alternative policy goals and action strategies in pursuit of an alternative democratic order. In some instances, governmental organizations have also been influenced to adapt and change through their interaction with NGOs. However, statutory constraints and often narrow targets imply limitations on the scope of NGOs to have a major impact on the new technocratic developmental discourse. Yet the success of their micro-models and widely credited expansion of democratic spaces do imply a constructive role in altering the terms of developmental politics. In this vein, NGOs as reflexive organizations are engaged in developing strategic alliances to have a wider impact in the contested domain of public policy.[42]

★ ★ ★

The field of policy research in India has received attention from different scholarly persuasions and institutions. While, initially, policy research was state-sponsored and had a narrow economic orientation, the successive waves of research institutions helped move towards a more interdisciplinary enterprise. The alternative development discourse broadly engendered by NGO-type policy research institutions moved policy research from an interdisciplinary focus towards the very reconceptualization of the meaning of democracy. The dominant

[41] Roy et al., 'Demanding Accountability.'

[42] Fernandes, 'An Activist Process around the Draft National Rehabilitation Policy', p. 291.

mainstream in India is still an economics-technology discourse but has much more intellectual and practical expertise to contend with. Concurrently, policy studies scholarship has also moved on from a predominantly programme evaluation orientation to the utilization of a variety of other approaches, including neo-Marxist approaches where emphasis is placed on the nature of the (bourgeois) state and the outcomes of class struggles in society to explain emerging policies. Predominantly positivist in orientation, the pluralist approaches account for policy outcomes in terms of contextual incentives, informal and formal rules, and individual and group level bargaining and rational action. In an assessment of the literature, we find that institutionalized policy analysis still maintains a substantially rationalist character, and is less engaged with making a practical contribution to the emerging discourse of a participatory democracy. Expertise and knowledge is defined through the dominant frames of information technology and global management, and sanctioned by state institutions as well as research disciplines. At the same time, NGO activity in a dynamic interaction with state and non-state institutions have been the sources for alternative policy research and alternative sources of expertise. It is to this transformative space that policy research should (and has begun to) pay greater theoretical attention, going beyond the limitations of the traditional policy research orientations towards a postpositive approach.

Our account of the changes in the field of policy analysis in India draws upon the post-positivist critique of the dominant empiricist orientation of policy analysis and converges with its analysis of trends in the West. The post-positive perspective in policy studies seeks to provide an improved reflection of the world of practice as far as policy process is concerned. Instead of attempting to insulate decision-making from everyday politics, it attempts to show that policy problems are defined in a subjective fashion and are dependent on the values and beliefs of the actors involved.[43] Policy changes can then be as due to the dynamics of complex relationships between societal actors that produce new constellations of social forces. Thus, policymaking can be recognized as a dynamic process occurring in a network society

---

[43] Fischer, *Reframing Public Policy: Discursive Politics and Deliberative Practices*, p. 25.

rather than one within hierarchies.[44] The emergence of the concept of governance brings into focus a new range of multi-level relationships among various governmental institutions, civil society organizations, and international organizations. Policy analysis would then move away from the pretense of objective and value-neutral policy analysis assumed in the scientific approach and would open the door to a participatory democracy where citizens can take part in meaningful debates and contest policy issues that deeply affect them.[45] The movement we have identified in this chapter in the Indian policymaking approach is of this order. As a normative project, the participatory imperatives seek to inform the kind of democracy that should evolve in India, rather than seeking to make corrections in programmes alone. Moving beyond identifying incremental solutions to merely augment the skills of the politician and bureaucrat, this research orientation seeks to empower citizens to participate in decision-making and to engage in a transformative democratic policy analysis.

[44] Hajer and Wagenaar, *Deliberative Policy Analysis: Understanding Governance in the Network Society*, pp. 4–18.

[45] Fischer, *Reframing Public Policy: Discursive Politics and Deliberative Practices*, p. 15.

3

Policy Research Organizations in South Asia*

With the rise and growth of relatively autonomous policy research organizations in the countries of South Asia, there has been considerable interest not only in their activities, but also in the role that they play in public policymaking. There is increasing recognition of the fact that government does not choose policies in a vacuum, nor do leaders decide without any basis. They seek policy advice and now do not restrict themselves to internal governmental institutions. Policy research organizations have proliferated because governments have sought advice from alternative sources, and also because civil society has become more active and finds space to influence public policy. However, South Asian scholarship has paid little attention to this dimension of the policy process. It is true that considerable social science research has been devoted to investigating policy outcomes and its impact. However, it is also true that considerably less is known on how and when social science research influences policy and why.

The purpose of this chapter is to broadly understand the factors that have led to the rise of policy research organizations in South Asia and the kind of role that they have performed. The chapter will examine the general socio-political environment and character of social science

* Kuldeep Mathur, 2009, 'Policy Research Organizations in South Asia', *IDRC Canada and CSLG Working Paper*, New Delhi: IDRC, pp. 1–37.

research context that shapes the characteristics of policy research organizations. These contexts differ in the countries of South Asia and the chapter will attempt to delineate how this difference has shaped these organizations.[1]

That the character of the political system is the key to the way public policy is deliberated, formulated, and implemented, is a widely accepted notion. The two extremes of open- and closed-ended political systems are associated with a distinctive policy process. Closed political systems are more likely to have a policy process that is centralized, secretive, and unresponsive; whereas open political systems are likely to be associated with a reverse set of characteristics: decentralized, consultative, and responsive. However, these are ideal types, and characteristics associated with a closed political system are not limited to authoritarian regimes but may continue to persist in new democracies in the developing world.[2] There can also be variations of policy processes as a political system evolves from a formal democratic system to a more meaningful participative democracy.

Policy process is also influenced by the strategy of economic development. A closely directed and state-led economy leaves little space for alternative policy advice. Much of the advice emanates from the government establishment itself. On the other hand, as liberalization of the economy takes place, policy processes tend to be more open to critical evaluation. Essentially then, democratization, participation, and liberalization have a strong influence on the role that relatively autonomous policy research organizations play.

Weaver and Stares suggest that the nature of representative government is also changing.[3] With the rise of many political parties, and formation of coalition governments, the nature of democratic process is becoming fractured. As a result, the demand for alternative policy advice is growing. In addition, civil society is increasingly becoming active; demanding greater transparency and accountability

---

[1] The discussion is based on the broad trends in each country. Some prominent institutions are mentioned. This does not purport to be an exhaustive list of policy research organizations in each country.

[2] Robinson, 'Democracy, Participation, and Public Policy: The Politics of Institutional Design', pp. 150–86.

[3] Weaver and Stares, *Guidance for Governance: Comparing Alternative Sources of Public Policy Advice*, pp. 1–4.

in the functioning of the government. This has further increased the demand for imaginative and impartial sources of policy advice. The response has been in terms of more policy research organizations and more research-based advocacy groups.

Economic liberalization has also led to the increasing role of multilateral institutions in a country's social and economic development. Before deciding on aids/grants, these institutions are interested in analyzing economic performance of the recipients, and seek advice on how this performance could be improved if found inadequate. Consequently, they sponsor studies to help them formulate their aid/ grant policies. This demand is also helping policy research organizations multiply.

SOUTH ASIA

India and Pakistan emerged as independent nations in 1947, which saw the partition of British India into the present two countries; while Bangladesh declared its independence from Pakistan in 1971. The history of the birth of these three nations was marked by severe social and political turmoil, the memories of which continue to influence public perceptions of each other till today. Independence came to Sri Lanka in 1948. One characteristic common to all these countries, is the heritage of British colonial rule which is discernible in their rules, laws, and institutions. Nepal is the only country of the region that was untouched by colonization and has been a monarchy till only a few months back.

Countries of South Asia have followed different political paths. India has remained a vibrant democracy since it declared itself a republic in 1950 and held its first national elections in 1951–2. Fourteen elections have followed, and the transitions of governments have been largely peaceful and orderly. The period of 1975–7, however, was an exception when fundamental rights were suspended and Emergency provisions of the Constitution were invoked to govern the country. The elections of 1977 restored democracy.

Pakistan began as a democracy, but after the assassination of the first Prime Minister, it declared itself as an Islamic Republic in 1956. Soon after, there was a coup and the army took over the reins of government under the leadership of Marshal Ayub Khan. He was replaced by another Army General, Yahya Khan, in 1969, after which came the

Indo-Pakistan war that led to the secession of Bangladesh in 1971. This was followed by a spell of civilian rule under Zulfiquar Ali Bhutto, following which the army again took over under the leadership of General Zia-ul-Haq. The general died in an air crash in 1988, making way for another spell of civilian rule, which again, was cut short by General Musharraf taking over in 1999. The country has gone through turbulent times and even the return of civilian rule in 2008 was marked by violence and the assassination of a popular leader of a political party that was fighting the national elections.

Bangladesh was plunged into army rule soon after independence with the assassination of the leadership that had led the country to freedom. A series of bloody coups and counter-coups in the following three months culminated in the ascent to power of General Ziaur Rahman. He was assassinated in 1981 by elements of the military, and Bangladesh's next military ruler was General H.M. Ershad, who gained power in a bloodless coup in 1982 and ruled until 1990. Bangladesh reverted to democracy with keen contests from parties led by the daughter of its founder and the widow of its past ruler. Military rule has been interspersed with civilian regimes; and as of 2008, the leaders of the two national contending parties have been released from jail but no political activity is permitted by the military rulers. In early 2009, elections were held and democracy was restored.

The name of Ceylon was changed to Sri Lanka when it declared itself a republic in 1972. It had become independent in 1948 and was granted a dominion status within the British Commonwealth. It has continued as a democracy since its birth as an independent nation. However, since 1983, the country has been battling severe civil strife due to a separatist militant organization fighting to create an independent state named Tamil Eelam in the North and East of the island.

Each one of the above mentioned four countries has had one stable feature—a unified civil service. Often, members of the higher civil service tended to occupy most of the critical positions in government in these countries. They were the single most important group of advisors in all sectors of economic, social, and security policies. In Pakistan and Bangladesh, military advisors replaced these civil service advisors in many cases, but they usually worked together. In India, armed forces have not entered any civilian positions. Higher civil service has been powerful in influencing policy and has also been the sieve through which alternative advice is filtered. In all these countries, the civil service remains influential as gatekeepers of all information reaching the decision-makers.[4]

Nepal has been a traditional monarchy. The monarchs have ruled with some semblance of people's participation, but the final authority has been the king. In recent years, Nepal has witnessed national struggles for adopting democracy. For some time, it was in the midst of militancy propagated by Maoist groups. In 2007, an Interim Parliament was formed and a bill was passed which declared Nepal as a Federal Democratic Republic. Elections were held in 2008 and a democratic government took over.

With this thumb-nail sketch of the political history of South Asian countries, it also needs to be mentioned that these countries are among the poorer countries of the world. The United Nations has placed them in the following positions in its rankings on Human Development in 2007:

TABLE 3.1: Human Development in South Asia

Countries	Human Development Rank*	Life Expectancy (Years)	Adult Lit. (%)
India	128	63.7	61.0
Pakistan	136	64.6	49.9
Bangladesh	140	63.1	47.5
Sri Lanka	99	71.6	90.7
Nepal	142	62.6	48.6

Source: UNDP Human Development Report http://hdr.undp.org/en/statistics/.
Note: * Out of 177 countries.

What must be noted is that Sri Lanka has done better than all other countries of South Asia in the field of human development. India has had a higher rate of economic growth in the last decade or so, surpassing its own trend of 1951–91, but has not done so well in the human welfare sector.

---

[4] All these South Asian countries have adopted varying forms of parliamentary system of government, giving a preeminent advisory role to the permanent civil service.

In short, countries that are poor and have gone through, or are undergoing political turmoil since their independence, are the focus of this study. The process of policymaking as well as the nature of policy research institutions have been influenced to a great extent by the continuities and discontinuities in the strategy adopted for social and economic development and for meeting political challenges.

INDIA

Centralized Planning Effort

An institution that has had significant impact on determining the direction and content of public policies in India is the Planning Commission. Established as a technical body of experts and commanding a certain amount of autonomy from everyday political pulls and pressures, the Planning Commission often heavily influenced economic decisions. During the years of its primacy, the role of technocrats and experts rose. The institutionalization of the role of the Planning Commission was one of the major influences in establishing a technocratic policy environment in which government used technical advice to legitimize its policies. Many policies were defended only for technical reasons and not put to public debate.[5]

Professor Mahalanobis, who headed the Indian Statistical Institute in Calcutta, played the most important role in shaping the Planning Commission and influencing public policies. The Indian Statistical Institute (ISI) became a prominent player in research backup for the Planning Commission; a close associate of Mahalanobis headed the Perspective Planning Division. There was a steady stream of international economists, and the Perspective Planning Division together with the Indian Statistical Institute was host to many of their research endeavours.[6] With the return of more and more brilliant Indian economists from abroad, the Planning Commission was looking for ways of utilizing their expertise. The concern was also to create national capability for policy research and not concentrate all efforts in Delhi or in the Planning Commission alone.

[5] Chatterjee, 'Development Planning and the Indian State', pp. 82–103; and Khilnani, *The Idea of India*, pp. 85–8.

[6] George Rosen, 1985, *Western Economists and Eastern Societies: Agents of Change in South Asia, 1950–1970*, New Delhi: Oxford University Press.

'The need to strengthen capabilities of institutions outside the government in the field of economics in order to provide independent sources of economic data and of evaluation of planning and to improve management, especially for what would be a growing public sector' was recognized by the Planning Commission quite early, during the First Five-Year Plan. A Research Programmes Committee, consisting of leading social scientists, was established in the Planning Commission to determine priorities for government support of institutional research relevant to planning.[7] At the same time, the Ford Foundation came forward to strengthen existing institutions or help establish new institutions. The Institute of Economic Growth was established in 1958. A grant was given to the Gokhale Institute to expand its facilities. The National Council of Applied Economic Research was established in 1956 with the support of Ford Foundation.

What is most significant about this Nehruvian period is that the influence of experts (read economists) and technocrats rose significantly as they moved effortlessly in and out of the government. They carried through the three Plans formulated under the leadership of Nehru without much dissension or debate. In general, experts either joined the government or chose to remain outside with adequate support to conduct policy-oriented research. Usually, the policy advice emanating from this research fell within the planning framework that had been adopted. During this phase, government funded and helped develop some research institutes that conducted policy-oriented research. These institutions had close links with government and the Planning Commission, and they brought academic expertise to monitor and evaluate development programmes and provide data that would be direct inputs for the formulation of public policies.[8]

The period after Nehru was a period of transformation in the role of the Planning Commission. While the practice of preparing Five-Year Plans continued, the Finance Ministry played a greater role in financial allocations; and other ministries, in setting sectoral targets. As more

[7] Ibid., p. 88.
[8] In any case, there were few alternatives articulated to the dominant planning paradigm. The only dissent came from the Gandhians; but their influence could not counter the dominance of the 'modernizers.' A lone economist, Dr Shenoy, dissented on fundamental grounds of opposition to planning and spoke for free enterprise.

and more state governments began to be led by political parties not necessarily in harmony with the party/coalition ruling at the Centre, the influence of the Planning Commission in determining state plans and priorities also declined. So, while in Nehru's time (1950s) critics were known to label it as 'super cabinet'; Rajiv Gandhi (1980s), in a hurry to liberalize the economy, saw the institution as a 'bunch of jokers'.

In the period after the economic reforms were introduced in 1991, the Planning Commission began to play a role in identifying the dimensions of policy environment that needed changes to support the private sector. In some sense, as Ahluwalia points out, the Commission acts as a think-tank for the government by proposing policy initiatives that are necessary to achieve Plan targets and by providing advice and critical evaluation of the effectiveness of policies in all sectors.[9]

Whatever transformation may have taken place in the role of the Planning Commission and in economic policies, the belief in the superiority of technical expertise or economic reasoning continues to dominate policy formulation even though the membership of the Planning Commission has diversified.

The Growth of Policy Research Institutions

Centralized planning and the wide ranging role of the state in promoting social and economic development demand phenomenally large amounts of data and information. Because the Planning Commission alone could not generate this information as inputs to policymaking, Government of India began to build a series of institutions that could perform this task in specialized sectors. Over the years, such institutions proliferated and diversified. The Planning Commission contracted out research studies and sought help in procuring data as inputs into the work of many of its committees. When the Planning Commission dominated policymaking, most research institutions in turn sought support for their research projects. Thus, the policy research institutions of this phase were financially dependent on the government through

[9] M.S. Ahluwalia, 2008, 'Planning Then and Now', *Seminar*, no. 589, September, pp. 18–24. Montek Singh Ahluwalia, currently Deputy Chairman of the Planning Commission, is a close confidante of Prime Minister Manmohan Singh and was a member of Manmohan Singh's team that introduced economic reforms in 1991.

the Planning Commission, and incorporated government functionaries in their policymaking bodies. Having government representation on an institution's governing bodies ensured that the government's policy research concerns were met. Institutions also did not object to this practice because it gave them hope that their work would be accepted. Many of the institutions so established, have outgrown this dependence. In the past quarter-century, more institutions that claim autonomy from government funding, and act as independent think-tanks and advocacy groups, have emerged.[10]

An important task undertaken by the government-supported research institutions was that of evaluating the implementation of policies and programmes. The Planning Commission had a Programme Evaluation Division that undertook such studies; but more and more of such studies began to be farmed out to these institutions as demands for independent evaluation grew. Such project-based research funded by the government was an added financial support for the research institutions. Research institutions found themselves linked with the Planning Commission in at least the process of policy analysis, if not direct policymaking.

Early in the era of planning in India, the ISI emerged as the most influential research institution. Founded in Calcutta in 1931 by P.C. Mahalanobis, who had gained Nehru's trust and confidence, it was the main catalyst for basing India's strategy of development on heavy industry during the Second and Third Five-Year Plans (1955–65).[11] The ISI was a pillar of excellence in India's still sparse academic

[10] These institutions are in addition to the nodal statistical agencies like the Central Statistical Organization or the National Sample Survey Organization, both part of the government and which periodically generate information. Almost all departments of the central government have units or directorates to compile data, monitor developments, and advice on policy.

[11] In 1940, Jawaharlal Nehru asked Mahalanobis to prepare a statistical commentary on the reports of the National Planning Committee of the Indian National Congress. Nehru visited the Institute in 1946 where, impressed by its activities and performance, he began to take keen interest in its work. In 1949, Nehru asked Mahalanobis to work as Honorary Statistical Adviser to the Cabinet, Government of India. This led to a closer connection of the Institute with national planning activities and, on 17 March 1955, Mahalanobis submitted to the Government of India a Draft Plan Frame that was accepted

landscape.[12] During this period, the ISI became the hub of economic analysts; and the ties with the Planning Commission became so close, that it established its unit on the premises of the Planning Commission. Mahalanobis invited foreign as well as Indian economists to the ISI in order to exchange ideas and offer guidance on the direction of movement of India's planning framework. Visitors included John Kenneth Galbraith, Paul Baran, Nicholas Kaldor, Paul Streeten, Ragnar Frisch, and John Sandee.[13]

The decade of 1956–65 saw the establishment of many institutions, the motivation for which seems to have been a need to compensate for the absence of a policy research environment in Indian universities. Early research institutions were also established to supply data (because the reason for failure of policies/plans was considered to be the lack of data interlinked with consequences of poor implementation). The establishment of many departments of public administration in universities shifted attention to problems of implementation and not policy analysis. During these years, key problems were framed as gaps in implementation; lack of coordination; and poorly developed roles of policymaking and implementation professionals.[14]

The more prominent of these early institutions were the National Council of Educational Research and Training and the Indian Institute of Public Administration in 1954; the National Council of Applied Economic Research in 1956; the National Institute of Education Planning and Administration (now a deemed university); the National Institute of Family Planning and Health (now Family Welfare and Health); the Institute of Applied Manpower Research; the National Labour Institute; and the Institute of Economic Growth in 1958. A prominent institution not connected with economic research emerged as the Centre for the Study of Developing Societies in 1962. Some of these institutions were fully funded and controlled by the government.

---

as the basis for the formulation of India's Second Five-Year Plan (available at www.vigyanprasar.gov..in/comcom/develop83.htm).

[12] J. Adams, 2006, 'Economics, Economists and the Indian Economy', *India Review*, vol. 5, pp. 37–61.

[13] Rosen, *Western Economists and Eastern Societies: Agents of Change in South Asia, 1950–1970*, p. 59.

[14] Mathur and Mathur, 'Policy Analysis in India: Research Bases and Discursive Practices', p. 605.

Ford Foundation provided financial grants for institution-building and for supporting specialized programmes to many of these institutions.

The second phase of the growth of policy research institutions began with the establishment of the Indian Council of Social Science Research (ICSSR), that today funds 27 research institutes. During the time that the Planning Commission acted as the 'think-tank' for the country, it funded research and encouraged scholars who had not joined the government to conduct research on issues on which it placed high priority. Funds came through its Research Planning Committee (RPC) that had been established during the First Plan period. As planning came under a cloud, and when a 'plan holiday' was declared during 1966–8, the formulation of the Fourth Five-Year Plan encountered difficulty. At this time, a proposal appeared to transfer funds administered by the RPC to an autonomous institution that would promote research institutes and sponsor independent research. The ICSSR was therefore established in 1969 to establish research institutions on a regional basis. All the institutions established during the first phase had been located in Delhi. Many of the strong institutions outside Delhi were started with the explicit intention of countering the centrifugal attractions of the capital. The aim was to provide substantive inputs to regional policies, as well as the evaluation and interpretation of central mandates at the regional level.[15]

Establishing policy research institutions outside the universities was also a commentary on the state of social science research in them. They were seen burdened by teaching and less concerned with research. Within the science sector, a model of establishing research institutes that could support industrial innovation under the Council of Scientific and Industrial Research had been accepted. This model came in handy for social science research too.

Another spurt of organizational growth appeared in the 1980s, a decade that saw a shift towards greater liberalization in Indian macroeconomic policy as well as in the use of foreign funding. This period was characterized by fewer state funds for research, but an

[15] R. Sudershan, 2001, 'New Partnerships in Research: Activists and Think-Tanks—An Illustration from NCAER', in Diane Stone (ed.), *Banking on Knowledge: The Genesis of Global Development Networks*, London: Routledge, pp. 87–103.

increase in donor and private domestic funding. These factors, along with the availability of a generation of Indians who had been involved in policymaking by post-independence governments, lay behind the creation of 'second-wave' institutes. Notable among these are the Indian Council for Research on International Economic Relations in 1981, the Research and Information Systems in 1983, the Indira Gandhi Institute of Development Research in 1986, and, earlier, in 1973, the Centre for Policy Research.

The third phase can be identified as a period when civil society organizations and privately supported institutions emerged as research-based policy advocacy groups. Think-tanks with sectoral specializations and an advocacy stance were set up at different times. Some of these specialized institutes have played crucial roles in defining policy and advocacy. These include the Indian Institute of Population Studies in Mumbai in 1956; the National Institute of Rural Development in Hyderabad in 1958; and in Delhi, the Indian Institute of Foreign Trade in 1963, the Institute of Defense Study and Analysis in 1965, the Tata Energy Research Institute in 1974 (now The Energy and Resources Institute—TERI), the National Institute of Urban Affairs in 1976, the Centre for Science and Environment as well as the Centre for Women's Development Studies in 1980, and in 1982, the Society for Participatory Research in Asia.[16]

These institutes aimed at providing opportunities to non-economic social sciences to address policy needs, and were also meant to serve as centres for multidisciplinary research. The names of most of these institutes underlined the multidisciplinary nature of their academic interests. Thus, there was a Centre of Development Studies in Trivandrum, a Madras Institute of Development Studies in Chennai, an Institute of Social and Economic Change in Bangalore, and a Sardar Patel Institute of Social and Economic Research in Ahmedabad. Eminent economists like V.K.R.V. Rao, K.N. Raj, Malcolm Adisesasiah, and D.T. Lakdawala led many of these institutes. But, aspirations to the contrary notwithstanding, major research projects continued to be dominated by economists, who also filled most of the faculty positions. However, as more studies began to focus on evaluation and on the

---

[16] The policy research and advocacy institutions mentioned here do not provide a full listing of such institutions in India.

impact of government programmes, inputs from other social sciences began to rise and the character of the faculty also changed.

In 2006, there were around 500 members of faculty in the ICSSR-supported institutes. Institute of Social and Economic Change in Bangalore and the Institute of Economic Growth in Delhi were among the largest institutes with faculty exceeding 40 members. The smallest were those located in Dharwad, Bhubaneswar and Guwahati where the faculty numbered between five and nine persons. Exact data about the specific social sciences represented in the faculty are not available; although, from the output of books from these institutes classified by disciplines in the *2007 Review Report*, economists seem to be most productive. Of 69 books published by the faculty through selected publishers, 29 are from Economics, 19 from Sociology, 14 from Political Science, 6 from History and 1 from Geography.[17]

The manner in which these institutes emerged influenced the space that they came to occupy in their relations with the government. How much notice the government took of their research findings depended greatly on the role and influence of their respective leaders. Working as members of important government committees, the leaders acted as 'policy brokers' to promote the research findings of their institutes and mobilize funds for more research. As the founders left the scene, the bridges that these institutes had built with the government weakened. For other reasons too, most of these institutes no longer command the status and prestige that they once had. Many institutes that emerged after 1989 are struggling to establish themselves. In most cases, they are inadequately funded and have been unable to attract alternative sources of funding.

In a perceptive study of ICSSR-sponsored research, Weiner acknowledged the wide variation in the quality of research conducted at these institutes and their kinds of policy-oriented work.[18] However, he stressed that even 'though these institutes have not yet made a conspicuous impact on public debates over policies, several have made state governments—at least some officials, if not politicians aware of the value of research for policy and programme development, and for

[17] ICSSR, 2007, *ICSSR Review Committee Report*, New Delhi, Annexures I and II, pp. 74–129.

[18] Weiner, 'Social Science Research and Public Policy in India'.

assessing the consequences of governmental interventions'.[19] Many years later, the Fourth Review Committee of the ICSSR expressed the following opinion:

Operational and policy-centric studies have been and will remain an important component of social science research. It will continue to attract substantial funding from government, business and international organizations. Even if it needs larger funding, it is necessary to pay more attention to improve quality; make the studies available in the public domain open to professional scrutiny; and utilize them to widen and deepen the knowledge base.[20]

It is difficult to assess the actual role of these institutes in the policy process. A director of an eminent institute emphasized that their main role has been in the generation of ideas. Sometimes, politicians and bureaucrats pick them up; but, to make an impact, the ideas require constant repetition like the chanting of a 'mantra'. He had found politicians to be more receptive to change than bureaucrats. A member of another institute noted that bureaucrats needed a great deal of convincing, a process that takes time. Then, when one bureaucrat who can make a difference gets convinced, he is transferred to another post. His replacement may be unwilling to pick up the thread from where it had been left, and another round of convincing must begin.

A prominent member of the faculty at an Indian Institute of Management, working in the area of urban governance echoed similar views. He felt that sponsoring a research study is seen only as a formality, and the usual comments of bureaucrats ignoring findings of a study are 'not relevant' or 'not feasible'. He went on to add that public policymaking in India is 'individual-centric' and bureaucrats do not pursue any systemic change.

Furthermore, rarely do the researchers interact and discuss the findings and policy recommendations of their study with decision-makers. Bureaucrats act as gatekeepers and allow only such information that they perceive useful for policymaking to go through. This is usually a behind-the-scene process and has disheartening effects on most staff in these institutes. An ICSSR administrator, long involved in monitoring the work of these institutions laments that 'today, neither

---

[19] Weiner, 'Social Science Research and Public Policy in India', p. 315.
[20] ICSSR, *Review Committee Report*, p. 37.

policy relevance nor excellence in research is the identifying feature of these institutes'. It is fair to say that few institutes have developed an ideological identity. Influential views were more often expressed on an individual basis by policy-oriented scholars spread across these institutes.

Due to this increased awareness, many institutes outside the ambit of the ICSSR have appeared. Some have partial support from the central government. Others have raised funds through endowments from state governments. Still others have received support through international funding. Most do not depend on a single source of funds. Among the institutes that promote alternative policies are the National Institute of Public Finance and Policy, the Centre for Science and Environment, the Tata Energy Research Institute (now The Energy and Resources Institute—TERI), and the Institute of Social Sciences. A characteristic of these institutes is that, apart from conducting research, they play an important advocacy role by publicizing their studies in the media and holding seminars for relevant policymakers. Replying to an interview question by a newspaper, the Director of TERI defined his role by asserting that '(the institute) has generated a wealth of information and data and it is our job to bombard policymakers through letters, workshops, and individual meetings. I think the challenge starts from here'.[21]

Today, India boasts of a large network of research institutes supplemented by university departments. Despite the large output of research studies, the debate in India centres around the extent to which these studies influence public policies, as well as the nature and quality of this research.

Research-Policy Dynamic

There are several ways of conceiving the research-policy dynamic. Stone identified ten ways, but concluded that the impact of research is uncertain and depends on social and political contexts.[22] She further argues that the normative dimension of research and policymaking

---

[21] *Express Newsline*, 24 February 2000, interview.

[22] Diane Stone, Simon Maxwell, and Michael Keating, 2001, 'Bridging Research and Policy: An International Workshop', Warwick University, 16–17 July, p. 4.

cannot be ignored. Reference to 'knowledge' or 'research' does not signify a single body of commonly recognized and accepted thinking, data or literature. However, although research may not directly influence specific policies, it is widely recognized that the production of research still exerts a powerful indirect influence by introducing new terms and shaping policy discourse.[23]

Concerning the role of economists in public policymaking, Reddy distinguishes between economic ideas and economists' ideas.[24] He suggests that one role of a trained economist in public policy is to clarify and dispel notions that intuitively appear to be right, but actually cause adverse consequences (that is, counterintuitive but rational). S/he also evaluates the consequences of lobbies for various causes (-neutral analysis or counting the cost). To describe the role of economists in policymaking, Reddy uses the term 'technopols'. A successful technopol needs to combine two very different types of skills. One is that of a successful applied economist, able to judge what institutions and policies are needed in specific circumstances in order to further economic objectives. The other is that of a successful politician, able to persuade others to adopt the policies that s/he has judged to be appropriate.

From the strength of the discipline as well as the needs of public policy, economists have been the most important policy advisors in India. During the early days of planning, Indian economists were joined by many Western economists. Rosen provides a comprehensive account of the interactions between American and Indian economists that were mediated by the Centre for International Studies at the Massachusetts Institute of Technology, and funded by the Ford Foundation.[25] Another facet of the involvement of Indian economists in policy deliberations came through internal participation. Most of them joined government at various points in their careers and mobilized research support for

[23] M. De Vibe, I Hovland, and J. Young, 2002, *Bridging Research and Policy: An Annotated Bibliography,* London: Overseas Development Institute.

[24] Y.V. Reddy, 1997, 'Economists and Public Policy', Valedictory Address of the Deputy Governor, Reserve Bank of India, at the 80th Annual Conference of the Indian Economics Association, Osmania University, Hyderabad (29 December).

[25] Rosen, *Western Economists and Eastern Societies: Agents of Change in South Asia, 1950–1970.*

the institutions to which they belonged. This involvement helped to strengthen the institutions in their policy focus, and establish linkages with government departments.

The role of research institutes in policymaking has depended on who carried their findings to government. Convincing arguments and scientific consensus are not sufficient to shift policy. During the 1950s and 1960s, the dominant ideology of planning was not questioned; attention was focused on finding ways to devise strategies that would improve the performance of planning. In her study of NCAER, Sudershan states that in the earlier decades, the Council did not question the government's approach to development.[26] The policy environment changed after 1980, when economic reforms were introduced. Greater disputation of the policies followed, and alternatives were suggested. A different genre of research institutes appeared. Some of them were headed by neo-liberal economists; others responded to the impacts of environmental degradation. Institutions of the former type included the National Institute of Public Finance and Policy; the Centre for Science and Environment was among the latter type.

Policy Research Institutes and Social Science Research

An important reason for the Planning Commission favouring the establishment of new research institutions was the perception that universities in India were not yet at a level of competence suitable for policymaking. Because universities could not provide adequate research, a decision was made to support institutions outside the university system. The institutions would focus on research rather than on teaching and examinations, emphasize policy issues rather than theory, and be allowed flexibility in personnel and salary scales that would permit them to attract able young Indian social scientists who were being trained in India and abroad.[27] The ISI, already working outside the university system, provided the model for government-supported institutions that were established after the First Plan. The years after the Fourth Five-Year Plan (1965–70) featured much

[26] Sudershan, 'New Partnerships in Research: Activists and Think-Tanks—An Illustration from NCAER', pp. 87–103.

[27] Rosen, *Western Economists and Eastern Societies: Agents of Change in South Asia, 1950–1970*, pp. 101–46.

discussion on the role that these research institutes played in contributing to policymaking and building social science knowledge. Weiner was among the earliest to consider these issues.[28]

In a study sponsored by the Social Science Research Council in New York, Chatterjee comments on the state of social science research in India.[29] His report notes that scholars at the research institutes; referring to their connections with training programmes and dissemination efforts by reaching out to decision-makers, movements and activists; agreed that their institutes were appropriate places for serious academic research in the basic as well as applied social sciences. The major issue, however, remains the quality of research. A recurrent theme in discussions of social science research in India is that the institutions and practices of social science are on the verge of irretrievable collapse. Other social scientists lament the poor quality of research output and indifferent impact on policymaking.[30]

More often than not, the non-university research institutes set up with government support decline due to lack of adequate financial support. Faculty positions lie vacant, facilities including libraries deteriorate, and funds are not available for research. Project funds, whenever available, respond to the immediate concerns of a client agency. Suffering from gross under-funding, the research institutes have to seek alternative sources of funds. 'Social support and respect cannot be assumed; it needs to be earned. As a research community, our ability to influence state policy and society will improve only if we can also put our own houses in order'.[31] The President of the Centre for Policy Research echoes similar sentiments in a comment in a newspaper. Pointing to

[28] Myron Weiner, 1979, 'Social Science Research and Public Policy in India', *Economic and Political Weekly*, vol. 15, pp. 1579–87 and 1613–28 (15 & 22 September).

[29] Partha Chatterjee et al., 2002 'Social Science Research Capacity in South Asia: A Report', vol. 6, New York: Social Science Research Council Working Paper Series, p. 94.

[30] Harsh Sethi, 2000, 'Social Science Research: Dark Days Ahead', *Economic and Political Weekly*, vol. 35, no. 40, 30 September, pp. 3549–50; A.V. Vaidyanathan, 2001, 'Social Science Research in India: Some Emerging Issues', *Economic and Political Weekly*, vol. 36, no. 2, 13 January, pp. 112–14.

[31] Harsh Sethi, 2002, 'Social Science Research: The Real Challenge', *Economic and Political Weekly*, vol. 39, pp. 3113–4 (18 August).

the lack of a robust, serious, and deep culture of academics, think-tanks, and a vibrant university system, he doubts that engagement with the outside world will be as effective as the situations demand.[32]

Autonomy

Unlike the early days of planning, social scientists in contemporary India feel hesitant to associate too closely with government. Given a severe ideological divide, working for the government, labels the social scientists. Consequently, the former easy movement of social scientists between their research institutions and the government has been affected by the phenomenon of 'commitment'. This commitment recently became contentious when some objected to the appointments of the Planning Commission to its many committees alleging that the appointees owed allegiance elsewhere because they had previously served international agencies. Such an issue had not appeared in the 1950s when the Planning Commission served as a sounding board for development economics by allowing all economists—national and international—to serve together on its committees. The political environment thus, has changed considerably.

Associated with this situation, many social scientists underline the need for autonomy from the government in order to conduct quality research. 'Autonomy' is linked with the perception that government support generally focuses a little too sharply on policy relevance and takes the researchers away from theoretical concerns. In the academic pecking order, work on theory ranks higher than that on practice. Thus, by inviting far closer scrutiny and rigorous examination, policy-related research discourages many. There is also the feeling that as the institutes move towards multiple sources for funding for their research, policy demands tend to displace the concerns of quality research. This is particularly true with increased project funding.

The demand for well-researched advice is declining from the government's side as well. Political leaders and administrators look for quick-fix solutions; preoccupied as they are with day-to-day problems. Even if they do commission research, their interest wanes by the time

[32] Pratap Bhanu Mehta, 2008, 'Not So Credible India: Why the World Sees India's Foreign Policy as Non-Serious and Whimsical', *Indian Express*, New Delhi, 24 April, p. 10.

the research gets completed. In addition, their successors sometimes do not evince that kind of interest.

One other dimension of autonomy, that is not discussed so often, is the freedom of the professional faculty led by the head of an institute from the unwarranted control of the governing board.[33] It was pointed out that the role of an academic leader belongs to the head of an institute and the governing boards should not usurp it. It was further argued, that most directors want a non-interfering board that looks at broad policy and helps the institute follow the vision it has set for itself.

Research Utilization for Policymaking

The model of research utilization for policymaking in India presents a haphazard picture. Initiative taken by the government in establishing research institutions at the beginning of the planning period indicates recognition of the fact that research can contribute to policymaking. During that early phase, government aligned itself closely with the ISI and some other institutes that it had established. One characteristic of these institutes had been their academic orientation; they sought to influence public policy through the excellence of their research. Unlike 'think-tanks' in the US or the UK that play avowedly advocacy roles, these institutes try to project an image of 'neutral' research that is internationally recognized. Professionalism in research and recognition in the academic world are actively sought values. The expectation is that the government will pick up research findings for policy use because of these attributes.

Another characteristic of the research-policy dynamic in India is the prominent role of economists. They were appointed to advisory positions in the government and their advice was eagerly sought. Economists within and outside the government have played a significant role as policy advisors. No other group of social scientists has achieved the prominence that they have acquired.

Changes in the policy environment began when planning went into decline and policies were contested. Institutions within the government also improved and began providing better quality data

---

[33] Discussion at the IDRC Round Table on 'Policy Environment', Puducherry, 25 January 2009. Invited social scientists from India participated in this Round Table.

that administrators considered more reliable. While the government-supported institutes pursued goals of social science research that were not of particular short-term relevance to the policymakers, other institutes funded by NGOs or private business groups conducted research in order to contest existing policies and to provide alternatives. Since the 1990s, the government has chosen its 'own' research to formulate policy. It is widely recognized that although research institutions may have influence on specific policies, they lack, in general, the direct influence that existed in the first decade after independence. Contemporary research indirectly influences policies by introducing new terms and shaping the policy discourse.

An indicator of the diminishing interest of public policymakers in utilizing research in their policy decisions has been the gradual decline of financial support to government-sponsored research institutes and to the ICSSR. The research gap appears to be filled by an increasing number of NGOs and independent policy analysts. International agencies are becoming major sponsors of policy-relevant research to support their programmes of aid and advice to governments. These agencies often fund projects and hold the policy research organizations accountable for them. In other cases, individual academics are supported by them. Some Indian academics find this channel rewarding to pursue their policy interests. Rarely have the international agencies supported policy research institutions through endowments. What is significant is that the results of such research find a more favourable echo in policy channels, than those of research having local sponsors. At the aforementioned IDRC Round Table in 2009, some concern was expressed about the way policy research is getting increasingly directed through international funding.

PAKISTAN

Pakistan's commitment to economic development emerged at the same time as that of India as they both became independent together. As already pointed out, Pakistan's political history has been one of democratic regimes interspersed with military rule. As a consequence, there are discontinuities in economic policy. In narrating the experience of the Ford Foundation and the role of the Harvard Advisory Group, Rosen has pointed out that different regimes had different priorities, and more attention was given to consolidation of power than long-term plans of development.[34] Conflicts were engendered because of strong political regional differences between the two provinces of West and East Pakistan. Any rational policy analysis floundered on the issues of regional imbalances, and the tussle over division of resources was essentially political rather than economic. The East–West tensions also coincided with the period when the Pakistani elite were fighting their internal battles between those who had migrated from India and those who were native-born in Pakistan. Both of these struggles had a significant impact on the way staffing of the Planning Commission was approached and particularly on the working of the Pakistan Institute of Development Studies that emerged as a policy research organization to support its work.

The relationship between economic decision-making and research was tenuous. The First Five-Year Plan was prepared in 1955. At this time, much of the work was done by the Harvard advisors; the Pakistani staff was either not available or not of the required level of competence. An advisor described the procedure of allocation of resources as highly subjective—'very arbitrary…decisions…reached almost exclusively by economists though not really on economic grounds…'[35] The greatest limitation on economic decision-making based on research was the domination of political interests. Commitment to economic development became the main plank for the Ayub Khan regime and the Second Plan was prepared on time in 1960. The Planning Commission was strengthened and an able administrator took over as chairman. However, by the time the need to prepare the Third Plan came, the political differences between the two provinces had become acute. The east Pakistani elites felt that the Ayub regime was moving far too slowly to bridge the widening disparity between the two provinces; they wanted each region to control its economy. The Ayub Khan regime rejected this as a prelude to political separation.[36]

This conflict spilled over into issues of professional staffing in the policy planning institutions. Economists appeared to be better trained in the University of Dacca (now Dhaka), which had a strong economics

[34] Rosen, *Western Economists and Eastern Societies: Agents of Change in South Asia, 1950–1970,* pp. 149–99.

[35] Ibid., p. 154.

[36] Ibid., p. 188.

department. Unable to find too many jobs in government departments, these economists tended to move towards research positions. However, the need for trained economists was very high. The whole discussion about the strengthening of the Pakistan Institute of Development Economics through a Ford Foundation grant revolved around the kinds of economists needed and training programmes required to fill research positions. The institute did excellent work and came to be known for its policy research. Its work till the country was split (in 1971) has been an important legacy for the institutes that emerged in different forms in the two countries.

One dimension of the legacy is the pre-eminent role of economists in the policy setup. As argued by Zaidi, 'in terms of number, prominence, power and privilege, influence, and visibility, economics dominates social sciences collectively, by a large multiple.'[37] This has also meant that over the years, economists have become powerful members of the state providing advice and formulating policies.

Policy Research Institutes[38]
One consequence of the discontinuities in policy regimes is the depleting space for policy debates in the public domain. Most social scientists reviewing the development and growth of social sciences in Pakistan have lamented the fact that the government, over the years, has not done enough for funding higher education and research.[39] We will discuss the state of social sciences later, but the point is 'the influence of the armed forces has dispossessed analysts and academics of the ability to conduct deeper analysis and become stakeholders in the field. Sadly enough, retired diplomats and military officers have emerged as analysts'.[40]

---

[37] Akbar S. Zaidi, 2002, 'Dismal State of Social Sciences in Pakistan', *Economic and Political Weekly*, vol. 37, no. 35, 31 August, pp. 3644–61.

[38] The listing of policy research institutes and limited information on them is based on the website of each of these institutes.

[39] Inayatullah, Rubina Saigol and Pervez Tahir (eds), 2007, *Social Sciences in Pakistan: A Profile*, Islamabad: Council of Social Sciences.

[40] Ayesha Siddiqua, 2005, 'The Development of Strategic Studies in Pakistan', in Inayatullah, Rubuna Saigol, and Pervez Tahir (eds), *Social Sciences in Pakistan: A Profile*, Islamabad: Council of Social Sciences.

Some Prominent Policy Research Organizations

As research input into policymaking is embedded in the wider context of the state of social science research, it may be useful to identify distinctive phases of the history of Pakistan that may have had an impact on the growth of social sciences. Zaidi has identified five phases.[41] The period 1947–58 was one of continuation of pre-independence history and efforts for planned strategies for development were initiated. The second phase was the period 1958–71, when there was a rise in US influence in policy sectors and in the education sector. The period 1971–7 was marked by the first democratic era in Pakistan and the expansion of public space for debate and discussion. The period 1977–88 was marked by the assertion of Islamic ideology and had a tremendous impact on the education system. From then on, the impact of globalization and influence of multilateral institutions on public policy became salient.

In this way of presenting Pakistan's history of political economy, Zaidi highlights two or three kinds of phenomena.[42] One is that in the initial period, teaching and research was limited to a small number of institutions and continued the pre-independence traditions of work. Later, some significant features impacting on the research environment emerged. These were the rise of American influence; the regional conflict and ultimate division of the country; rise of Islamic ideology; and finally, the continuing period of globalization and heightened influence of multilateral institutions. Each of these dimensions has had a profound influence on the direction of research in the country.

The Institute of Development Economics, established in 1957 in Karachi, was one of the earliest policy research institutes. It was established with the support of the Ford Foundation and supported the activities of the Planning Commission. 'The focus of research was very significantly on solving young Pakistan's numerous economic problems, and the institute played an active role in giving policy relevant advice'.[43] It was accorded an autonomous status in 1964, when it came to be known as the Pakistan Institute of Development Economics. It went through severe strain during the period preceding the regional conflict in the country. In 1970, the Institute had shifted to Dhaka, but after

[41] Zaidi, 'Dismal State of Social Sciences in Pakistan', pp. 3646–8.
[42] Ibid.
[43] Ibid., p. 3646.

the country was split in 1971, a new institute of the same name was established on the Quaid-i-Azam University campus in Lahore in 1972. The Institute was granted a degree-giving status in 2000; it trains people towards the award of Ph.D. Apart from this, keeping policy-oriented research in focus, it continues its training programmes for the country's civil servants.

The Applied Economics Research Centre was established at Karachi University in 1973. Since its inception, the Centre has undertaken research on issues in applied economics, with special interest in the areas of agriculture, human resources, urban and regional economics, and public finance. With the subsequent growth of the Centre, its activities broadened to include the advanced training of economists from all parts of Pakistan. Institutionally, this growth in capacity, size, and scope has led to the Centre being awarded the title of 'Institution of National Capability in Applied Economics' by the University Grants Commission of Pakistan.[44] The Centre's research is policy-oriented, with emphasis on areas such as the economics of agriculture, public finance, urban and regional economics, trade, human resources, health and environment, poverty, and social issues. As the Report of the American Social Science Research Council points out, contract research has rapidly become one of the major activities of AERC.[45] There is considerable demand from international agencies and government departments for policy-oriented quantitative research, and the Centre possesses the capacity to provide it.

The Sustainable Development Policy Institute was founded in August 1992 on the recommendation of the Pakistan National Con-servation Strategy (NCS), also called Pakistan's Agenda 21. The NCS placed Pakistan's socioeconomic development within the context of a national environmental plan. This highly acclaimed document, ap-proved by the Federal Cabinet in March 1992, outlined the need for an independent non-profit organization to serve as a source of expertise for policy analysis and development, policy intervention, and policy and programme advisory services. SDPI is registered under the Societ-ies Registration Act, XXI of 1860. Its mandate provides for:

[44] Chatterjee et al., *Social Science Research Capacity in South Asia: A Report.*
[45] Ibid.

- Conducting policy advice, policy-oriented research, and advocacy from a broad multidisciplinary perspective.
- Promoting the implementation of policies, programmes, laws, and regulations based on sustainable development.
- Strengthening civil society and facilitating civil society-government interaction through collaboration with other organizations and activist networks.
- Disseminating research findings and public education through the media, conferences, seminars, lectures, publications, and curricula development.
- Contributing to building up national research capacity and infrastructure.

SDPI provides policy advice to a number of organizations in the public, private, and voluntary sector on issues and themes related to different aspects of sustainable development. This policy advice emanates from SDPI's research programme and identifies alternatives for existing policies and practices. SDPI also plays an active role in providing advice and suggestions on contemporary issues such as the government's Devolution Plan, problems related to the Kalabagh Dam, or those related to education, and even on the environmental policy in general.

In its role as one of Pakistan's most active and successful advocacy and networking organizations, SDPI has played a key role in raising awareness about environmental and social issues in Pakistan, particularly in the Islamabad region. In its advocacy role, SDPI has played a 'reactive' role on such issues as human rights, gender, academic freedom, peace, religious tolerance, the nuclear issue, and other themes pertaining to justice, freedom, and development. In addition, it undertakes studies on the basis of its research findings. SDPI uses its research output to advocate policies by participating in conferences and workshops and through contributions in local newspapers and magazines. It also has strong links with many NGOs in Pakistan as well as with several networks of NGOs, both locally in the South Asian region and internationally.

The Institute of Policy Studies was established in Islamabad in 1979. It has focused mainly on research on Pakistan society and politics, education, economy, foreign policy and security issues, regional and global developments related to Pakistan and the Muslim World, and issues with regard to Islamic Studies and Islamization. It has produced around 200 publications and over 1,000 unpublished reports. Seminars and conferences are a regular feature at IPS. Besides research activities, the Institute has a training programme for both corporate and social sectors.

The Islamabad Policy Research Institute (IPRI) was founded in 1999 as an autonomous body to produce well-analyzed inputs and ideas to formulate responses. It is a research institute dedicated to undertaking analyses and evaluations of important national and international politico-strategic issues and developments affecting Pakistan, South Asia, and world affairs. The Institute projects an independent viewpoint and provides well-considered options to policymakers. IPRI freely interacts with similar national and international organizations, networks, and scholars to benefit from the exchange of ideas and views.

The Collective for Social Science Research was established in 2001 with a small core staff of researchers in social sciences, having extensive experience in conducting multidisciplinary research, both in Pakistan and internationally. Their areas of research interest include economics, education, development policy, gender studies, health, labour, migration, poverty, and urban governance. The Collective collaborates with a number of local and international academic organizations, the Government of Pakistan, and international development organizations, to conduct this research. It is recognized for three main areas of innovation in the practice of applied social sciences in Pakistan: the introduction of a political economy perspective in macro- and micro-issues; the attention to informal collective action and social networks; and the combination of quantitative and qualitative research methodologies. The Collective's objective is to produce high quality academic research in the social sciences and to foster informed debate on social, political, and economic issues and policies. However, it must be recognized that most of the research projects are consulting assignments for development organizations or collaborative partnerships with local and international academic organizations. Only some are self-generated by the Collective in pursuit of its own research agenda.

The Social Policy Development Centre is an organization in the private sector engaged in policy research. Since its inception in 1995, it has been giving policy advice to the public sector. Its research is focused on analysis of policies, pilot project monitoring, and evaluation. It also serves as the database for the social sector, and disseminates information.[46]

These are only some of the policy research organizations that have emerged in Pakistan. PIDE and AERC are among the oldest institutions; while others came into being after the 1990s. A study that surveyed non-profit organizations in Pakistan has identified around 7,815 such organizations involved in what it calls 'civil rights and advocacy'. This is around 18 per cent of the total non-profit organizations so identified. The majority of these are community-based organizations working at the local level, conveying day-to-day problems to various levels of government, and assisting their communities in resolving issues concerning water supply, electricity, sewerage, etc. The category 'civil rights and advocacy' also includes organizations that work at the national level and provide advocacy on national issues.[47]

Context of the Status of Social Sciences

The Council of Social Sciences, Pakistan, sponsored an evaluation of the status of various social science disciplines in Pakistan universities. The period chosen was from 1947 to 2003. All the contributors to the volume expressed deep dissatisfaction with the state of their respective disciplines. In spite of a phenomenal increase in the actual number of departments and teachers, the quality of academic output has been mainly from low to average.[48] A major reason for this state of affairs, as Saigol points out, is that 'the overwhelming ideological orientation of teachers across the disciplinary spectrum revolves around religious and nationalist thinking.' The result is that 'the absence of debate and controversy, discussion and contention, makes most of the universities

[46] Anwar Shaheen, 2007, 'Contribution of NGOs to Social Science Research in Pakistan' in Inayatullah, Rubina Saigol, and Pervez Tahir (eds), *Social Sciences in Pakistan: A Profile*, Islamabad: Council of Social Sciences, p. 445.

[47] Aisha Ghaus-Pasha, Haroon Jamal, and Muhammad Asif Iqbal, 2002, 'Dimensions of The Nonprofit Sector in Pakistan', *SDPC Working Paper No. 1*, Islamabad: Social Policy and Development Centre, accessed pcp.org.pk.

[48] Rubina Saigol, 2007, 'Conclusions' in Inayatullah, Rubina Saigol, and Pervez Tahir (eds), *Social Sciences in Pakistan: A Profile*, Islamabad: Council of Social Sciences, p. 471.

very dull and insipid places where received knowledge from old books is transmitted from generation to generation.'[49]

Most contributors to this volume have underlined the lack of an independent environment in which free enquiry can be carried out. Ahmed points out 'that social sciences are nourished on debate, on the testing of existing knowledge, and on discovery and innovation. This is possible only in a democratic society and with democratic institutions of governance and justice.'[50] Similarly, Hasan suggests that another factor that has reduced the importance of social sciences in the country is the fragility of democratic culture and weak democratic structure.[51] Social sciences flourish in an environment of freedom of expression, which only a democratic system can ensure. In the last few years, business management and information sciences have attracted more recognition and funds. The private sector has joined in to support institutions in these areas. Zaidi also points out that there is an agreement amongst social scientists regarding the depressingly decrepit condition of social sciences in Pakistan.[52] The reasons for such a state of affairs are embedded in the lack of independent inquiry and social sciences being dominated by politically motivated public themes.

Thus, policy research faces a challenging environment. There is lack of demand from government and also restricted public space for debate and contestation. Quality of social science research also, is not of high order. It does appear then, that most of the institutes mentioned here do more of training than policy research.

One other issue that has impacted the nature of policy research has been the role and influence of multilateral agencies in funding research. At a recent discussion, a concern was raised regarding the ability of these agencies to push research in directions that are of interest to them. Such directions may not reflect local conditions. As a participant pointed out, 'funding and donor agencies are determining the research agenda and

---

[49] Ibid., p. 477.

[50] Ahmed Syed Jaffar, 2007, 'Pakistan Studies: A Subject of the State and State of the Subject', in Inayatullah, Rubina Saigol, and Pervez Tahir (eds), *Social Sciences in Pakistan: A Profile*, Islamabad: Council of Social Sciences, p. 308.

[51] Hasan Mehdi, 2007, 'Journalism and Mass Communication', in Inayatullah, Rubina Saigol, and Pervez Tahir (eds), *Social Sciences in Pakistan: A Profile*, Islamabad: Council of Social Sciences, p. 279.

[52] Zaidi, 'Dismal State of Social Sciences in Pakistan', p. 3660.

in many cases, this is irrelevant to the local people.'[53] The extent of this influence depends on the involvement of the international community in the country's development. In Pakistan, security issues have now taken precedence over social issues.

SRI LANKA

The Chairperson of the Social Science Research Committee (SSRC) of the National Science Foundation (NSF), speaking at a symposium on 'The Potential Role of Social Sciences in National Development: Challenges and Opportunities', commented that 'Sri Lanka, absorbed in the critical social issues of relief, reconstruction, and rehabilitation of internally displaced people and children deprived of education, requires the expertise of social sciences to fully achieve its objective of rebuilding.' There is a need to sensitize the government about the potential role of the social science community. The Chairman added that social scientists could serve as a 'think-tank' to the government and provide feedback on the effectiveness of these (policy) processes.[54]

The above remark was made in the context of the prevailing relationship between research and policy in Sri Lanka. Generally, the feeling is that 'by and large, policymaking remains quite divorced from the inputs of research organizations; and there appears little interest on the part of ministries to get research organizations more involved in that process.'[55] Some research institutions focusing on peace and conflict have arisen in response to internal strife; these include the International Centre for Ethnic Studies, Centre for Policy Alternatives, and others.

In the earlier days, the Marga Institute attracted considerable attention from researchers and policymakers. Set up in April 1972, it started as a civil society initiative in the early 1970s and developed over a span of three decades. The ideas leading to the establishment of the

[53] IDRC Round Table on 'Policy Environment', Khatmandu, 5–6 March 2009. Social scientists from Pakistan, Bangladesh, and Nepal participated in this Round Table.

[54] Jayanthi Liyanage, 2003, 'Social Scientists Not Consulted on Public Policy', *Sunday Observer Magazine*, Colombo, 4 May, available at http://www.sundayobserverlk/2003/05/04/fea22.html.

[55] Dushin Weerakon, Deputy Director and Fellow, Institute of Policy Studies, Colombo, in a personal communication with the author.

Marga Institute took shape in the late 1960s, among a group of public officers, academics and professionals.[56] It has been recognized as a leading institute that has contributed to the formulation of development policy. However, this influence declined with the devaluation of planning as a strategy of development. During the tenure of President Jayawardene, there was a deliberate effort to push out the use of the word 'plan' and replace it by the word 'programme'.[57]

The website of the South Asian Research Network[58] mentions the Institute of Policy Studies as one of the major policy research organizations in the country. This Institute was set up by an Act of Parliament in 1990 as a policy 'think-tank' that engages in socioeconomic research to supplement the research capacity of the Ministry of Finance and Planning, the Central Bank, and others. IPS is funded by the Royal Netherland's Government and the Government of Sri Lanka. Over the course of the last two decades, it has been able to develop its own endowment fund and has claimed autonomy from foreign funding. In the early years, the Institute's programme focused on macroeconomic policy issues. More recently, the research portfolio has been extended to other areas, such as social and economic infrastructure, health policy, gender, poverty alleviation, energy policy, and government reforms.

Another prominent policy research organization is the International Centre for Ethnic Studies (ICES). This Centre was established in 1982 on the initiative of Sri Lankan scholars, supported by the Ford Foundation. Its website mentions that 'it functions as an international centre of excellence located in the global south to conduct research and develop policies and mechanisms to address issues of ethnicity, pluralism, and the prevention and management of conflict. ICES has played two roles, one of research and one of policy advocacy. Following extensive academic, legal, and political involvement in the constitutional process and policy formulation in Sri Lanka and strong advocacy in the areas of gender, human rights, and minority rights, ICES is well-known in the international community for its capacity to generate high quality research, which is politically relevant, nationally, regionally, and

[56] Available at http://www.margasrilanka.org/History.html.
[57] Conversation with Godfrey Gunateilleke Emeritus Chairperson, Senior Advisor Marga Institute, 21 January 2009.
[58] Available at http://southasia.ssrc.org/centers/srilanka/.

globally. It has also always provided space for and encouraged creative expression as a vehicle for political and social change.'

The Centre is actively supported by international scholars and funded by several multilateral agencies like CIDA, IDRC, etc. It has a culture of working collaboratively and conducts its projects with partners in Asia, Africa, Europe, and North America drawn from academic institutions, policy institutes, women's organizations, and community-based groups, among others. Since its establishment in 1982, ICES has undertaken a series of research and policy formulation programmes and projects in areas such as ethnicity, minority protection, and multiculturalism.

Commenting on the kind of social science research conducted for policy in Sri Lanka, Wikramsinghe comments that one overarching theme in the expansion of social science research in Sri Lanka since 1982 is related to 'ethnic conflict'.[59] In the last twenty years, the focus of social science research has been on the roots of ethnic conflict, studying its various manifestations, and trying to find solutions. The result is that even new areas of research like devolution, comparative federalism, minority rights, et al., have emerged in response to these queries.

However, the policy environment, after the intensification of the ethnic conflict in Sri Lanka, has not been very conducive to the development of social sciences per se, and to the acceptability of research findings as policy inputs. At a Round Table in 2009,[60] a group of social scientists noted that the public space for debate and contestation of policies was increasingly getting constricted. Security concerns dominate policymaking. This has created a situation in which the larger policy framework cannot be questioned. What can be brought into the public domain for debate and discussion has got to pass the test of what has come to be known as a 'sensitive issue'. A participant pointed out that the dictum among academics of 'publish or perish' has been replaced by 'publish *and* perish'. Both the government as well as the

---

[59] Nira Wickramsinghe, 2008, 'The Production of Knowledge on Peace, Security, and Governance in Sri Lanka', Paper presented at a Conference on Knowledge on the Move: Research for Development in a Globalizing World, The Hague, Netherlands: Institute of Social Studies, p. 6, available at http://www.nuffic.nl/home/ newsevents/docs/events/kotm/abstracts-andpapers/.

[60] IDRC Round Table Discussions on 'Policy Environment' in Sri Lanka, Galle, 21 January 2009. Invited social scientists from Sri Lanka participated in this discussion.

militants resent dissent and the fear of reprisals is very high. The long period of violence and conflict has taken its toll on public opinion, and divisions in society have become deeper and sharper than ever before.

A view was also expressed, that pan-country research was not possible as data of at least two provinces in the country was not available since the conflict started in 1982. For other provinces, data is not wholly reliable, and interviewing is usually out of bounds. So if there is a research-policy space, it is increasingly getting limited to the domain of hard or medical sciences.

BANGLADESH

The Bangladesh Planning Commission has its roots in pre-independence Bangladesh. In the mid-1950s, a Provincial Planning Board was established under the United Front Government of the then East Pakistan (present Bangladesh). It was an important agency for formulating investment programmes, and negotiating with the Central Government of Pakistan for an adequate share of the financial resources for the development of East Pakistan. After liberation, the Planning Commission was established in 1972. However, from the start, it got into conflict with the ministers and this could not be resolved through negotiations. Gradually, the Planning Commission lost its authority and by the time of the collapse of the government after the assassinations of its leaders, the Commission had completely lost its influence and credibility.[61]

The Bangladesh Institute of Development Studies was established as a successor to the Pakistan Institute of Development Economics in 1972. As mentioned earlier in the section on Pakistan, this Institute was officially shifted to Dhaka in what was then East Pakistan. Through an Act of Parliament, it was renamed Bangladesh Institute of Development Studies. Initially, it was fully-funded by the government; but in 1983, the government created an endowment fund making it functionally autonomous and eligible for donor funding.

The link between research and policy is sometimes tenuous. Although, it is not necessarily so in Bangladesh where researchers from the IDRC's Micro Impacts of Macroeconomic and Adjustment Policies

---

[61] Stanley Kochanek, 2004, Review of 'Making of a Nation—Bangladesh: An Economist's Tale', *Asia Pacific Development Journal*, vol. 11, no. 2, pp. 124–8.

(MIMAP) programme have been working closely with the government since the project's inception in 1992. Dr Mujeri of the Bangladesh Institute of Development Studies, the leader of this research team, emphasizes that the close relationship between research and policy is a recent development. He claims that the Planning Commission has based its policy on poverty, primarily on the findings of this research. Exchanges are facilitated in Bangladesh because the research community is small. 'We know what others are doing and what the scope of their work and policy influence is,' says Mujeri.

I think it is important that, at the end of the day, it is not whose research has got to the policymakers, but whether policies have been developed or not and if they are the right policies. As researchers we feel that if our research has been used, we have done something that is at least useful.[62]

The Bangladesh Institute of International and Strategic Studies (BIISS) was established in 1978. It undertakes, encourages, and promotes independent research to advance objective understanding of all aspects of international relations and strategic studies. The Institute carries out policy research on how developing nations, like Bangladesh, can survive in the complex international system and strengthen regional and international cooperation.

There appear to be many other institutions that have some role in providing inputs into policy. Usually, such institutions have been established by military or civil bureaucrats who have access to decision-makers in the country.[63] These institutions tend to become more influential in influencing policy and also in determining the directions of policy research. However, a participant referring to them at the IDRC Round Table (in 2009) pointed out that the advice from them was not necessarily based on quality research.

NEPAL

Nepal has seen rapid political changes in the last two decades. Around 1990, political reforms began to be introduced and some form of parliamentary system began to take shape. The succeeding democratically

[62] Michelle Hibler, 'From Research to Policy in Bangladesh', http://www.idrc.ca/en/ev-26053-201-1-DO_TOPIC.html.

[63] Discussion at IDRC Round Table on 'Policy Environment' in Kathmandu, 5–6 March 2009.

elected governments had short tenures and the King continued to play a key role in the politics and administration of the country. However, there was a revolutionary Maoist movement brewing, and in 2006, the King was made to give up his powers and an interim constitution was promulgated. This however, was followed by a quick progression of events during 2006–8, with the Prime Minister declaring himself Head of State and the King abdicating and being forced to leave the country.

This political environment has not been conducive to establishing firm foundations of social science research in the country. Tribhuvan University was the prominent university where several centres were created to pursue teaching and research.

The Centre for Economic Development and Administration (CEDA) was established in 1969 under a tripartite agreement between His Majesty's Government of Nepal, Tribhuvan University, and the Ford Foundation. Started as an autonomous institution, the Centre was integrated into Tribhuvan University and given the status of a research centre in 1975 after the National Education System Plan (NESP) was implemented. CEDA has been serving as a policy-research centre, contributing to national development policies and strategies. The Centre's activities are basically confined to research, consultancy, and training programmes. To its credit, the Centre has publications that are well-received by both national and international agencies. Its basic goal is to contribute to nation-building through analytical and problem-solving works in the areas of socioeconomic and administrative development.[64]

Another institution that came up around the same time was the Institute of Nepal Studies. It was established in 1969 and was renamed the Institute of Nepal and Asian Studies in 1972, with the responsibility of both teaching and research. In 1977, the Institute was converted into a purely research centre, and renamed Centre for Nepal and Asian Studies (CNAS). CNAS is a statutory and multidisciplinary research centre under Tribhuvan University with a team of about 19 fulltime

[64] Centre for Economic Development and Administration, http://www.tribhuvan-university.edu.np/faculty/ceda.htm, Tribhuvan University, Nepal.

110 Public Policy and Politics in India

researchers for conducting independent research and deliberation on issues and studies in social sciences.[65]

Subsequently, a large number of NGOs established advocacy groups that were registered as Trusts. The Institute for Policy Research and Development (IPRAD) is a non-profit organization established in 1995, composed of economists, management experts, engineers, social and political scientists, and lawyers. The specific objectives of the organization are:

- to undertake research on economic, social, management, institutional, legal, and environmental issues;
- to conduct trainings and workshops in areas which directly enhance the skills and awareness of low income and disadvantaged groups;
- to evolve and draw up policy alternatives for ensuring a sustainable development process.

The Institute for Social and Environmental Research (ISER) is another prominent non-governmental, non-profit, research and development organization registered under the Non-Government Organization Registration Act 1977 of Nepal. Established in 2001, ISER is the successor to the Population and Ecology Research Laboratory (PERL), Nepal, founded in 1995. ISER is governed by a General Council composed of individual and institutional members. An Executive Committee is elected by the General Council and it is the apex body of the organization, responsible for the overall management and conduct of ISER. ISER aims at contributing towards instituting high quality research, human resource development to conduct such research, implementation of programme interventions, and policy advocacy in major social, environmental, and development challenges facing Nepal.[66]

One other such institution is the Institute for Integrated Development Studies (IIDS) established in 1990 as the successor organization to the Integrated Development System (which was established in 1979). It is a non-government organization with a vision to become Nepal's leading private, independent, non-partisan research institute committed to holistic and sustainable development based on human values. The

[65] Centre for Economic Development and Administration, http://www.tribhuvan-university.edu.np/faculty/ccnas.htm, Tribhuvan University, Nepal.
[66] Institute for Social and Environmental Research, http://iser-nepal.org/, Nepal.

mission of the Institute is to contribute to the identification, analysis, and understanding of major development policy issues facing the country and provide responses to them.

Another feature of recent developments in the field of policy research has been the rise of research-based consultancy firms. They conduct research on contract for government as well as international agencies. Many of the non-profit organizations as well as the consultancy firms have been initiated by bureaucrats. They have access to decision-making bodies in governments and are acquainted with processes of decision-making. The result is that large amounts of research funds from multilateral agencies and the government are directed towards them. In this way, donors and multilateral agencies play a more significant role in influencing policy than the university-based research institutions.

* * *

Traditionally, governments in South Asia have sought inputs into policy decisions from the bureaucrats in their line ministries. Whether these inputs are based on research or on their personal experience has not mattered much. Thus, an administrator working in the Ministry of Civil Aviation or Education becomes the resource for any change in policy in those sectors. The critical element is that of reliability and it is for this reason too, that when a specialist is needed, s/he tends to be incorporated in the government bureaucracy.

The strategy of planned economic development began to change this relationship when the demand for expertise, not necessarily available in bureaucrats, grew. The first effort was to incorporate experts within the government hierarchy. It was only later that outside experts began to be recognized as resources for policymaking. Policy research organizations began to develop after the governments accepted this kind of relationship.

However, South Asian countries do not present a common model for the growth of such institutions. Democracy, strategy of economic development, and an open sociopolitical system have greatly influenced the way policy research organizations emerged in these countries. In Pakistan, democratic regimes were interspersed with long spells of military rule. The strategy of economic development adopted at independence, did not endure for long. Regional politics was a factor in eroding the idea of rationality in planning. Economic neglect, among many other factors, led to the movement of separation, and Bangladesh was born. Here too, democracy was unable to sustain itself and spells of military rule became part of its political history. A political environment of uncertainty was not conducive to the emergence of alternative sources of policy research. However, what must be emphasized is that the nature of military rule in Pakistan differed from regime to regime. This meant that the freedom to articulate alternatives varied among regimes, allowing for diverse policy research organizations to emerge. Areas of strategic studies and international relations were of interest in all the regimes, and research institutions working on these themes found easy recognition. Another reason for their recognition was the interest that bureaucrats—civil or military—took in them, and the initiatives they took to establish institutions to promote policies.

Sri Lanka has been mired in violent ethnic conflict since 1982. Since then, the agenda of national consolidation and integration has superseded any other; the result being the inability of policy research institutions to transcend the boundaries and constraints of 'ethnic studies'. In Nepal, the King has played a critical role in all appointments, and powers were concentrated in the office of the Prime Minister for a long time. Opportunities for the articulation of alternatives were few and far between. A democratic regime has taken over only recently and therefore the growth of policy organizations has been stunted.

India has been fortunate in this regard. The persistence of a strategy of planning and orderly democratic change led to a conducive political environment for the growth of policy research in institutions outside the government. In the early years of planning, the need for data, information, and analysis was so great that the Planning Commission encouraged new institutions to take on this job. As dominance of the idea of planning declined in the 1970s, opportunities for presenting alternatives emerged. Policy research institutions multiplied, and the existing ones responded by adding more policy relevant sectors of research to their portfolio. Due to the size of the country and its diversity, policy research institutions delved into multiple areas of public concern.

Even though there is diversity in the growth pattern of policy research organizations in South Asia, due to the unique political and economic history of each country, it appears that the challenges they face are not too dissimilar.

Initially, policy research institutions in all these countries were promoted and funded by the government. At this time, the Ford Foundation was very active in supplementing government funds. Gradual decline in government funding affected most institutions, but many succeeded because they were able to find alternative sources of funding. Other sources not only meant multiple ministries, but also included funding from multilateral agencies. Most of such funding was project-based. In all the three IDRC Round Tables, there was little acknowledgment of any large endowments that helped establish institutions or supported their revenues. Funds came in for financing such things as buildings or a library, but these were one-time grants. Large, project-based funds have raised some serious concerns among social scientists in South Asia. It was pointed out that project funds tend to determine priorities and these priorities do not necessarily reflect local concerns. Such a tendency also diminishes the capacity of an institution to choose its own research directions.

With liberalization and increased interest of international agencies in policy research, civil society and advocacy groups have also taken the initiative to form their own institutions. In all the countries of South Asia, such institutions have multiplied, and those that reflect donor interests have attracted greater amount of funds. Many of these institutions have also taken the form of consulting firms/corporate bodies. Governments have often turned to them for quick results and for the reliability of adhering to a contracted time schedule due to their corporate culture.[67] A consequence of this diversity and dispersal of policy research in varied types of institutions is that of uneven development of capability of research institutions. Government-funded institutions, most of the time, are unable to face the competitive challenge of

---

[67] The Review Committee Report of the Indian Council of Social Science Research points out: 'Government departments and public sector organizations and more recently, UN agencies, aid agencies of foreign governments, international financial agencies, and private foundations also have shown increasing interest in funding research on socioeconomic development and policy issues. This has led to a mushrooming of nongovernmental "research" institutes and an increasing presence of private consulting firms and NGOs in surveys and "research". This trend has gathered momentum with the progressive liberalization and globalization of the economy.' ICSSR, 2007, *ICSSR Review Committee Report*, New Delhi, p. 12.

remuneration and facilities offered by some of these agencies and begin to suffer from paucity of talent.

Bureaucrats—civil and military—have found this new space amenable to float their own policy research institutions. Thus, another breed of institutions has emerged. These institutions are based on the influence commanded by a single bureaucrat or a group of bureaucrats on the government. Because of that influence, they are able to get donor support for their activities. Many social scientists across South Asian countries feel that such institutions neither reflect local social needs nor high standards of social science research.

It should also be mentioned here that the bureaucrats in the South Asian countries, emerging from colonial tradition, have continued to play a significant role in advising their respective governments. This role has often been to restrict opportunities to outsiders in giving policy advice. In Bangladesh, however, the government was very open to international experiments; to the extent that 'it stifled local ways of thinking.' The bureaucrats probably had to accept opening up to external advice due to peculiar politico-economic conditions prevailing in the country.

With concerns about diminishing autonomy to determine research priorities, social scientists across South Asia lament the deterioration in quality of social science research. The standards of policy research are embedded in the general quality of social science research in the country. Policy research organizations were established independent of the universities because it was felt that universities were so involved in teaching, that research was neglected. Thus, the argument was that if academics devoted all their time on research, the quantum of research would increase and so would its quality. In the process, talent moved to these institutions from the universities. Universities became even more vulnerable to the same charge. The process does not seem to have stopped at the level of institutes. With liberalization and globalization and increased funding from multilateral institutions, opportunities have expanded and research institutes, facing a resource crunch, are grappling with issues of retaining talented faculty.

The fact that there is diversity in the way policy research organizations have been established and later multiplied, needs to be emphasized. This diversity is embedded in the unique political and economic history of each country. However, some of the challenges these institutions face are not too dissimilar across countries. There is some amount of commonality though the details may be different. Therefore, in looking at the future of these organizations, we need to understand the historical context in which they have evolved, the capability of social scientists to do quality research, and how global factors have come about to influence their vision and performance.

4

Battling for Clean Environment

Supreme Court, Technocrats, and
*Populist Politics in Delhi**

D uring the early 1990s, Delhi had been declared one of the most
polluted cities in the world. The hazardous industries were
located right in those areas where people lived; the river Yamuna on
the banks of which the city stood was full of toxic industrial effluents
making the water unfit for use, air heavily laden with particulate matter
and poisonous gases made the people vulnerable to many respiratory
diseases and open to many kinds of cancer and heart diseases. Motor
vehicles had multiplied phenomenally and were using fuel that did
not adhere to emission norms. Many environmental groups launched
campaigns for Clean Delhi, but the governments showed little interest.

In September 1986, in response to an appeal from concerned citizens,
the Supreme Court directed the Delhi administration to file an affidavit
specifying the steps taken to implement laws concerned with the
control and prevention of water and air pollution in the city. From this
year begins the saga of the Court passing various orders for enforcing

* Kuldeep Mathur, 2004, 'Battling for Clean Environment: Supreme Court,
Technocrats and Populist Politics in Delhi', *CSLG Working Paper*, New Delhi:
Jawaharlal Nehru University, pp. 1–28. Among many colleagues who willingly
gave their time to comment on the paper, my special thanks are to Rakesh
Jayal without whose help, research for this paper could not have been possible.

measures for clean air and seeing that its orders are implemented. The ultimate triumph of the Supreme Court came in introducing Compressed Natural Gas (CNG) as a single mode of fuel for public transport in April 2002 in the midst of considerable social and political conflict. Technocrats were not unanimous about accepting CNG as the cleanest fuel. Commuters wanted an efficient transport system and were not much concerned about the dispute on choice of fuel and its impact on health.

This chapter narrates the role of the Supreme Court in controlling air pollution in Delhi in the face of political contestation and government reluctance in implementing what had already long been on the statute books. This narrative focuses attention on the transport vehicles and their contribution to air pollution and therefore will not refer to pollution caused by hazardous industries and the government's performance in shifting them out from congested areas of Delhi.

NATURE OF ENVIRONMENTAL POLITICS

When environmental protection and conservation came on the global agenda, environmentalists, mostly in Europe and elsewhere in the West, took the route of electoral politics to bring about changes in the social and economic order that would be conducive to a healthy living, free from the polluting technologies. The primary efforts of the advocates of such strategies were devoted to political debate over issues, influencing legislative processes through electoral contests, development of policy, and the shaping of policy implementation. The principal assumption underlying such activities was that liberal democratic decision-making processes were sufficiently open to allow for the environmental agenda to be carried out through them.[1] However, they were disappointed at the pace that this happened. Legislative acts were not always implemented but allowed to languish on statute books. In such cases, democratic processes stalled the translation of policy into action. Laws became symbols of intention and not of action. They acted to enhance a government's prestige among those who pushed an agenda of sustainable development.

---

[1] Frank Fischer, 1995, *Evaluating Public Policy*, Chicago: Nelson-Hall Publishers, p. 194.

In the field of environment, the gap between policy and implementation is especially noticeable. The political leadership may agree to
the enactment of laws but block their implementation. When activist
environmentalist groups do not see enough action in the enactment
of laws, they search for ways that can force the government into
implementing laws. Realizing that it is futile to work through political leadership that has already demonstrated its resistance, they began
to search for state institutions outside the electoral arena that enforce
implementation.

In a way, this impasse has sought to depoliticise environmental conflict. In elaborating on the concept of 'ecological modernization', Hajer
points out that the 1980s saw the emergence of a new policy discourse
that portrayed environmental protection as a 'positive-sum game'
where economic growth could be reconciled with ecological problems.[2]
Environmental protection was possible within the existing socio-
political structures and the obstacles related to problems of collective
action because environmental pollution reflected inefficiency in the
choice of technologies and their use. What was needed was to upgrade
the technologies. Hajer emphasizes that 'ecological modernization
does not call for any structural change but is, in this respect, basically a
modernist and technocratic approach to the environment that suggests
that there is a techno-institutional fix for the present problems.'[3] This
means that ecological modernization set off the environmental movements of the 1970s that called for alternative social arrangements and
economic policies for development. The move away from electoral
politics and reliance on legislative action, thus, signifies a move towards
a new role for science and technology in political decision-making,
stressing that the goals of economic growth and that of environmental
protection are compatible.

Within the realm of politics, another event signalled a move
towards a technocratic solution of environmental problems in the
West. Termed as 'professionalization of reform' by Moynihan while
referring to the scientifically oriented policy discourse during the Great

[2] Maarten A. Hajer, 1995, *The Politics of Environmental Discourse: Ecological
Modernization and the Policy Process*, Oxford: Clarendon Press, pp. 24–41.
[3] Ibid., p. 32.

Society period,[4] it is widely believed that the technocratic discourse in policy process dominated that time. The idea that political issues can be transformed into technically defined ends, which can be pursued through administrative means, was very influential. Technically trained elites took upon the role of influencing policies most enthusiastically and there arose a new technocratic class striving for political power. Technocratic experts were portrayed as social engineers who were also changing the policy process by transferring power from the corrupt and self-serving politicians to virtuous and the technically trained experts.[5]

The United States was not alone in seeing the growth of policy institutes that sought to influence public policy. Expert advice began to be offered on an institutionalized basis in several countries.[6] However, the proliferation of such institutes contributed to the emergence of a new kind of policy discourse where differing and conflicting advice was offered and the government had to make a choice. The policy discourse took 'an argumentative turn'[7] where technical advice was not necessarily unanimous. There were many dimensions to this lack of unanimity. One was the quality of research and its validity. The other was the political orientation of the experts and their institutes whose advice was cloaked in a political garb that supported or opposed the government of the day. In both the US and Britain, policy institutes represent diverse ideologies and compete for political influence.[8] They also tend to set the public agenda even before political parties take up an issue.

POLICY DISCOURSE IN INDIA
The policy discourse in India bears heavy technocratic influence from the time the country embarked upon its strategy of planned economic

[4] Quoted in Fischer, 'Policy Discourse and the Politics of Washington Think Tanks', p. 25.

[5] Ibid., pp. 22–7.

[6] Weaver and Stares, *Guidance for Governance: Comparing Alternative Sources of Public Policy Advice.*

[7] Fischer and Forrester, *The Argumentative Turn in Policy Analysis and Planning*, pp. 22–42.

[8] Fischer, 'Policy Discourse and the Politics of Washington Think Tanks', pp. 32–6; Diane Stone, 2001, 'Bridging Research and Policy', paper presented at the International Workshop, Warwick University, 16–17 July.

development. The leadership that took over the reins of government when the country became independent identified its future with the development performance of the West. Of particular significance in this view was the perception of the significant role that science and technology played in transforming society. Nehru was further impressed by the strides that Soviet Russia had made through judicious planning and the rational use of resources, and he envisioned India quickly attaining the levels of economic development achieved by Western nations through industrialization and modernization. To pursue such goals, the services and advice of experts and technocrats were very necessary. As Khilnani points out, Nehru's intention was to establish the superior rationality of scientists and economists in policymaking.[9] Very soon, the Planning Commission became the exclusive theatre where economic policy was formulated.

The result was that the public and its representatives had little say in wider deliberations about India's future. This lack of participation was justified by the argument that the economic strategy demanded 'technical evaluation of alternative policies and determination of choices on scientific grounds'.[10] Participation in policy deliberations would also have opened up the whole debate about the directions that India should take—a debate symbolized by the widely known different views of Gandhi and Nehru. Committees of experts became an important instrument of resolving a political debate and, even though the Planning Commission did not have a long life in this powerful role, the idea of technical conceptualization and resolution of problems of social conflict has come to stay.[11]

As policy and research institutes multiplied in the last two decades, research-based arguments to shape public policy began to emerge. Policies began to be contested on technical grounds. Apart from other reasons, diverse sources of funding and sponsorship also led to different policy recommendations. Government, earlier restricted to its own institutions for research inputs, now had varied and alternative sources

[9] Khilnani, *The Idea of India*, p. 81.

[10] Partha Chatterjee, 1997, 'Development Planning and the Indian State', in P. Chatterjee (ed.), *State and Politics in India*, New Delhi: Oxford University Press, p. 274.

[11] Bjorkman and Mathur, *Policy Technology and Development: Human Capital Policies in the Netherlands and India*, p. 5.

of policy advice. Alternatives also provided opportunities to experts with different political orientations to influence policy. Technocrats competed with each other for 'expert' political space and research findings were not necessarily neutral. The garb of expertise helped in offering policy advice that had political overtones. But the debates were confined to the 'knowledgeable' and the technicality of arguments restricted widespread participation.

ENVIRONMENTALISTS AND THE SUPREME COURT

In spite of this technocratic orientation, environmental politics in India did not follow the route that it took in the West. Initially, it was concerned with the use and control of renewable natural resources where the issues revolved around communities dependent on nature. The struggles were centred on control of common property resources and revolved around critical issues of equity and justice. Environmentalism began as an integral part of local level activism for social justice.[12] The early years were dominated by forests, dams, degradation of land by mining, indiscriminate use of pesticides, the unsustainable extraction of groundwater, etc. It was only in the decade of the 1990s that attention turned to urban environment.[13] Different waves of environmentalism brought in different actors with varying social projects. If the earlier movements were akin to social movements, the concern about urban environment was expressed by more technically-oriented individuals searching for alternative answers in modern science and technology.

The urban environment policies were framed within the technocratic discourse of economic planning. The issue was not so much about shaping policies but that of implementing those that had already been enacted. For, since the time of the Stockholm Conference, the government began to enact a series of laws for environmental protection. The problem was that most of the time they just remained on statute books. This happened in spite of the fact that the number of administrative and institutional structures bearing environmental responsibility within the government grew from less than a dozen to more than 120

[12] Jayanta Bandyopadhyay, 2002, 'Between Local and Global Responsibilities', *Seminar*, vol. 51, no. 516, August, pp. 21–5.

[13] Harsh Sethi, 2002, 'The Problem', *Seminar*, vol. 51, no. 516, pp. 12–14.

after the Stockholm Conference.[14] Under the Acts passed in 1974, several Pollution Control agencies were set up. The Bhopal gas tragedy in 1984 provided further impetus to such legislation and to the setting up of institutions. But as stressed by Singh, the implementation structures are so fragmented and sectoral that administrative commitment and accountability become extremely compromised.[15] Institutions also lack teeth by design and not ignorance alone.

Such a situation highlights one other important characteristic of the Indian policy discourse that has made environmental politics follow a different route than in the West. And this is as true of environment protection as any other policy area where state intervention tends to upset the prevailing relationships of power and pelf. There is vast evidence to show that wherever administration is involved in the implementation of redistributive policies, the operational process is left ineffective. Little linkage is established between policy objectives and capacity to implement these objectives. During the Plan era, the political leadership and those representing specific interests did not bother to wield influence to shape policy, for they knew that they could scuttle its implementation. Policy planners went on to frame policies that won accolades at international forums or pleased the intellectual constituencies within the country. When these policies did not show results, alibis were found in poor implementation.[16] The result is that the government does not hesitate to formulate the most forward-looking policies; opposition, confident of scuttling them if implemented, allows them on the statute books and thus little debate takes place at the policy formulating stage. Much less attention is paid to strengthening the capacity of the implementing system. The poor record of administrative reform shows how the urge for change remains more in government documents than in reality. Water and Air Pollution Control Acts were passed in 1974 soon after the Stockholm Conference in 1972, but there was little to show on the ground.

[14] Amita Singh, 2000, *The Politics of Environmental Administration*, Delhi: Galgotia Publishers, pp. 77–108.

[15] Ibid., p. 83.

[16] See Kuldeep Mathur, 1995, 'Politics and Implementation of Integrated Rural Development Programmes', *Economic and Political Weekly*, vol. 30, no. 41/42, pp. 2703–8; Gunnar Myrdal, 1968, *Asian Drama: An Inquiry into the Poverty of Nations*, New York: Pantheon Books.

In this situation, environmentalists were more concerned about implementation than in the enactment of laws. They began to turn towards the courts to direct the government to enforce laws. This reliance on courts has increased substantially after the Supreme Court allowed petitions made on behalf of affected parties to enforce Constitutional obligations on the state. Since the 1980s in particular, the judiciary has taken upon itself a more activist role. The way the Supreme Court emerged as a protector of the interests of those who could not approach the Court because of the high cost or lack of legal support is a story of the evolution of what has popularly come to be known as judicial activism. The Court started its activism by insisting that the executive implement the laws that it had initiated through legislation. The government accepted this insistence because it was merely asked to do what it promised to do through legislation.

The cases of environmental degradation that have been filed before the Court were really speaking cases against inaction of the state or wrong action of the state. Where issues of environmental pollution caused by industrial units were raised, the Court made it clear that these were failures of the state's responsibility to protect the rights of the residents to life and liberty, as guaranteed by Article 21 of the Indian Constitution.[17] Together with this interpretation, the Court also expanded on the concept of 'locus standi'. Traditionally, a person who petitioned the Court should show that s/he has been affected adversely by state action and that the conflict is justiciable. But the Court took the view that persons with sufficient interest could challenge government action or inaction. If public duties are to be enforced and public interest served by their enforcement, then public spirited persons and organizations must be allowed to move the Court in furtherance of group interest even though they may not be directly injured in their own rights and interests.[18] It is this reinterpretation of its role that has allowed the Court to accept petitions that are made on behalf of the poor, the underprivileged or those who cannot mobilize themselves. In doing so, the Court has emerged today as redresser of public grievances and in the eyes of many as an agent of social change.

[17] S.P. Sathe, 2002, *Judicial Activism in India: Transgressing Borders and Enforcing Limits*, New Delhi: Oxford University Press, p. 224.

[18] Ibid., p. 202.

However, by its very nature, the Court is unable to resolve a political dispute, and so in environmental cases it has relied on experts and research institutes to help it to take decisions. As the Court sought advice from experts, those involved in the movement for environmental protection also began to seek their support. In this way, the interests of experts defining pollution problems as those of inappropriate or outdated technology converged with those of the environmental activists in their search for alternative technologies to resolve environmental problems. However, the problem of the Court became complex when there was no unanimity on technological advice. In choosing a particular advice, the issue of law or its interpretation is not under consideration. The choice becomes dependent on its own understanding of the problem and its conviction, and may reflect its political or technological orientation.

AIR AND WATER POLLUTION IN DELHI

Environmental concern for air and water pollution began to be expressed in India in legislative terms after the Stockholm Conference in 1972. The Water (Prevention and Control of Pollution) Act was passed in 1974 and Air (Prevention and Control of Pollution) Act in 1981. A Central Board for the Prevention and Control of Water Pollution was constituted in 1974 for the purpose of implementing this Act. This Board was also given the powers to exercise and perform the functions of the Central Board for the Prevention and Control of Air Pollution Act. In 1988, the Board was renamed as Central Pollution Control Board and noise pollution was also brought under the ambit of its activities. Among its many functions, it was enjoined a research function of collecting, compiling, and publishing technical and statistical data relating to water and air pollution. The Board is a technical body entrusted with the task of setting standards and advising the government on technical matters. It does not have a statutory function of enforcing standards and depends on its advisory role to the Ministry of Environment to see that its standards are met.

The Environment Protection Act, an umbrella legislation, was also passed by the Government of India in 1986. This Act empowered the Government of India to 'take all such measures as it deems necessary or expedient for the purpose of protecting and improving the quality of the environment and preventing, controlling and abating environmental pollution.' It also authorized the central government to constitute an authority with powers to perform such functions as laid down in the Act.

At this point of time, various studies were showing that water and air pollution were increasing at a rapid pace in Delhi and in all other metropolitan towns, and there was growing frustration with the fact that the government was doing little to check and control the situation.

A public interest appeal was filed in the Supreme Court in 1985 by an environmental lawyer Mr M.C. Mehta in his capacity as chairman of a non-governmental organization 'Environment Protection Cell' of Hindustani Andolan, an NGO that he helps run. The Bhopal tragedy had taken place in 1984 and there was growing concern about hazardous industries that emitted toxic gases which were located in densely populated areas of Delhi. On 5 December 1985 gas leaked from Shriram Foods and Fertilizers Ltd. Thousands of people fled for safety, a large number was hospitalized and one person died. A chlorine based industry, Hindustan Insecticides, was located right in the middle of a densely populated area. The factory used about 70 tonnes of chlorine every day for the manufacture of DDT. According to a survey conducted by another NGO at the time, around 110 factories in Delhi lacked minimum safety measures and were hazardous to health. The appeal also pointed to the impact of innumerable transport vehicles that ply in and through Delhi. Taking support from many studies, the appeal contended that the emissions were above dangerous limits and were responsible for increasing illness and death from respiratory and other diseases. The appellants requested the Supreme Court to issue a writ, order, or direction to the Government of India, Delhi administration, Delhi Electric Supply Undertaking, and Delhi Transport Corporation:

1. To close down the hazardous industries/units located in the densely populated areas of Delhi or shift such hazardous units far away from the population.
2. To shift its most hazardous units which emit smoke/ash or toxic substances into the air.
3. To take action against those vehicle owners who emit noxious carbon monoxide, oxides of nitrogen, lead, and smoke from their vehicles.

The vehicles plying in the capital should be checked periodically for emission of smoke and pollutants and standards be fixed to control the exhaust, especially of commercial vehicles, and register only such vehicles that are found in order.

4. To close down the thermal power plant or fix electrostatic precipitators.

What the appeal, filed by Mehta and his group, demanded of the Supreme Court was to issue a writ of mandamus to the various authorities to implement the laws enacted to prevent and control pollution of air and water in Delhi. The laws already existed, but the Government of India and the Delhi administration were not making sufficient efforts to implement them. It pointed out that the pollution was taking place because of hazardous industries emitting dangerous gases into the air and effluents into the Yamuna River and due to emissions from the motor vehicles owned by the government as well as private individuals. The basic argument was that the state was not fulfilling its constitutional obligations. Articles 39(e), 47, and 48(a) of the Constitution cast a duty on the state to secure the health of the people, improve public health, and protect and improve the environment. The appeal demanded that the Court direct the state to fulfill its constitutional obligation of environmental protection to the people.

CONTROL AND PREVENTION OF AIR POLLUTION

The campaign against vehicular pollution gained momentum only after the Government of India constituted the Environment Pollution (Prevention and Control) Authority for the National Capital Region under the Environment Protection Act, 1986, in 1998. This is popularly known as the Bhure Lal Committee, named after its Chairman who was then a member of the Central Vigilance Commission. Among others, members of the Committee included Anil Agarwal from the Centre for Science and Environment, which was spearheading a campaign for cleaner Delhi; Jagdish Khattar from Maruti Udyog (car manufacturer) representing the automobile industry; D.K. Biswas, Chairman of the Central Pollution Control Board; and Delhi's Transport Commissioner, K. Dhingra. This Committee was a statutory body and the Court enjoined that its directions were final and binding on all persons and organizations concerned. With reference to vehicular pollution, the

Government, in its notification, enjoined that the Authority 'shall take all necessary steps to ensure compliance of specified emission standards by vehicles, including proper calibration of the equipment for testing of vehicular pollution, ensuring compliance of fuel quality standards, monitoring, coordinating action for traffic management and planning'.[19]

In its First Report,[20] the Committee drew attention to the fact that several steps had been taken by the government to control and prevent pollution, but their impact had been limited because of old vehicles in use and quantum increase in new vehicles. Therefore, the Committee proposed a priority of measures that needed to be completed on a previously laid time schedule. This schedule is discussed in Table 4.1.

The critical part of these measures was concerned with the conversion of public and private transport vehicles to single fuel mode of CNG (Compressed Natural Gas) and phasing out of vehicles that were more than eight years old. Deadlines were set for implementing these measures. This Report was accepted by the Supreme Court, which passed orders to implement it according to the deadlines set. These orders were passed in July 1998. The Court also directed that the number of buses should be increased from the 6,600 to 10,000. The critical deadlines that raised a political storm were for the replacement of old vehicles with those that ran on clean fuel, the adoption of single fuel mode of CNG, and augmentation of public transport buses. These measures were to be implemented by 31 March 2001.

Public transport in Delhi is provided by both the public and the private sector; hence the costs of conversions would fall on both. Increase in the number of buses would lead to greater competition among the private operators. The public sector—Delhi Transport Corporation (DTC)—was sustaining continuous losses which climbed to Rs 2.02 billion in 1996 and further to Rs 8.5 billion in 2001. Besides, the Corporation borrowed about Rs 7.2 billion from the state government but defaulted on repayment, not having paid even a single installment

[19] Government of India, 1998, *The Gazette of India Extraordinary Part II, Section 3, Subsection 2*, New Delhi: Government of India Press, p. 4.

[20] Environment Pollution Authority for the National Capital Region, 1998, *Report on Monitoring and Priority Measures Proposed by the Authority for Air Pollution and Control*, New Delhi: Government of India.

TABLE 4.1: Priority Measures for Completion

Priority Measures	Deadline
Augmentation of public transport to 10,000 Buses from existing 6,000	01.04.2001
Elimination of unleaded petrol from Delhi	01.09.1998
Installation of pre-mix dispensers for the supply of only pre-mix petrol in all petrol stations to two-stroke engines	31.12.1998
Replacement of all pre-1990 autos and taxis with new vehicles using clean fuel	31.3.2000
Replacement, with financial incentives, of post-1990 autos and taxis with new vehicles on clean fuel	31.03.2001
Ban on plying of buses more than eight years old, except on clean fuels	01.04.2000
Entire city bus fleet (DTC and private) to be steadily converted to single fuel mode on CNG	31.03.2001
New Inter State Bus Terminus to be built at North and South-west borders of National Capital Territory Delhi to avoid pollution due to entry of inter-state buses	31.03.2000
Gas Authority of India to ensure availability of CNG by increasing CNG supply outlets in the city from nine to 80	31.3.2000
Two autonomous fuel testing laboratories to be established for monitoring fuel quality specifications and adulterations	01.06.1999

Source: Environment Pollution Authority for the National Capital Region, *Report on Monitoring and Priority Measures Proposed by the Authority for Air Pollution and Control*, available at cseindia.org/challenge_balance/.../LeapfrogFactor_Delhistory.pdf.

in five years.[21] The Court orders were an additional burden on such a loss-making corporation which could implement them only if the state or central government bailed it out. The private operators of buses were not inclined to make the necessary heavy investment or allow more operators to enter the market; rather they looked to avenues that could at least postpone the implementation of the order. Thus, the public and the private sector found common cause in making attempts to delay the implementation of the orders of the Supreme Court.

As the time approached for the phasing out of publicly or privately owned old diesel buses and the adoption of the single mode of fuel of CNG, the Supreme Court began to be approached by the Government of India and the Delhi administration to give more time to meet the requirements of deadlines. Time was first extended to 30 September 2001, then to 31 January 2002, and then till 31 March 2002. Till now, postponement was argued on the plea that the preparations for the switch-over were taking time and that commuters will be put to great difficulty for there would be an insufficient number of buses on the streets. There may be virtual anarchy on the Delhi roads. The plea was also taken that bussing of school-children will be affected if all diesel buses are taken off the roads because of lack of replacement. The Delhi government began to announce how the school vacations may have to be staggered. Private operators threatened to go on strike unless the Delhi government provided them with financial incentives through low interest loans and higher fares. The central government, responsible for the supply of CNG, argued for more time to establish dispensing and feeder stations and to divert the supply from other uses to public transport in Delhi.

Till this time, though, the basic order that CNG would be the single fuel for public transport was not disputed. However, the Court was provided with a discordant note on this ground after a Committee, appointed by the Government of India on 13 September 2001 to reconsider the single fuel decision, submitted its report. A Committee of experts drawn from the fields of environment, energy, vehicular technology, et al., and headed by Dr R.A. Mashelkar, Director-General, Council of Scientific and Industrial Research, was appointed

---

[21] *Times of India*, 2001, 'TNN: IIT Study Based on Assumptions', *Times of India*, 18 August.

to recommend an appropriate auto fuel policy to the government. The Committee set for itself several guidelines for its work. An important one that set parameters for its deliberations was, 'Rather than a rigid prescriptive policy, a flexible policy which allows multi-fuel and multi-technology option for reaching prescribed emission norms was considered desirable.' The Committee assigned studies on urban road traffic and air quality to specialized institutes like the Central Road Research Institute, National Environmental Engineering Research Institute, and the Institute of Petroleum.

The Interim Report of the Committee[22] made some major recommendations that in some ways were counter to the Supreme Court directives. It began by acknowledging that public health is of prime concern and air quality is a crucial factor in determining it. It also set itself the task of improving air quality through measures that were cost effective and at the same time practical for reducing pollution from in-use vehicles and setting realistic/achievable standards for new vehicles. The Committee emphasized that, 'auto fuel policy needs to be guided by evidence-based analysis, based on sound scientific principles, and should also be based on cost effectiveness'. Then it went on to recommend that 'the government should decide only the vehicular emission standards and the corresponding fuel specifications without specifying vehicle technology and the type of fuel'. The Committee, thus, did not endorse the idea of a single fuel being clean and that public and private transport should be run only on CNG.

The recommendations of the Mashelkar Committee prompted the Government of India to appeal to the Supreme Court not to insist on CNG as the only clean fuel. As a matter of fact, it made the plea that buses should be permitted to run on low sulphur diesel. It was contended that in some countries ultra low sulphur diesel (having sulphur content of not more than .001 per cent) was now available. The battle was being redrawn for up to now neither the Government of India nor the Delhi administration was contesting the Court's insistence on a single mode of fuel of CNG, but asking for time to implement its decision. Now, the Court's insistence on CNG as a single mode of fuel was being questioned. In its order of 26 March 2001, the Court asked

[22] Government of India, 2001, *Interim Report of the Expert Committee on Auto Fuel Policy*, New Delhi: GOI, 28 December.

the Bhure Lal Committee to examine this question and permit various parties to submit their representation to it. The Court then demanded a report from the Committee indicating which fuel can be regarded as 'clean fuel' that does not cause pollution or is not otherwise injurious to health.

Several organizations and associations made representations to the Bhure Lal Committee. Among these were the Ministry of Petroleum and Natural Gas, Government of India, Society for Automobile Manufacturers, several associations of transporters, two major manufacturers of CNG chassis buses (Tata Engineering and Ashok Leyland), petrol dealers association, et al. The Committee also solicited the opinion of Prof. Dinesh Mohan of the Indian Institute of Technology (IIT), Delhi and the Tata Energy Research Institute (TERI), now renamed The Energy and Resources Institute.

In terms of the clean fuel controversy, the technical views of TERI, IIT, and the Centre for Science and Environment were important. In its representation, TERI argued that while the Government may continue with its programme of introducing CNG buses, it should not insist on CNG as a single mode fuel. It suggested that there is a need to explore retrofit options of less than eight-year-old diesel buses with diesel oxidation catalyst with 500 ppm sulphur. More studies were needed to compare the emissions of Indian buses powered by alternative fuels like ultra low sulphur diesel and CNG. R.K. Pachauri, Director-General of TERI, argued that the decision in favour of CNG was taken without any trials being carried out under operating conditions with this as well as substitute fuels.[23] He underscored the point that there is overwhelming evidence now that CNG is not even the best fuel for reducing pollution, quite apart from its practical problems. Based on the IIT study findings, he supported the ultra low sulphur diesel as an alternative fuel.

IIT's Professor Dinesh Mohan also argued that specific fuels should not be prescribed and that choice should be based on technologies available or expected in the future and on a sound cost-benefit analysis. Even for Euro-IV and Euro-V standards in Europe, there is no agreement on the fuels to be used in a widespread manner. He cited the study conducted by IIT which argued that CNG is no better than

[23] R.K. Pachauri, 2001, 'Clearing the Air: Many Roadblocks on the CNG Route', Times of India, 1 September, p. 6.

ultra low sulphur diesel as an automotive fuel. 'Contrary to popular perception, CNG vehicles emit more carbon monoxide and nitrogen oxide than those running on .05 per cent ultra low sulphur diesel. Use of CNG does reduce particulate matter (PM) emissions but increases CO and hydrocarbon emissions from buses.'[24] The bus fleet in Delhi should be converted gradually, allowing for new technologies to move in. He also raised the issue of costs for the operator of bus services and to the commuter in deciding the maximum subsidy that the government should pay for public transport. In accepting 'the polluter pay principle', taxes on car users have to be raised to subsidize the bus fares.

Anil Agarwal of the Centre for Science and Environment disputed the contention that the CNG buses were more expensive. He also contested the view that ultra low sulphur diesel could be considered as an alternative fuel. He cited evidence to show that reduction of sulphur in diesel fuel, even as low as 10 ppm, does not make it a clean fuel. On the basis of the Swedish experience, he argued that to make diesel somewhat as clean as CNG, a package of fuel and technologies is needed—very low sulphur and PAH diesel together with good engines, oxidation catalysts, particulate traps, and certain kinds of catalysts. The cost of the above package is very high and cannot be recommended.

The representation of the Ministry of Petroleum and Natural Gas, Government of India, made the plea that adequate amount of gas is not available if the entire bus fleet will have to be run on CNG. It contended that there will be a serious crisis when the CNG supply will have to be diverted from other gas-based industries like power and fertilizers, et al. It also argued that there could be uncertainties in supply because of breakdowns of the gas processing facilities or the pipelines, dependence one single fuel may not be viable. The oil companies as also the Society of Indian Automobile Manufactures represented that low sulphur diesel may be considered a clean fuel. The chassis manufacturing companies, Ashok Leyland and Tata Engineering, supported the use of low sulphur diesel too. The transporters' associations joined the same chorus to argue that CNG is not available in places outside where their transport also plies and

[24] Dinesh Mohan, 2001, 'IIT Research Drills Holes into "Clean" CNG Theory', Press Interview, *Times of India*, 17 August, p. 3.

therefore, demanded subsidies for buying new buses to ply in Delhi in the shape of raised bus fares, etc.

In its recommendations to the Supreme Court submitted in August 2001, the Bhure Lal Committee rejected hydro-carbon fuels as clean fuels and accepted CNG, LPG, and Propane as environmentally acceptable fuels for Delhi.[25] It then made several recommendations for preparing plans of supplying adequate quantity of gas, providing subsidies to operators for changeover, supply schedule from bus manufactures, and ultimately heavy fines for those operators who continue to ply diesel buses after a stipulated date.

The Supreme Court considered the Bhure Lal Committee Report on Clean Fuels and passed orders on 5 April 2002, which were to be complied with by the transporters, Delhi administration, and the Government of India. This was a landmark judgment for the Court chose to comment upon various facets of public life apart from upholding the case of CNG as single mode of fuel for the National Capital Region of Delhi. A former Chief Justice of India who was in the forefront in leading the judiciary towards activism called it a seminal and historic judgment.[26] The Court reiterated its concern for the health of the people in Delhi and reminded the governments of their constitutional obligations. It quoted World Bank data to show the extent of correlation of air pollution with respiratory and cardiovascular diseases in India and abroad, and felt that the health cost should be taken into account while considering costs of controlling air pollution. It underlined a World Bank estimate that suggested, using 1992 data, that the annual health cost to India was to the order of Rs 55.5 billion due to ambient air pollution while the cost to Delhi alone was to the order of Rs 10,000 million. It justified its intervention by emphasizing the lack of effort in controlling pollution and protecting the environment by the enforcement agencies, even when adequate laws were in place.

The Court chided the Government of India for not taking effective steps to halt or control this deterioration in air quality. The Court termed it 'baffling' that first the Delhi administration and then the

[25] Environment Pollution Authority for the National Capital Region, 2001, Twelfth Progress Report June–July 2001, New Delhi: Government of India, August.

[26] P.N. Bhagwati, 2002, 'A Seminal Judgment', Down to Earth, vol. 10, no. 24, 15 May, p. 50.

Government of India were not prepared to implement the Court orders in spite of postponement of deadlines and extension of time given by the Court. It is worthwhile to quote what the Court said in this regard, '... leaves us with no doubt that its (government's) intention, clearly is to frustrate the orders passed by this Court with regard to conversion of vehicles to CNG. The manner in which it has sought to achieve this object is to try and discredit CNG as the proper fuel and, secondly, to represent to the Court that CNG is in short supply and, thirdly, delay the setting up of adequate dispensing stations.' The Court disapproved the appointment of the Mashelkar Committee and saw it as a ruse to bypass its orders. It thought that the Committee was not serious in its concern for public health for the government had not even appointed a doctor or an expert in public health on the Committee. It further strongly disapproved of this Committee's recommendations by noting that norms of emission had been established long ago and choice of the fuel was left to the users, but the air of Delhi continued to deteriorate for there was no compliance. The Court used strong words to say that recommending emission norms 'is a clear abdication of the constitutional and statutory duty cast upon the government to protect and preserve the environment and is in the teeth of precautionary principle'.

The Court rejected pleas of shortage of CNG or inability to provide an adequate number of dispensing stations, and saw them as the government's low priority in fulfilling its constitutional obligations regarding public health. This low priority was expressed in the fact that the Government was continuing to supply CNG at low prices to commercial units while denying it to public transport which was willing to pay higher rates. The Court emphasized that 'If there is a short supply of an essential commodity, then the priority must be of public health, as opposed to the health of the balance sheet of a private company. To enable industries to cut their losses, or to make more profit at the cost of public health, is not a good sign of good governance, and this is contrary to the constitutional mandate of Articles 39(e), 47 and 48(a).' It also rejected the idea of multiple fuels and did not accept the findings of studies that showed that it was possible to have an alternative in low sulphur diesel. Then the Court went ahead to pass orders regarding the phasing out of buses run on diesel, penalizing those that continued to ply on diesel after a particular date, directing the government to frame plans to supply CNG in adequate quantities, and also plan financial incentives schemes to encourage the private operators to convert their diesel fleet into CNG.

It is clear that the Supreme Court was fighting a battle with government agencies that were either not interested in environmental issues or were prompted by other interests to take up cudgels on behalf of groups that saw the status quo as a profit-making enterprise. Research studies were pitted one against the other and torn out of context; none of the specialists tended to integrate and simplify findings to mobilize opinion or to raise public debate. Where were the consumers of public transport and how were they reacting to technical decisions being taken in their (read public) interest? It is this aspect of policy contestation to which we now turn.

THE POPULAR RESPONSE

As the deadline of April 2001 approached, the Delhi administration, which was primarily responsible for converting the diesel buses into those of CNG, began seeking the alibi of crisis on the roads of Delhi in order to seek postponement of the date for conversion. The diesel buses went off road and the operators went on strike on the streets of Delhi. Three years had passed since the Court's order and the Delhi administration had acquired only 400 CNG buses to run on city roads. This number would bear the burden of around 10,000 buses running in Delhi. When the diesel buses went off the roads, the commuters became angry, burnt buses, and stoned policemen on the city's streets. In response, the Chief Minister dared that she would face any punishment for contempt of Court in the interest of the people of Delhi. And this interest was in their commuting in diesel buses. No reference was made to the health of the people of Delhi. If this were not enough, the Chief Minister went on to add in the Delhi Assembly that the Supreme Court did not understand the ground realities.[27] Such a posture of the Delhi government sought to gain popularity for the Chief Minister. The message that emanated from the floor of the House caught the people's imagination and in public perception, the stock of the Chief Minister went high. The commuters were in particular all praise for

[27] Pankaj Vohra, 2001, 'CNG Fiasco: Chief Minister Backtracks as Problem Worsens', *The Hindustan Times*, 15 April, p. 3.

the Chief Minister who not only empathized with them but was also willing to go to jail for their cause.[28] Without taking any blame for the lack of preparation in the three years since the Supreme Court set the deadline, the Delhi government took up cudgels on behalf of transport associations that were demanding postponement of the deadline.

The central government took a similar stand by arguing that extreme hardships were being caused to the citizens of Delhi because of supply bottlenecks. The dispensing stations had not been placed and public transport vehicles were standing in long queues for long hours to get CNG. The Government of India also pleaded shortage of supply of gas and therefore argued that CNG should not be made mandatory for all public vehicles. The media was full of stories about how the inadequate number of dispensing stations was harassing vehicle drivers who had to work during the day, spend nights to fill CNG, had little to eat or sleep, and could not return home to see their children.

Political leaders who were sitting in the opposition came to support the cause of the transporters. The Congress Party was the elected government of Delhi while the BJP ruled at the central level. The Congress Party had come to power by defeating the BJP that was now in search of causes to regain popularity. It found one in the CNG issue. Knowing that its party ruled at the centre, it led transporters' demonstrations against the Delhi government for relaxation of the deadline. The Congress Party held its own rallies against the BJP and challenged them to debate. After various postponements, when the deadline in April 2002 approached, the local BJP Party led the transporters to believe that it could get an Ordinance passed by the central government declaring diesel as a clean fuel. The central government refused to do so because this would have brought it in direct conflict with the Supreme Court. But the political parties did not make any effort to educate the people about the aims of the Supreme Court's decisions in promoting a healthy environment. Health, disease, and polluted air did not figure prominently in public debate and discussion. Public debate, carried out in the media, pointed more to the travails of the commuters rather than on the need for clean air for the citizens of Delhi. For example, a reader, in a letter to the editor of The Hindu newspaper said, 'The common man who depends on the buses alone will pay the price for "clean air"... As

---

[28] Vohra, 'CNG Fiasco: Chief Minister Backtracks as Problem Worsens'.

things stand, it will take a long time to add more CNG buses and put in place adequate number of CNG-filling stations. In the intervening period, it is the poor who will continue to suffer.'[29] Sentiments expressed in the letter captured the mood of public debate and discussion at the time.

RESEARCH INSTITUTES AND TECHNOCRATS

As already mentioned, the two leading environmental research groups—TERI and CSE—cited research studies whose findings were pooh-poohed by the other. A Professor of Transport from IIT also joined the fray. While CSE continued to be the most vocal supporter of CNG and hailed the decisions of the Apex Court, TERI adopted a view that was supportive of the government's stand of multiple fuel policy and for allowing ultra low sulphur diesel too. The IIT expert also insisted on greater flexibility and did not want the options of new technology to close by adopting a single mode of fuel. CSE conducted a strong public campaign discrediting the other two opinions and casting doubts on their sincerity in promoting public interest because of one's affiliations with manufacturers of diesel buses and the other's sponsorship of the professorial chair he held by funds from a car manufacturing company. Research findings were used to support one position or the other. Allegations were made that the full picture was not emerging.

The most prominent role in the campaign for CNG was played by the Centre for Science and Environment. While TERI had been bringing out studies on levels of pollution in Delhi and its findings found place in the petition submitted by Mehta in 1985, the CSE adopted a more active advocacy role. In its series on the State of Environment, it brought out a report titled 'Slow Murder: The Deadly Story of Vehicular Pollution in India' in 1996. The Report carried considerable data to show how pollution levels were rising in Indian cities and argued that vehicular pollution is the result of a combination of bad vehicular technology, poor fuel quality, poor vehicular maintenance, and non-existent traffic planning. The Report became the basis of its public campaign.[30] The Director of CSE was appointed to the Bhure Lal Committee, which

---

[29] 'Letter to the Editor', *The Hindu*, 10 June 2002, p. 3.

[30] Anil Agarwal, Anju Sharma, and Anumita Roy Chowdhury, 1996, *Slow Murder: The Deadly Story of Vehicular Pollution in India*, New Delhi: Centre for Science and Environment.

provided the Centre further opportunity to conduct a more vigourous campaign for adopting a clean fuel for Delhi.

In this campaign, CSE's Anil Agarwal did not mince words. He was a spirited and bold advocate of CNG and effectively used his membership of the Environment Pollution Control Authority (Bhure Lal Committee) to press the choice of CNG. Accusing the detractors of CNG of various kinds of ulterior motives, Agarwal pointed out that the unseemly politicization of the CNG issue in Delhi, with rival parties busy accusing each other for the ongoing mess and demanding an alternative fuel, shows how little India's leaders care about the environment, public health, and just plain commitment of purpose.[31] He then hammered on saying, 'the question that we should ask, especially in India where private interests rule over public interests, is, whose interest is CNG stepping on? Does the answer lie in the fact that CNG, unlike diesel, cannot be adulterated, cannot be siphoned off, and there is no money in its spot purchases?'[32]

★ ★ ★

The Court passed its final orders in April 2002 that upheld the recommendations of the Environmental Pollution and Control Authority, popularly known as the Bhure Lal Committee. The Committee rejected multiple fuel policy, which would have allowed the use of ultra low sulphur diesel, and chose a single fuel policy by recommending CNG and other gases like LPG or propane. This choice contradicted the recommendations made by the technical committee of the Government of India and various research institutes. The choice was, however, the same as the one advocated by the Centre for Science and Environment. The Director of CSE, who was a very vociferous advocate of this choice, was also member of the Bhure Lal Committee. It is obvious that the Committee was effectively persuaded by Agarwal who dissuaded it from considering any other alternative presented by others—research institutes, government committees or associations of transporters or vendors of oil!

The Supreme Court did not hesitate to pass severe comments on the motivation of governments and in effect said that they did not

[31] Anil Agarwal, 2001, 'Smell the Air, Minister', *Indian Express*, 20 August.
[32] Ibid.

work in public interest. It did not accept the plea that CNG was in short supply. It pointed out that, if it was so, then the government had wrong priorities for CNG was still being supplied in adequate quantity to private industries which were paying less than what public transport was willing to pay. The motivation for setting up the Mashelkar Committee was questioned and, despite the fact that it was chaired by the top government technocrat, its report was dismissed for echoing the government voice and not reflecting a sound technical advice. The Court went on to say that 'it is naive of Mashelkar Committee to expect merely laying down fresh emission norms will be effective or sufficient to check or control vehicular pollution.' Similarly, the Court did not hesitate to say explicitly that the governments were not ready to accept its orders.

The political leadership, whether in government or in opposition, showed limited perspective for short-term electoral gains. Little mobilization to seek support for policies that would improve the environment and make for healthy living took place. Instead, the leadership sought support from the people to fight the Supreme Court. Panic spread among the parents of school children when the Delhi administration made an uncalled for announcement that it would close all schools till the issue of choice of fuel was decided.

The advice from technocrats was not unanimous. Different perspectives were articulated. Reference to 'research' or 'knowledge' does not signify a single body of thinking, data or literature that is commonly recognized and accepted.[33] The normative dimension of research cannot be ignored. Research agendas can reflect the interests of those who want to influence the way they would like the policy discourse to proceed. In many ways, research legitimizes those who commissioned or funded it. Thus the citing of different research findings reflects a struggle between different 'world views' or 'regimes of truth'.[34] In efforts to bridge research and policy, different 'knowledges' compete, leading to a techno-political struggle. In this case of adoption of CNG as a single fuel public transport in Delhi, the Supreme Court became the final arbiter rather than the political bargaining process. But the Court's

---

[33] See the discussion in Stone et al. (eds), *Banking on Knowledge: The Genesis of Global Development Networks*, London: Routledge, pp. 87–103.

[34] Ibid.

decision was not an interpretation of law; it was a choice of 'world views' that opted for one kind of technology.

Another reason for the rise of techno-political struggles is the indeterminacy of science in finding single solutions or decisive answers to environmental problems. The concept of 'clean fuel' had political overtones, primarily because scientific evidence was not conclusive. The indeterminate nature of the relevant scientific evidence opened the door for competing interpretations of the same evidence.[35] In addition, the Director of CSE laments the fact that most scientists are employed with government agencies in India and are not ready to speak out.[36] Despite the high levels of particulates in India's urban air, the Centre has not been able to find a single scientist who has studied the health effects of this pollutant. In such a situation, the easiest technique is to find a problem in every solution. She goes on to plead for the environmental movement to find its own scientists—those that are not influenced by bureaucrats and politicians.

In ushering in a new social order, the environmentalists have been critical of the way technocratic discussions tend to avoid democratic politics with its political parties and interest groups. They were against the way the technocrats were impatient with political problems that block implementation of rationally determined solutions and perceive technocratic policy discourse as antithetical to democratic processes. However, the battle for clean air for Delhi to provide healthy living to its citizens was fought on technocratic grounds. The arena of policy discourse was monopolized by technical findings to prove the superiority of fuels. In its public campaign, CSE labelled all opposition to CNG—whether coming from other technical think-tanks or from transporters, governments, political parties or even principals of affected schools—as political obstacles to a rational decision. Various leaders of these groups were termed as 'saboteurs'.[37]

The way the Supreme Court, the technocrats and experts, and the political leadership in opposition and in government played their roles in the battle for clean environment has many implications for the

---

[35] See Frank Fischer, 2000, *Citizens, Experts, and the Environment: The Politics of Local Knowledge*, Durham and London: Duke University Press, Chapter 5.

[36] Sunita Narain, 2002, 'Changing Environmentalism', *Seminar*, vol. 51, p. 18.

[37] See the various issues of *Down to Earth*, 2001 and 2002, vols 9 and 10.

functioning of democracy and the emerging system of governance in India. The increasing incidence of judicial activism reflects the growing insensitivity of the government to the problems of those who do not have strong political voice. It also reflects the inability of the institutional processes to resolve conflicts in society. More and more groups that do not have organized strength to influence political decisions are taking recourse to judicial processes to get their grievances redressed. The perception that political decision-making works on partisan interests and that the judicial process is neutral and transparent has grown over the years. Courts have begun filling policy gaps and stepping in where powerful groups in society cannot be contained through political methods. The land mafia, polluting industries, and the transport lobby could be ordered only by courts to adhere to laws and thus work for a clean Delhi. In this process, new policy directions have emerged that encourage the government to legislate appropriate policies. This has in some ways devalued political institutions because people welcome the court's intervention, even in areas that strictly fall in the domain of the executive or the legislature.

In the environmental sector, the government probably finds it convenient for the Apex Court to find solutions to social conflicts that it cannot easily handle. If the conflict persists, then it has an alibi to escape responsibility. The risk is that the role of the Court may become devalued if there is an accumulation of decisions that find partial implementation or that legitimately belong to the political realm and have less to do with legal interpretations. Ironically, de-politicization of an issue by the Court may lead to its own politicization.

5

Does Performance Matter?
Policy Struggles in Education*

W hile considerable work has been done on the availability of policy alternatives and why they are articulated, much less attention has been devoted to explore how the actual choice among varying alternatives was made and who among policymakers contributed in what way. There is a lack of adequate attention to the processes of public policy and this neglect emerges from the kind of explanations that are offered for the reasons why a state pursues some activities and not others. These explanations have much to do with what the state is perceived to be and what it is supposed to do.

Within a traditional Marxist analysis, the basic proposition is that politics is a manifestation of class conflict in society. This basic proposition leads to the argument that the primary function of the state is to ensure the legal, institutional, and ideological hegemony of the dominant class or class alliance over the subordinate classes.[1] Briefly, two important consequences flow from this reasoning. One is that policy change occurs when there is a shift in relationship among the social classes and therefore research analysis should concentrate on

* Kuldeep Mathur, 2001, 'Does Performance Matter? Policy Struggles in Education', *Journal of Educational Planning and Administration*, vol. 15, no. 2, 1–18 April, pp. 225–40.

[1] M. Grindle and J. Thomas, 1991, *Public Choices and Policy Change: The Political Economy of Reform in Developing Countries*, Baltimore: Johns Hopkins University Press, pp. 20–2.

when and why these shifts occur. The second follows from this. The role of policymakers is not central to understanding the processes of policy change because all that they are doing is to represent their class interests.

If individual policymakers are inconsequential in the Marxist tradition, the pluralist approach regards them as neutral arbitrators in negotiating compromises among diverse conflicting groups. In this tradition of thought, the state is a political arena where the groups fight their battles for scarce resources or attempt to influence policies that determine the way the resources will be shared. The principal role of the public officials is to facilitate the process of bargaining and compromise and be neutral arbitrators. Research analysis tends to understand the rise of interest groups, their access to policymakers and their strength in the bargaining processes. Little significance is attached to individual policymakers in this mode of thinking too.

Both of the above approaches tend to explain policy outcomes through societal dynamics. What happens in state institutions and whether state actors have the capacity to influence policy outcomes is really not part of their consideration. The present analysis assumes that the role of policymakers goes much beyond what is portrayed in these approaches. One important reason is that policymakers as individuals bring with them not only their social background, but professional training too. Experientially evolved social perspectives can deviate from the straitjacket of their social background.[2] Their roles can be conditioned by the institutions of which they become a part and their decisions cannot be torn out of the procedures and processes laid down in those institutions. State institutions have their own dynamics and momentum, which sometimes quickly engulf the actors in them and facilitate or restrict their autonomy in decision-making.[3]

The purpose of this chapter is to focus attention on the processes determining educational policy in India and explore the role of various actors in shaping the outcomes. It is assumed that policymakers do have room to manoeuvre and can shape policy outcomes. Their motivations

[2] Kuldeep Mathur and J.W. Bjorkman, 1994, *Top Policy Makers in India: Cabinet Ministers and their Civil Service Advisers*, p. 14.

[3] Ashutosh Varshney, 1995, *Democracy, Development, and the Countryside: Urban-Rural Struggles in India*, Cambridge: Cambridge University Press, pp. 57–60.

and perspectives are imbued by personal and professional values that can counter societal pressures. This is not to say that the social context or the play of social power groups is of no consequence. Both are. But the interactions in the state apparatus have an influence that cannot be completely marginalized. For an adequate understanding of policy outcome, we need to consider the institutional processes and the capacity of the policymakers. In the field of education, like many other fields, technical advice has come to play an increasing role in decision-making. Within state institutions, more often than not, technically trained professionals get pitted against bureaucrats and politicians. Sometimes, they challenge the assumptions of these groups, at other times they provide support to their formulations. However, legitimacy of a policy is drawn from some professional expertise or the other. It is important to identify these processes to understand the nature of policy outcomes.

COLONIAL EDUCATION

In terms of its historical context, the education system of India owes little to the traditional Hindu or Muslim systems of education that prevailed before the advent of the Europeans on the subcontinent. As a matter of fact, the colonial education system was not a modernized transformation of any traditional system of Indian education. It was established outside the traditional systems and without any relationship to them. During British rule, the Charter Act of 1813 had permitted missionaries to go to India in order to educate and proselytize, while the East India Company had accepted responsibility to educate Indians in Western knowledge. In 1823, a General Committee on Public Instruction was set up to give shape to an education policy that the Government of India needed to pursue. This Committee consisted of Orientalists and Anglicists, and the ideas of both groups were put before Lord Macaulay who at the time was Law Member of India. Macaulay rejected the ideas of the Orientalists and, through a forceful and now well-known Minute, made a vigorous plea for Western learning taught through the English language.

In 1837, English was made the language of administration, and a government resolution of 1844 threw subordinate positions open to Indians. The result was that institutions of oriental learning declined as English was made the main language of study and the medium of instruction after the primary stage. Rapid expansion occurred of schools and colleges that taught English education, with the higher stratum of society adopting and patronizing it. The system of English education had taken root. Concentration, since 1835, on the urbanized upper and middle classes led to the neglect of mass education.[4] The education system emerged from the needs of the colonial power.

It was this restrictive system of education that India inherited at the time of independence. The post-colonial history of reform has been a struggle to unshackle the system from its past by making it accessible to all sections of society and correcting its bias of emphasizing the study of language and humanities. Mahatma Gandhi whose vision sharply differed from the one that was offered in the modern and industrial societies of the West was a powerful influence on nationalist reformers. There has since been a continuous struggle between the modernizers and the Gandhians, and the modernizers have usually won.

FIRST POLICY REVIEW

The Education Commission of 1964–6 provided the first comprehensive effort to look at the educational system in India after independence. The 1948–9 University Education Commission and the 1952 Secondary Education Commission had respectively looked at university and secondary education in a compartmentalized fashion but, despite extremely low literacy rates in India, neither committee nor commission had been established to specifically review primary and adult education. In addition to its mandate to look comprehensively at education, the 1964 Commission was charged with the responsibility to suggest a national education system for the country. In a perceptive analysis, the member-secretary of the Commission, J.P. Naik, suggests that the Commission raised a debate on education that had not occurred earlier and sharpened reaction to many issues that were more political than educational in nature. For example, the use of regional languages as media of instruction at the university level raised a storm in political circles. It was not the main recommendation and neither was it being suggested for the first time. In fact, the University Education Commission 1948–9, the Emotional Integration Committee

[4] For elaboration of the argument, see A. Basu, 1982, *Essays in the History of Education*, New Delhi: Concept Publishing Co., p. 19.

of 1962, and the Vice-Chancellors' Conference 1962 had made the same recommendation. The political situation was such that the opposition to this recommendation tended to influence much of the reaction to the Education Commission.[5] And this was lukewarm to outright negative. For various reasons, as a Report, it did not last much in national discussions and debate. But it had a strong influence on all subsequent policies. Since the Commission submitted its report in 1966, all educational policies that came later have been either heavily influenced by its recommendations or have deliberately designated their departures from it.

COMPOSITION OF THE COMMISSION

In its resolution laying down the terms of reference for the Commission, the Government of India emphasized that 'it is desirable to survey the entire field of educational development as the various parts of the education system strongly interact with and influence one another'. It suggested that what 'is needed is a synoptic survey and an imaginative look at education considered as a whole and not fragmented into parts and stages'. It further went on to say that:

While planning of education for India must necessarily emanate from Indian experience and conditions, the Government of India is of the opinion that it would be advantageous to draw upon the experience and thinking of educationists and scientists from other parts of the world in the common enterprise of seeking for the right type of education, which is the quest of all mankind, specially at this time when the world is getting closely knit together in so many ways.[6]

UNESCO provided three international experts on the Commission. They were Jean Thomas, Inspector General of Education in France and formerly Assistant Director General of UNESCO; Anatoly Shumovsky, Director, Methodological Division, Ministry of Higher and Special Secondary Education in the Russian Soviet Federated Socialist Republic and Professor of Physics at Moscow University; and Sadatoshi Ihara,

[5] See J.P. Naik, 1982, *The Education Commission and After*, New Delhi: Allied Publishers, p. 38.
[6] Ministry of Education, 1966, *Report of the Education Commission, 1964–66: Education and National Development*, New Delhi: Ministry of Education, Government of India.

Professor of the Faculty of Science and Technology at Waseda University, Tokyo. The Government of India also hoped that the collaboration of other eminent scientists and educationists would be available as consultants.

Dr D.S. Kothari, Chairman of the University Grants Commission, headed the Commission. An eminent scientist and Professor of Physics at Delhi University, he had worked closely with the team that advised Nehru about science matters. Other than the chairman and the three foreign members, there were eleven more members, plus a member-secretary. All of them were connected with the profession of education in one way or another. The Member-Secretary was J.P. Naik, Head of the Department of Education Planning, Administration, and Finance at Poona's (now Pune) Gokhale Institute of Politics and Economics. Naik had made a name for himself as an educational activist and had established the Indian Institute of Education in Poona. A prolific writer, he was the moving spirit behind the Commission and its recommendations. He had joined the national liberation movement under Gandhi's leadership and had served a prison sentence too. Gandhi had perceptible influence on his ideas and work.

In addition, there were two foreigners apart from those seconded by UNESCO. H.L. Elvin was Director of the Institute of Education at the University of London and Roger Reville was the Dean of Research at the University of California. Of the 16 members, five were foreigners and represented the educational systems of France, Soviet Russia, Japan, the UK and the USA. All of these countries were in the developed world. However, there were no experts from countries, which were either experimenting with innovative systems or struggling to achieve education for all.

The remaining nine members were also connected with education in one capacity or the other. Among the academic administrators were A.R. Dawood, former Director, Extension Programme for Secondary Education; R.A. Gopalaswami, Director of Institute of Applied Manpower Research; V.S. Jha, former Director of the Commonwealth Education Liaison Unit in London; P.N. Kirpal, Educational Adviser to the Government of India; K.G. Saiyidain, former Educational Adviser to the Government of India; and B.P. Pal, Director of Indian Agricultural Research Institute. Among those connected with universities were M.V. Mathur, Professor of Economics and Public Administration at Rajasthan University; S. Panandiker, Head of the Department of Education, Karnataka University; and Triguna Sen, Rector of Jadavpur University outside Calcutta.

To understand the nature of the recommendations and the working of the Commission, it is necessary to stress that the Commission consisted of people who were intimately involved in the field of education and its administration. Nearly all had some relationship to a University or an institute of higher education. There was a strong bias towards specialization in the fields of science and technology. A weakness, pointed out by Naik himself, was that even though the Commission called its report 'Education and National Development', it had little to say on development or on society.[7] He felt that this happened because there were no social scientists on the Commission. Naik subsequently became founding member-secretary of the Indian Council of Social Science Research and believed that no education planning is possible without substantial inputs from the social sciences. Other significant weaknesses included the absence of a gender perspective since the Commission had only one woman member, and the heavy reliance on foreign experts in its deliberations.

In the course of its work, the Commission travelled the length and breadth of the country, holding discussions and seminars, visiting schools, colleges and universities. Two conferences with student representatives were also held. According to the calculation of the Commission itself, over 900 persons were interviewed and the total number of notes and memoranda sent to the Commission was around 2,400. About 20 international consultants also met the Commission. These included eminent persons like Professor Edward Shils and Lord Robbins. The Commission set up twelve task forces on:

1. School education
2. Higher education
3. Technical education
4. Agricultural education
5. Adult education
6. Science education
7. Teacher training and teacher status
8. Student welfare

[7] Naik, *The Education Commission and After*, p. 57.

9. New techniques and methods
10. Manpower
11. Educational administration
12. Educational finance
    In addition, it set up seven working groups on:
1. Women's education
2. Education of backward classes
3. School buildings
4. School–community relations
5. Statistics
6. Pre-primary education
7. School curriculum

The task forces and the working groups made a detailed study of the specific problems assigned to them and presented their reports to the Commission. Each task force or working group included two or three members of the Commission and, on an average, consisted of around a dozen members. Many sub-groups were also appointed. The result was that more than 250 experts and educational administrators participated in these deliberations. Agencies like the UNESCO and the British Council provided support by supplying international members and consultants. In addition, UNESCO provided the Associate Secretary, Mr McDougall, as well as office support.

THE IMPLEMENTATION PROCESS

The Education Commission submitted its report in June 1966 after a labour of two years. Indira Gandhi had become the Prime Minister in January 1966 after the death of Lal Bahadur Shastri in whose tenure the Commission had been appointed. But there was some continuity because M.C. Chagla had remained Education Minister in both Cabinets. When the Report was submitted, Chagla held a press conference and made its recommendations public for wider discussion and debate. The copy of the Report was available in September 1966 and was distributed to the state governments, the Vice-Chancellors' Conference, the Central Advisory Board of Education (CABE), and members of both Houses of Parliament. The expectation was that, after comments had been received, the Government of India would issue a statement on Education Policy.

However, elections were announced in early 1967; so the processes of consultation continued until a new government under Mrs
Gandhi came to power in March 1967. The Cabinet was changed and
Dr Triguna Sen, who was a member of the Commission, took over the
portfolio of education. But as Naik pointed out, Dr Sen—though dedicated to the implementation of the Report—lacked a political base, and
therefore found it difficult to carry the state governments and others
with him, particularly when he ceased to command the confidence of
the Prime Minister.[8] Undaunted and committed to the Report, Sen proceeded to appoint a Committee comprised of Members of Parliament,
which represented all the different political parties. He expected that,
based on a report of this parliamentary committee, he could prepare a
draft for a national policy and place it before Parliament.

The new parliamentary committee was asked to:

1.   Consider the Report of the Kothari Commission,
2.   Prepare a draft statement on the national policy on education, and
3.   Identify a programme for immediate action.

However, discussions in the committee were contentious; the wide
differences of opinion can be gauged from the fact that no less than nine
of the thirty members wrote minutes of dissent, which ran into twenty-
three pages against a Report of twenty-six pages. The discussions centred
on only a few issues that related to 'selectivism' in admissions or in
choosing universities for special funding or the medium of instruction.
Most other issues were ignored.

Unfazed, the Education Minister took the Report of this parliamentary committee and that of the Commission for discussion to the
Central Advisory Board of Education as well as to the Vice-Chancellors'
Conference. While the Board spent most of its time debating the
issue of the medium of instruction, the Vice-Chancellors' Conference
debated the proposal on choosing major universities for special funding.
As a result, the 1968 policy document was a very watered-down version
of the Kothari Commission Report. Subsequent Education Ministers,
all of whom belonged to the Congress Party, through assurances of
implementation, kept the recommendations of the Commission alive,
but even this pretence was dropped as the country moved to more immediate concerns during the 1970s.

[8] Naik, *The Education Commission and After*, p. 31.

THE INTERREGNUM

The decade of the 1970s was a period of political turmoil in the country. There was a war and an adventure into a semi-authoritarian rule through a state of emergency. When Mrs Gandhi lost the elections in 1977, the new government was formed by a coalition of all people who had led the movement against her rule. What united the coalition was its anti-Gandhi stand and not specific policy programmes. But some interest was taken to reformulate education policy. This interest emerged from the initiatives of a group known as Citizens for Democracy. Justice V.M. Tarkunde led this group and the motivating force of their Report on 'Education for Our People: A Policy Frame for the Development of Education over the Next Ten Years (1978–87)' was the well-known educationist J.P. Naik (who had, as mentioned earlier, served as the secretary of the Education Commission). Around 44 Indians appended their names to this document and their professional background was varied and diverse, though they were all connected with one educational institution or another. The recommendations in this Report were greatly influenced by the ideas of J.P. Naik who in turn owed much to the philosophy and ideas of Mahatma Gandhi. J.P. Narain, who had spearheaded the struggle against Mrs Gandhi and who himself was a follower of the Mahatma, endorsed the Report. It called for a radical reconstruction of education under the auspices of a social movement, which would take away the state monopoly and compel it to work towards reforming the system in favour of the poor and the deprived.

Soon after, the government, led by the coalition, presented a Draft National Policy on Education in 1979. This Draft Policy was inspired by the earlier Report, but even before any national debate could take place, the government fell and this draft was forgotten.

NATIONAL EDUCATION POLICY, 1986

The adoption of the 1968 Education Policy based largely on the recommendations of the Kothari Commission led to considerable expansion in education facilities throughout the country at all levels. Perhaps the most notable development was the acceptance of a common structure of education wherein most of the Indian states implemented the 10+2 model for schools and three years for an undergraduate degree. Another significant development was the institutionalization of the leadership role of the central government. While the Kothari Commission was conducting its deliberations and when the 1968 Policy was enunciated, the federal system had specified education as a subject within the sole responsibility of the states. A 1976 constitutional amendment, however, reassigned education to the concurrent list. This shift had substantive implications because it required that governmental responsibility for education would be shared. It also enjoined the central government to accept a larger leadership role by providing guidance in innovative programmes and by supporting the states with finance and administration (if required by the states) for implementing those innovative programmes.

From the time that Rajiv Gandhi took over as Prime Minister on the death of Indira Gandhi, he began to refer to the need for a new education policy. In one of his first radio broadcasts after the assumption of office, he said that our 'educational system needs to be reconstructed as a dynamic force for national growth and integration. I intend to initiate a comprehensive review of the system and to build a national consensus on reform.' Soon after winning a massive mandate in the December 1984 elections, he again referred to education as having a dynamic role to promote national cohesion and the work ethic. In a speech on 5 January 1985, he proclaimed that 'I have asked that a new national education policy be drafted'. Speaking to the State Education Ministers Conference in August 1985, he not only underlined the need for a new education policy but also raised several questions that needed to be tackled with urgency. These included issues of values, questions of unequal opportunity, gender bias, and the role of education in smoothening social tensions. These issues and questions became the focus of debate and deliberations that followed later. Thus the Policy that emerged in 1986 was a product of strong commitment from the Prime Minister himself.

As preparation, two premier institutions—the National Council of Educational Research and Training (NCERT) and the National Institute of Education Planning and Administration (NIEPA)—were asked to provide a comprehensive appraisal of the existing educational scene. This appraisal was used by the Ministry to publish a document in August 1985 titled the 'Challenge of Education: A Policy Perspective' in order to elicit national debate. Recognizing the contributions of earlier committees, particularly the Kothari Commission, the document laid down its perspective by saying that 'perhaps the problems of today [are] more the result of tardy and haphazard implementation and a progressive decline in the allocation of resources'. It then went on to suggest that the 'new education policy should articulate the educational imperatives not only in terms of objectives, concepts and priorities but it should also spell out an operational strategy with associated financial, material, organizational and human requirements to achieve the long and short objectives laid down in the policy'. It argued that if radical change were accepted in education policy, equally radical instruments and organizational structures would have to be devised to give it a practical shape. This document became the basis for many seminars and workshops while comments were solicited directly from the public. National institutions like NCERT and NIEPA were harnessed to organize these meetings and to sift through the large number of individual comments. Consultations were also held with the Central Advisory Board of Education. The policy document, this time, was a product of a bureaucratic exercise though consultations with experts were held.

The National Policy of Education was placed before Parliament in early 1986. The major thrust of this enunciated policy was to develop a strategy of implementation, accompanied by the assignment of specific responsibilities for financial and organizational support. The most urgent tasks that it set itself to tackle were the problems of access, quality, quantity, utility, and financial outlay. It set these problems in the emerging phase of India's social and political life, which was increasingly characterized by inequality, and the lack of social justice. Speaking to the National Development Council in April 1986, the Prime Minister said that the idea is not to eliminate or destroy a system that has been in practice. The attempt is to guide the system in particular specific directions and to try to stop its drift. 'The thrust in all this,' he continued, 'is to eliminate inequalities, to liberate talents, and to achieve a national fulfilment.' The policy document was a brief twenty-nine pages that laid down a strategy of implementation.

While some organizational actions began to be initiated as a consequence of this policy, Rajiv Gandhi and his party lost the electoral mandate in 1989, and a new government led by V.P. Singh came into power. In May 1990, this coalition government appointed a Committee to review the 1986 Policy of Education—a review that was initiated even before the stipulated period of five years had been completed. The urgency reflected the nature of the coalition in power, which had the support of backward and minority communities and had on its agenda a contentious 'reservation' policy recommended by the Mandal Commission. In the announcement of the setting up of the Review Committee, the government provided its perspective when it said:

Government accords the highest priority to education both as a human right and as the means for bringing about a transformation towards a more humane and enlightened society. There is a need to make education an effective instrument for securing a status of equality for women and persons belonging to the backward castes and the minorities. Moreover, it is essential to give work and employment orientation to education and exclude from it the elitist aberrations, which have become the glaring characteristic of the educational scene. Educational institutions are increasingly influenced by casteism, communalism, and obscurantism and it is necessary to lay emphasis on struggle against this phenomenon and to move towards a genuinely egalitarian and secular social order. [Therefore] the National Policy on Education 1986 needs to reviewed, to evolve a framework which would enable the country to move towards this perspective of education.

The Review Committee itself pointed out that these concerns were not new but that it intended to give a new direction and to make a break from the past.

COMPOSITION OF THE COMMITTEE
To chair the review committee, the V.P. Singh Government appointed Acharya Ramamurti, a social worker and long-time associate of Jaiprakash Narain. An Additional Secretary in the Department of Education, Government of India, was appointed as Member-Secretary. Other than these two, the Committee consisted of 15 members. Most of the members (at least ten of them) were connected with universities or institutions of higher learning. One member was Chair of the National Open School whose background was with a Christian missionary society working for school education. Another member belonged to the DAV society concerned with college education. Another three members worked with NGOs running schools. The Committee was heavily loaded towards experience with higher education.

Two points need to be made about the membership. Acharya Ramamurti was part of the Sarvaodya movement of Mahatma Gandhi and ran a large number of schools on Gandhian ideas. He was part of the group that was critical of the elitist bias in the 1986 Education Policy and was also one of those who promoted the integration of work and education from the primary level itself. Another influential member of the Committee was Anil Sadgopal who had considerable experience in running schools for poor tribal children and had initiated several innovative methods. He shared the vision of a decentralized community-based education system where the people could assert themselves and make the system accountable. The Review Committee Report bore the imprint of the ideas of these two who sought to correct the 'elitist' aberrations of the 1986 Policy. The inspiration of Mahatma Gandhi resurfaced.

Following the practice of the Kothari Commission, the 1990 Review Committee adopted a procedure of wide-ranging consultations and discussions in order to finalize its recommendations. Six subcommittees were constituted for considering various subjects in detail. These subjects were:

1. Access, equity, and universalization.
2. Education and the right to work.
3. Quality and standards in education.
4. National unity, value education, and character building.
5. Resources and management.
6. Rural education.

Each subcommittee was authorized to co-opt additional members. While each subcommittee had four or five members, the number of co-opted members and special invitees for their meetings exceeded fifty. The subcommittees held formal discussions with as many people as possible. Some field studies were also conducted and NCERT presented a paper on citizen perceptions of the 1986 Policy. Many seminars and workshops were held in various parts of the country. However, the government had already become shaky towards the end of 1990 and there was a hurry to complete the work and present the Report. Sadgopal suggested in an interview that this hurry left out many recommendations and analysis that they had originally considered for incorporation.

THE POLICY PROCESS

The Ramamurti Committee submitted its Report in December 1990, which was tabled in both Houses of Parliament on 9 January 1991. At its March 1991 meeting, the Central Advisory Board of Education considered the procedure to be adopted for consideration of the Report and decided that its own Chairman (the Minister of Human Resources Development) should constitute a committee for this purpose. It must be pointed out that, by this time, the Ministry, which had appointed the Acharya Ramamurti Committee, had fallen and that a new government headed by P.V. Narasimha Rao had come to power. The government was again one of the Congress Party that had enunciated the 1986 Policy under the leadership of Rajiv Gandhi. In fact, Narasimha Rao was the Minister actively involved in the formulation of the Education Policy at the time of Rajiv Gandhi. It was natural for the 1986 Policy to be revived. A decision was therefore taken to review the Ramamurti Committee Report in a way that the threads of the 1986 Policy could be picked up again.

Following this decision, the Minister appointed a committee with sixteen members and chaired by Janardhana Reddy, Chief Minister and Education Minister of Andhra Pradesh. The Committee is popularly known by his name. The Joint Secretary in the Department of Education was appointed as Member-Secretary. There were six other ministers from Madhya Pradesh, Arunachal Pradesh, Bihar, Tamil Nadu, West Bengal, and Kerala. The other eight members of the Committee consisted of a member of the Planning Commission, Chair of the University Grants Commission, a university professor, chair of a development institute (long associated with UNESCO), principal of an innovative school, a scientist, a functionary of a social service organization and, most interestingly, a folk theatre personality. This Committee appeared to be the first in which there was a mix of political leaders, experts, and administrators.

The Janardhana Reddy Committee invited comments from the state governments on the Report of the Ramamurti Review Committee and asked the Department of Education to prepare detailed comments on each chapter of the Report. Other members of the Advisory Board as well as officials and non-officials commented on the Report. All these documents formed the basis for deliberations by the Reddy Committee. Although expected to submit its report within two months after its appointment in July 1991, the Committee took much longer and the Report was submitted in January 1992. The Committee found that, while the concerns of the Ramamurti Review Committee were unexceptionable, very few of its recommendations had policy implications. Therefore, it found little ground for revision of the 1986 Policy. Nonetheless, it recommended that the plan of action needed to be revised. The next task was to prepare a programme of action in order to revise the 1986 National Education Policy suitably.

In order to draft a Program of Action, a Steering Committee consisting of fourteen members was established. Chaired by a member of the Planning Commission, this Committee was comprised mostly of government functionaries like the UGC Chair and Secretaries to Government. Twenty-two task forces were constituted on different subjects comprising educationists as well as officials of state and central governments. The twenty-two subject areas were: (1) education for women's equality, (2) education of Scheduled Castes, Scheduled Tribes, and other weaker sections, (3) minorities' education, (4) education of the handicapped, (5) adult and continuing education, (6) early childhood care and education, (7) elementary education, (8) secondary education, (9) *Navodya Vidyalas*, (10) vocational education, (11) higher education, (12) open education, (13) rural universities/institutes, (14) technical and management education, (15) research and development, (16) media and educational technology, (17) delinking degrees from jobs and manpower planning, (18) cultural perspective and development of languages, (19) sports, physical education, and youth, (20) evaluation and examination, (21) teachers and their training, and (22) management of education. Many of the task forces included members of the Steering Committee but also at least 250 other experts and administrators. The task force reports were included as a chapter of the document. As the draft report was oriented towards implementation, it was first discussed at a conference of State Secretaries and Directors of Education. After incorporating the suggestions made at that conference, a draft Program of Action was placed before the CABE which, after due consideration, endorsed the document in 1992.

A follow-up to the 1992 Program of Action was further deliberation on decentralized management of education. Two constitutional amendments (73 and 74) had been adopted that placed the institutions of *panchayati raj* and urban governance on a constitutional footing.

Education was among the subjects included within the jurisdiction of *panchayats* and municipalities, and the state legislatures were expected to make suitable laws in this regard. The Program of Action had recommended that a CABE committee be set up to prepare guidelines on decentralized management of education in light of these amendments. Set up in 1993 and chaired by the Chief Minister of Karnataka, CABE approved its Committee's Report in the same year. Technical assistance for this Committee was provided by NIEPA.

INSTITUTIONAL NETWORK FOR POLICYMAKING

One characteristic feature of policymaking in education is India's federal system and the fact that education was initially included in the list of subjects reserved for the states. Only in 1974, through a constitutional amendment, did education become part of the concurrent list, which signified that both the Centre and the states could legislate in the field. Even after this amendment, however, the Centre never took unilateral decisions but rather undertook elaborate consultative processes before formulating any policy. In most cases, it developed guidelines and then through wide-ranging discussions cajoled the states to implement them. When necessary, the Centre provided funds to implement the schemes that it suggested.

Both policy as well as implementation processes are time consuming and always involve delay as well as require patience. Much of the central funding comes as plan expenditure. So, when the plan completes its five-year cycle, the responsibility for sustaining such schemes falls on the state governments. By accepting a central scheme and its money, states postpone their direct responsibility until the post-plan period. Some states hesitate to undertake such delayed responsibility or else fulfil their parts of the bargain inadequately. This situation is not conducive for full commitment to any scheme or policy, and state acceptance of Centre initiatives may only reflect the lure of extra funds. Many schemes that followed from the New Education Policy of 1986—like Operation Blackboard or the District Institutes of Education and Training (DIETs)—have reflected this hesitation when being implemented. Many of the states do not fulfil this responsibility and thus, most of the time these schemes suffer from shortage of funds leading to tardy achievement of goals and targets.

The probability of under-implementation leads to the need for continuous monitoring by central agencies over the performance of their schemes as well as maintenance of dialogue with state implementing agencies. A vast network of committees and visiting teams has thus appeared in order to oversee implementation of education projects. The Education Ministry of the Government of India finds itself drowned in problems of implementation without having the direct ability to resolve them. The national institutes that were supposedly established to plan and develop perspectives are drawn in the implementation muddle. They become part of the Ministry's teams to resolve field problems and spend considerable time and energy supporting such initiatives in government corridors.

In many cases, this process becomes quite contentious and appeals involve the political level. Hence, conferences of Chief Ministers and Education Ministers are frequently held in order to iron out differences or to legitimize the proposals of the Centre. The issue of making the right to free and compulsory education a Fundamental Right and to enforce it through suitable statutory measures is a case in point. After consultations with technical experts were exhausted, the proposal was discussed at a conference of Chief Ministers on 4–5 July 1996 and then at a conference of Education Ministers on 10 August 1996. The issue figured again in a meeting of experts with the Minister and then the decision was taken to appoint a Committee of State Education Ministers in order to consider the financial, administrative, legal, and academic implications of the proposal. This Subcommittee submitted its Report in January 1997. Subsequently, the political configuration of the government changed and little has been heard of the proposal since then.

On a regular basis, CABE holds meetings, which the Government of India's Minister of Education chairs and its members are the state Education Ministers. Among nominated members of this Board are state-level administrators and other experts. The Ministry seeks advice from this Board on all matters that concern the states. The Board also establishes its own subcommittees to examine issues in depth such as the case of decentralized management of education. The meetings of Education Ministers called by the central Education Minister have become controversial under the present central government which is wary to consult the states.

The Ministry draws on the expertise available at NCERT and NIEPA for advice on routine operational and policy issues. Involving others from different institutions in the country whenever wider consultation and discussions are needed widens this advisory support. As voluntary groups have become more involved in primary education and literacy programmes in recent years, their representation in the consultative process is also visible. While the central government tends to involve the state governments more in the policy planning process, the Education Department has lagged behind in consulting horizontally with other related central departments like those of Social Welfare or Tribal Development. The result is sometimes duplication of programmes and lack of coordination.

The style of policy formation involves extensive advice and consultation. The outstanding feature of policymaking is characterized by accommodation and settlement, involving political, administrative, and specialists' groups. Another feature of the use of committees is that a political committee processes the recommendations of an expert committee leading to further compromises and adjustments. The result is that the role of experts is not as salient as it appears to be. Thus, by its very nature, the policy process is built on compromises. As the membership of committees becomes more diverse, the search is not for 'best' solutions but for acceptable ones that are a considerable dilution of optimal ones. In order to stretch its probability of acceptance, a policy may have to make compromises in terms of its thrusts and its technical components. In addition, the content of policy will have to be consistent with the level of understanding that the concerned members may have of technical components. The committees do not provide reasons why some alternatives were accepted and not others.

* * *

In spite of this intense policy activity, educational performance in India suffers from many of the weaknesses that the country started with at the time of independence. Universalization of education is still a distant dream and after 65 years of independence, literacy rates are among the lowest in the world. The education style inherited from the colonial rulers still flourishes and the dream that education will be a system that promotes equality and national integration in society continues to be elusive. Instead of strengthening programmes on a continuous basis, each government introduces its own debate and formulates its own policy to show the difference from the past. The effort is to emphasize differences rather than to build on strengths. The result is that none of the political parties try to seek a national consensus. Indian politics is confrontationist and less concerned about reaching agreements for the fulfilment of long-term national goals.

Another feature of policy process in India has been that the debates that were part of the national struggle for independence are still yet not resolved. The Gandhian ideas still exercise a strong influence on activist educationists who do not accept that the bureaucracy-dominated, state-supported, centralized education system offering homogeneity can be a solution to eradicating illiteracy in the country.

Even though Nehru had considered a nationwide review of education policy, it was his successor Lal Bahadur Shastri who appointed an Education Commission chaired by Dr D.S. Kothari. By the time the Commission presented its Report, Indira Gandhi had become Prime Minister and was fighting for her political survival in both party and government. Education not being among her priorities, she left it to her Education Minister, Dr Triguna Sen, to steer the report through Parliament. Although Triguna Sen was well-intentioned and sincerely supported the work of the Commission, as he was its member too before becoming a Minister, he knew little about education and even less about primary education; and because Mrs Gandhi lacked extensive political support, it was necessary to create a political consensus. Some sort of consensus did emerge but, in the process, controversies were created over some recommendations. And these controversies tended to overshadow the common points of agreement.

Consequently, the 1968 National Education Policy was largely anodyne with few actions undertaken to ensure that the recommendations were implemented. Until 1986 when a new Education Policy was devised, only a few of the Kothari Commission's recommendations bore fruit. The new Education Policy was designed at the insistence of Rajiv Gandhi, the then Prime Minister, who was notably impatient. Although his civil service and political advisors counselled caution and advised widespread consultations to build consensus, the 1986 Policy was hurriedly formulated due to the personal involvement of the Prime Minister. At least, unlike earlier education policies, issues of implementation were not neglected and a Programme of Action was prepared.

The leadership of the Prime Minister plus the fact that a Programme of Action was prepared at the outset, helped lay the Policy on the ground fairly quickly. This was in contrast to the 1969 Policy, which had a much larger gestation period. It took more than two decades, for example, for the national education system of 10+2 for school and three years of undergraduate studies to become established. A distinguishing feature of the 1986 Policy was its emphasis on designing a plan of implementation and this bore the imprint of bureaucracy, which was primarily involved in formulating it.

The policy process described above conforms to the general perception that educational decisions in India are political decisions and rarely reflect technical expertise in education. The political economy of education has remained a dominating factor in determining educational programmes. Reports of expert committees and even those of this Commission were processed by political leadership and made available for public debate. If the problem lies in the state arena, state political leaders are consulted on a formal basis. Consequently, while there is undoubtedly a gain in political legitimacy, recommendations are considerably watered-down (if not altogether rejected), and considerable delay occurs before a policy document emerges from such deliberations. Many recommendations continue to linger, get included in other reports, or become debating points used for political advantage.

Despite the exception of several notable politicians, education has not been on the agenda of India's political parties. They have not focused on educational problems as technical problems but have been more concerned with the political consequences of educational issues. Little time is spent on an in-depth analysis of problems or understanding them. However, although political initiatives are rare, there is considerable reluctance to leave things to the experts. The result is that a hiatus between politicians and experts has grown into negative mutual perceptions. More often than not, educational propositions are turned into grist for the political mill from which emanates ultimate power. From the way state ministers are assigned the education portfolio, political parties do not consider it of great significance. Usually, the weakest among the ministers is given responsibility for education. At the central level, the record has been no different. In the last two decades, education has gone to political lightweights, or to those who have no interest in education other than using it to advance their own or their party's political fortunes in other fields.

A widely shared view is that education is fit only for academics and that politicians should keep their hands off it. When the Education Commission was appointed in 1964, the Union Education Minister M.C. Chagla boasted that he had not appointed any politician to it. But such splendid isolation made educationists blind to many aspects of educational reality which are basically political. As Naik argues, an issue like that of selective admissions cannot be solved except jointly by politicians and educationists.[9] On the other hand, because of this very isolation, the politicians remain largely ignorant of basic educational problems so that when they interfere with education—which they often do—they do more harm than good. In other words, the educationists desire full political support without any political interference (which is their concept of autonomy), while politicians interfere too frequently with education (which is their concept of accountability to the legislature) without committing themselves to provide any support.

[9] Naik, *The Education Commission and After*, p. 197.

6

Privatization as Reform

Liberalization and Public Sector Enterprises in India*

India is currently experiencing a pronounced shift in state form and governing practices. Since the initiation of economic reforms in 1991, it has come to be widely recognized among both critics and supporters, that the central planning model and the dominant role that the state had played in the economy and in society cannot survive the combined onslaught of economic crises and the processes of globalization. Even in western countries, the Keynesian welfare state is under pressure and is giving way to a restructuring of the economic and political systems. The New Right is leading the intellectual attack on the state and the public sector primarily through the enunciation of public choice theory. The emphasis on the virtues of the market is highlighting the weaknesses of the public sector and hence the need for its privatization. Political leadership promoting economic reforms in India, in which privatization and the slimming of the state is the major agenda, has articulated pragmatic reasons for reform. The purpose of this chapter is to examine some of the issues raised by public choice theory in questioning the efficient performance of the public sector and to also

* Kuldeep Mathur, 2003, 'Privatization as Reform: Liberalization and Public Sector Enterprises in India', in Gurpreet Mahajan (ed.), *The Public and The Private: Issues of Democratic Citizenship*, New Delhi: Sage Publications, pp. 276–95.

explore whether reforms in the public sector are possible without dismantling it. The first part of the chapter will look at some general theoretical issues, the second part at the characteristics and pattern of public enterprises in India, the third at the efforts of reform and possible reasons for their failure, and finally, the last section will conclude with the argument that wholesale privatization is not desirable and serves as a simplistic solution to a complex problem that requires a more nuanced response.

THEORETICAL ISSUES

Much of the discussion on the concept of a liberal democratic state is concerned with the questions of the public-private divide. The early liberal theorists took the old feudal order, which was grounded in impositional claims about natural hierarchies and the organic whole, and recast it as a 'world of walls'.[1] The Church was separated from the State so that the latter could be shaped and governed according to the principles of liberalism and later liberal democracy. The State was separated from the economy so that the market could develop according to its laws of supply and demand. Such division helped develop rules and practices of state or public terrain that could be distinguished from those of the private. But as Bowles and Gintis point out, the public-private partition is neither fixed, nor natural or obvious.[2] Historically, the boundaries have been drawn and redrawn. The Keynesian welfare state was one such attempt in the postwar years and now, another attempt is being made. The Keynesian state asserted the primacy of the public over the 'invisible hand' of the market and engendered expectations that the state was responsible for meeting the basic needs of the citizens.[3] The current attempt tends to reverse this formulation and seeks to rearrange public and private by shrinking the state and expanding the autonomy of the market. The neo-liberal agenda stresses the primacy of the market in generating a new social order.

---

[1] Janine Brodie, 1996, 'New State Forms, New Political Spaces', in Robert Boyer and Daniel Drache (eds), *States Against Markets: The Limits of Globalization*, London: Routledge and Kegan Paul, p. 384.

[2] Samuel Bowles and Herbert Gintis, 1986, *Democracy and Capitalism*, London: Routledge and Kegan Paul, p. 66.

[3] Brodie, 'New State Forms, New Political Spaces', p. 386.

Central to the concept of privatization is the idea of competition. Competition is accepted as a powerful tool and an essential dimension of economic, political, and social life. Competing for the efficient exploitation of natural resources and the generation of new means to satisfy individual and collective needs at lower costs and higher quality is seen to have contributed greatly to the improvement of both material and non-material levels of wellbeing. It is also seen as a driving force behind technological innovation. One might say that competition triggers market growth, cuts costs, and drives technological change. Competition and the market go together and it is widely believed that the public sector is inefficient because it does not face competition. Today, competition has been elevated to an ideology and represents an important reason for privatization. As The Group of Lisbon point out,

A new era of competition has emerged in the last twenty years, especially in connection with globalization of economic processes. Competition no longer describes a mode of functioning of a particular market configuration (a competitive market) as distinct from oligopolistic and monopolistic markets. To be competitive has ceased to be an end; competitiveness has acquired the status of a universal credo, an ideology.[4]

Market and competition go together in the new liberal state, which is then led to perform two important functions: promote the market, and create conditions for free and fair competition. Politics also gets redefined in this framework. The attempt is to depoliticize the economy by arguing that market-driven adjustment and regulation provide the greatest good to society. Critical governing instruments of a welfare state like public enterprises are seen as ineffective and inefficient delivery systems and should be removed from the realm of political negotiation. Much of this argument for depoliticization is based on an understanding of the way the rulers behave and why they do so. This can be subsumed under the broad rubric of what has come to be known as the theory of predatory rule. It is assumed that rulers play a critical role in determining state policies. Their power rests on coercion and also on raising revenues. Levi hypothesizes that greater the revenue of the

---

[4] The Group of Lisbon, 1995, 'Limits to Competition', mimeo, Cambridge, MA: MIT Press, p. xii.

state, the more is the possibility to extend its rule.[5] Revenue enhances the ability of the rulers to elaborate the institutions of the state, to bring more people within the domain of those institutions, and to increase the number and variety of public goods provided through the state. For reasons of self-interest to extend their rule and for state reasons, rulers attempt to extract as much revenue as possible. In the process of extraction, the rulers may line their own pockets and divert funds in their personal direction. The capacity of the rulers to serve their own interests increases with the size of the public sector. As the public sector is reduced, market regulation takes over, limiting the perfidious role of the rulers. Thus, it becomes important to keep politics and economic decision-making separate. A liberal state is a democratic state where competition takes place through elections without its impact being felt in the economic arena, which is governed by the market.

The motivation of rulers is at the heart of the public choice theory that provides the intellectual grist to the privatization mill. And this is what we turn to now. The public choice theorists have attempted to identify explanations of political and organizational behaviour on the basis of the motives of actors. Their central assumption is that human beings behave in the political arena in the same way as they do in the economic arena. They are rational maximizers of their self-interest. Their self-interest is defined purely in terms of material income or satisfactions derived from it. The stress in this theory is on mono-motivation in contrast to the generally understood diverse motivations of an individual's behaviour. In explaining political behaviour, then, values, culture or history are ignored.

The pursuit of self-interest works for wider social interests when regulated by the market. Thus, there are two important and basic assumptions: first, the market best regulates that individuals work for their material self-interest, and the second is the pursuit of self-interest. Advocacy for slimming the government and reducing the public sector follow from this formulation. While recognizing that individual self-interest is a powerful and pervasive motive, it is still open to question whether the market is the best way to regulate it to serve public interest.

[5] Margaret Levi, 1988, *Of Rule and Revenue*, Berkeley: University of California Press, p. 2.

Institutional discipline could be another method, which can harness self-interest for good purposes.

Emphasis on individual motivation has also led to the exploration of institutions as a source of discipline and re-examination of the bureaucratic design for state activities. Weber had contended that bureaucratic organization was the manifestation of rationality and a powerful mechanism to bring about efficiency. Well laid-down formal rules, hierarchy, and obedience to rule of law ensured that individual bureaucrats would respond with rational behaviour and work for public interest. According to the public choice theorists, the engine of rationality has lost its sheen. The case of state failure is based on how monopoly rents are created through the imposition of regulation and control over the economy. Political pressures dominate economic policymaking and execution leading to the misallocation of resources. Corruption and favouritism surround bureaucratic allocations of investment licenses, import licenses, and the award of government contracts. A consequence of this system is that government machinery is increasingly used to serve personal interests. Government bureaucratic organization has been discredited not only in theory, but also in practice, and therefore there is a search for alternative ways of implementing state activities.

The new institutional approach is based on the previously mentioned assumption that self-interested individuals, who pursue optimizing strategies, will require reference to appropriate sets of decision rules or decision-making arrangements in dealing with structures of events if the welfare potential of a community of individuals is to be enhanced. No single form of organization is presumed to be 'good' for all circumstances.[6] Public goods, because of their very nature, cannot be delivered through bureaucratic organizations. Gordon Tullock analyzes the consequences that follow when rational, self-interested individuals pursue maximizing strategies, in very large public bureaucracies.[7] A typical career-oriented bureaucrat will act to please his superiors because his advancement depends on their favourable recommendation. Distortion of information will take place because the tendency will

[6] V. Ostrom, 1991, *The Intellectual Crisis in American Public Administration*, Tuscaloosa: University of Alabama Press, p. 48.

[7] Gordon Tullock, 1965, *The Politics of Bureaucracy*, Washington, D.C.: Public Affairs Press, p. 167.

be to forward only favourable information. Large-scale bureaucracies will thus become error-prone and cumbersome in adapting to rapidly changing conditions. Efforts to correct the malfunctioning of bureaucracy by tightening control will magnify errors.[8] Control will engender 'bureaucratic free enterprise'[9] when groups and individuals within the organization set themselves up to formulate their own goals and to create opportunities for side payoffs leading to graft and corruption. Organization goals get distorted and they begin to work in contradiction to the public announcements of their goals and purposes.

Starting from these basic premises, the public sector has been attacked for the failure in its fundamental institutional design. The new public management perspective, shaped by neo-classical economic principles and the public choice theory, questions its size, roles, and structures. Asserting that public bureaucracies are unable to manage the production and delivery of goods where exclusion is not possible or difficult, or where monopolistic conditions prevail, the private sector is seen as having the managerial capacity, flexibility, and competitive drive essential for the efficient and effective provision of many activities previously assumed to be the province of the public sector.[10] Much of the discussion therefore is in terms of exploring alternative strategies for privatizing the public sector.[11]

This section has attempted to highlight the major contours of the intellectual attack on the public sector. Among its weapons is the economic theory of politics where the fundamental assumption is that a rational man is a maximizer and tends to be so whether he is involved in economic or political activities. Further, this theory suggests that the market is the best way to allocate public goods, manage public enterprises or, arrive at collective social decisions, or even to govern

[8] Ostrom, *The Intellectual Crisis in American Public Administration*, p. 53.

[9] Tullock, *The Politics of Bureaucracy*, p. 167.

[10] For an elaboration of this theme, see Martin Minogue, Charles Polidano and David Hume, 1998, *Beyond the New Public Management: Changing Ideas and Practices in Governance*, Northampton, MA: Edgar Elgar Publishing Ltd.

[11] David Osborne and Ted Gaebler, 1992, *Reinventing Government: How the Entrepreneurial Spirit is Transforming the Public Sector*, New Delhi: Prentice-Hall of India Pvt. Ltd.; Emanuel S. Savas, 1982, *Privatizing the Public Sector: How to Shrink the Government*, Chatham, NJ: Chatham House Publishers.

democratically. It also suggests that public bureaucracies have to be organized keeping the individual motivations in mind and the nature of goods and services that they seek to provide. Reform movements that have been subsumed under what has come to be known as new public management are inspired by diverse strategies that can privatize different kinds of public sectors.

CHARACTERISTICS AND PATTERNS OF PUBLIC ENTERPRISES

At the time of independence, the political leadership identified the future of India with developments in the West. Of particular significance was its perception of the role of science and technology in transforming those societies. Nehru was fascinated with developments in Soviet Russia and was impressed by the achievements made possible by planning and the rational allocation of resources. He saw India quickly attaining the levels of economic development achieved by the Western nations through industrialization and modernization. With the emphasis on rational allocation of resources and industrialization, planning and state intervention became central to the strategy of development initiated through the various Five Year Plans. In this strategy, public enterprises occupied a significant place. The reason was the limitations of the private sector at that time. There were private monopolies and there was little capacity to make large-scale investments. The stepping in of the state in areas of infrastructure development that required heavy investments was something that was welcomed by the private sector. It was only later, as a matter of fact in the 1956 Industrial Policy Resolution, that the ideological basis of the public sector was underlined: 'The adoption of the socialist pattern of society as the national objective, as well as the need of planned and rapid development, require that all industries of basic and strategic importance or in the nature of public utility services should be in the public sector'.[12] Thus at this time, the role of the public sector in the economy was defined more in terms of filling in the gaps of the limitations of the private sector even though a philosophy of socialist pattern of society had been enunciated. The Second Five-Year Plan was based on the now well-known Nehru-Mahalanobis

[12] Government of India, 'Industrial Policy Resolution', 1956, in *Guidelines for Industries (1982)*, New Delhi: India Investment Centre, p. 2.

model which recognized that irrespective of the ideological bias, the private sector would not find it attractive to undertake investments of the magnitude required under planning, when the new projects were likely to be more capital intensive, with long gestation periods and with unattractive rates of return.

It was the Indira Gandhi period from 1969 onwards that saw a strengthening of state controls and state entry into the service sector on a larger scale. The public sector played a leading role in the manufacturing sector during the Second and Third Plan periods. This was the period when the public sector walked into areas where the private sector was unable to or hesitant to tread. Public policy stressed regulation of monopolies and the public sector came to acquire a more ideological role of providing greater equity and justice in society. This led it into the realm of the service sector too. Even otherwise, the perspectives on the role of the public sector had begun to change. The Seventh Five-Year Plan saw the public sector as a 'pace-setter' in high technology industries and an institution to generate sizable resources for new investments. It also talked about the leading role of the public sector in stimulating development of efficient ancillary manufacturing, which in turn would strengthen the sinews of industry. A variety of justifications and objectives of the public sector have been documented.[13]

Indeed, there has been no formal government document like a White Paper that clearly lays down the rationale of the public sector in India. There have been suggestions from various committees.[14] The Administrative Reforms Commission of 1967 had recommended that the government should make a comprehensive and clear statement on the objectives and obligations of the public sector. Several parliamentary committees as also much later, the Economic Administration Reforms Commission headed by L.K. Jha said the same. As a result, the rationale of public investment or roles of public enterprises as perceived by the government have to be inferred from government documents and the kind and range of investments made. As a consequence, the public sector in India has developed with multiple objectives that are quite

[13] For a listing, see S.K. Goyal, 1986, *Public Sector in India*, New Delhi: Indian Institute of Public Administration, p. 80.

[14] Ramaswamy R. Iyer, 1991, *A Grammar of Public Enterprises: Exercises in Clarification*, Jaipur: Rawat Publications, pp. 9–11.

often contradictory. To assess it on one single criterion would be both unfair and inadequate. This becomes very clear from the listing of objectives given by the Public Enterprises Survey, 1995–6:

- To help in the rapid economic growth and industrialization of the country and create the necessary infrastructure for economic development;
- to earn return on investment and thus generate resources for development;
- to promote redistribution of income and wealth;
- to create employment opportunities;
- to promote balanced regional development;
- to assist the development of small-scale and ancillary industries; and
- to promote import substitutions, and save and earn foreign exchange for the economy.

It is obvious that the public sector means everything to policymakers and has become an umbrella concept that ultimately does not specify whether it is a business or a commercial proposition, and the manner in which it needs to be attended to.

Usually, the public sector refers to all activities funded out of the government's budget. In this chapter, we will restrict our attention to public enterprises of a particular kind. Public sector in India refers to all government activities that are run as departmental and non-departmental enterprises. Departmental enterprises form part of the government's financial systems but have separate accounts of income and expenditure. Their surplus or deficit is merged in the accounts of the departments of the government, for example, telecommunications, the postal department et al. In the case of the railways, a separate budget is presented. Highway construction and maintenance, irrigation, housing, health, and educational services fall into the departmental enterprises. Non-departmental enterprises refer to activities that are carried out by entities, which are legally separated from the government and are made to maintain a separate account of all their financial transactions and set them out in the form of a profit and loss account. These enterprises are set up under the Companies Act or under special statutory provisions. Public enterprises can be further classified into central government or state enterprises.

The public sector, then, comprises of three types of organizations: administration by a government department, the joint-stock company governed by company law and controlled by the government as a major shareholder, and autonomous public corporations. Our reference in this chapter is to central enterprises, which are either joint stock companies or statutory autonomous corporations. In the 1950s, there were only twenty-one public sector enterprises with an invested capital of Rs 810 million. This increased to eighty-five enterprises in the 1960s with Rs 39,020 million as the invested capital. The 1970s saw a near doubling of enterprises to 169 and the invested capital had grown four times to Rs 155,340 million. The increases accelerated in the 1980s with the number of enterprises growing to 244 and the capital to Rs 993,290 million.[15] As pointed out earlier, the reason for this expansion was the spread of the public sector in all sectors of the economy.

The size of the public sector can be gauged from another point of view as seen from Table 6.1. The share of the public sector in the total capital stock was 46 per cent while value added was only 26.8 per cent. Investments in the public sector formed 9.4 per cent of GDP, while savings were only of 1.6 per cent, thereby leaving a savings-investments gap of -8 per cent. As seen in Table 6.1, savings of both public and private corporate sectors are low, but those from the public sector are considerably lower in comparison to the private sector. In other words, the public sector works at very low levels of profitability.

The number of central government non-financial enterprises stood at 236 in 1997–8.[16] Some of these units are very large and the largest among them account for around 95 per cent of the total assets. Among these are Indian Oil, ONGC, and SAIL. Of the total capital employed, it appears the main share has been claimed by oil, steel, coal, and power. A good deal of investment has also gone into medium and light engineering industries. Most of these enterprises are the ones, which like the sick private textile industries had to be taken over as a rescue operation by the government.[17]

Even though the profitability of public enterprises is low, there has been an appreciable improvement in it during the 1980s. The ratio of gross profit to capital employed showed a marked improvement from

[15] K.P. Kalirajan and R.T. Shand, 1996, 'Public Sector Enterprises in India—Is Privatization the only Answer?', *Economic and Political Weekly*, vol. 31, p. 2683.

[16] Government of India, 2000–1, *Indian Economic Survey*, New Delhi: Aklank Publishers, p. 135.

[17] Goyal, *Public Sector in India*, p. 86.

7.79 per cent in 1980–1 to 11.4 per cent in 1992–3. The net return on investment improved from –1.11 per cent to 4.47 per cent between 1980–1 and 1989–90, although the ratio came down to around 2.4 per cent in the early 1990s.[18] The picture about the profitability of enterprises becomes clearer if we disaggregate the public enterprises into two categories of profit-making and loss-making enterprises. As can be seen from Table 6.2, the increase in profits has been accompanied by an increase in losses, but the net profit has registered a rise in 1992–3 over 1980–1. Out of the 104 loss-making enterprises, eighty were in manufacturing industries and the rest were in the services sector. The public enterprises in the manufacturing sector accounted for eighty per cent of the losses incurred by all loss-making public enterprises and also accounted for nearly 87 per cent of employment in such enterprises. It is this feature of profitability that dominates the larger perception of inefficiency and over-employment in the public sector.

Later figures for 1997–8 show considerable rise in profitability of central public enterprises. During this year, out of 235 operating units, 134 earned profits and 100 incurred losses. According to Gupta, public sector units earned a net profit of Rs 132.35 billion during 1998–9 after providing for income tax of Rs 64.99 billion and adjusting a loss of Rs 92.74 billion incurred by 106 enterprises.[19] Out of the 106 loss-making enterprises, 33 were already sick and were taken over by the government from the private sector. The government has acted as 'hospital' for failed enterprises, thus incurring losses when the turn-around was not possible.

Together with this question of profitability is the issue of employment, which has gradually acquired the characteristic of what is now commonly known as overstaffing. The trends in employment in the organized sector of the economy show that total employment in the public sector registered a relatively high growth rate of 2.4 per cent per annum between 1976 and 1991 as compared to the very low growth rate of 0.8 per cent in the organized private sector during the same period.[20] The share of the public sector in total employment in the

[18] S.N. Raghavan, 1994, *Public Sector in India: Changing Perspectives,* New Delhi: Asian Institute of Transport Development, p. 39.

[19] Asha Gupta, 2000, *Beyond Privatization,* London: Palgrave MacMillan.

[20] Raghavan, *Public Sector in India: Changing Perspectives,* p. 18.

TABLE 6.1: Public Sector in the Indian Economy

Public Sector	Share in Net Capital Stock March 1992 (Per cent)	Share in Gross Value Added 1990–3 (Average Per cent)	Saving (Per cent of GDP)	Investment (Per cent of GDP)
Administrative Departments	12.6	9.3	–2.2	1.9
Departmental Enterprises	13.6	4.0	0.7	2.0
Non-departmental Enterprises	20.0	13.0	3.1	6.2
Public Sector	46.2	26.8	176	–94
Private Sector	53.8	73.2	18.6	14.2
Total	100.0	100.0	21.8	23.8

Sources: Geeta Gouri, 1996, 'Privatization and Public Sector Enterprises in India Analysis of Impact of Non-Policy', *Economic and Political Weekly,* vol. XXXI, no. 48, 30 November.

TABLE 6.2:   Trends in Net Profit/Loss of Central Public Enterprises:
1981–93 (Rs million at current prices)

Category	1980–1		1992–3
Profit of Profit-making Enterprises	55.7		734.6
	(94)*	(131)	
Loss of Loss-making Enterprises	76.0		395.0
	(74)	(104)	
Net Profit/Loss of All Enterprises	−20.3		339.6
	(168)	(235)	

Source: Raghavan, *Public Sector in India: Changing Perspectives*, p. 41.
Note: * Figures in brackets relate to number of enterprises.

organized sector increased from 66 per cent in 1976 to 71 per cent in 1991. The average annual per capita emoluments of public sector employees were around Rs 105,879 in 1995–6 (as mentioned in the Public Enterprises Survey of 1995–6).

Over the years, a very comprehensive and complex system of relationships has emerged between the government and public enterprises. The government as owner and as an agency accountable to the Parliament has tended to administer, control, and monitor the performance of public enterprises very closely. Departmental enterprises were in any case under the government, but joint-stock companies and corporations also came to be controlled through administrative ministries where civil servants and not the managers of the enterprises became the decision-makers. Issues of autonomy and accountability have dominated the discussion about reforming the public sector. Increasing autonomy and reducing bureaucratic interference was the major recommondation of the Appleby Report that was brought out as far back as 1956 and has been a refrain taken up by parliamentary committees a s well as academic writings since then.

Little structural reform has followed, but since the 1990s, the idea of regulating the relationship between the government and public enterprise by means of a Memorandum of Understanding (MoU) has led some enterprises to sign contracts with the government, which clarify the objectives of the enterprise, identify responsibilities on either side, and provide a basis for evaluation of performance. This path of reform has not been easy because the enterprises come in various sizes and forms with different bargaining capacities. As mentioned by Iyer, who was Secretary of the Jha Commission, the role of government qua government tends to seep into that of owner, and it is rather difficult to persuade the government to forget its 'sovereign' aspect and accept a contractual relationship with an enterprise.[21] Second, while the Chief Executive is expected to make firm commitments to the government, the administrative ministry is unable to do so, on behalf of the government.

A neglected area of reform has been that of increasing productivity of the use of existing resources through technology upgradation. Kalirajan and Shand have argued that technical efficiency can contribute substantially to improving the performance of the public sector.[22] What has happened is that budget constraints in public sector enterprises, generally, are unduly soft, and political accountability prevails over performance accountability. Performance accountability requires that resources are not wasted and are used to their full capacity. A necessary condition for this is that the enterprises should not enjoy soft budgets which come in terms of subsidies, favourably administered prices, easily arranged tax reliefs, and easy credit availability and repayment. In essence, soft budgets allow enterprises to produce outputs by using inputs liberally and not using them to their full capacity. On the basis of data for 50 manufacturing public enterprises, Kalirajan and Shand show that on average these enterprises realized only 60 per cent of their potential output.[23] From their point of view, this carries the crucial implication that output in public enterprises can be increased without increasing levels of input (labour and capital), but just by improving technical and management practices.

Another theme in examining the working of public enterprises in India has been the issue of internal organizational structure and questions of incentives and motivations. While initiating debate on the Second Five-Year Plan in the Lok Sabha, Nehru had stated that the way a government functions is not exactly the way that business houses and enterprises normally function. He argued that normal government

[21] Iyer, *A Grammar of Public Enterprises: Exercises in Clarification*, p. 60.
[22] Kalirajan and Shand, 'Public Sector Enterprises in India—Is Privatization the only Answer?', pp. 2683–6.
[23] Ibid.

procedures, when applied to a public enterprise, would lead to failure of that public enterprise. Therefore, he preferred a system for public enterprises that had adequate checks and protections but had enough freedom to work quickly and without delay. This balancing act led to the designing of various kinds of organizational structures and their relationship with the government. But this search for a balanced organization has been an elusive dream. In the initial years, the differences among enterprises were seen only in terms of ownership and, therefore, it was argued that any professional manager could manage them. This allowed for movement of managers from the private sector to the public sector. At this time too, public enterprises were seen as part of the expanding domain of the civil service and thus civil servants also began to seek managerial positions in public sector enterprises. Very soon, the choice became clear and civil servants went on to man public enterprises and mold them according to their own experiences. The autonomy debate was a non-starter with both administrative ministries and public enterprises being headed by the same group of people whose incentives did not lie in the specific organization that they worked in, but in the larger civil service system.

Institutional autonomy without professional strength in the management of an enterprise was difficult to achieve. The debate about professionalizing the management was never resolved. The result was that there was no stop to making public enterprises resemble government departments in work and procedure. In an interesting formulation, DiMaggio and Powell have put forward a theory of 'institutional isomorphism', which aims at a general explanation of the development of institutional similarities.[24] Isomorphism is defined as 'a constraining process that forces one unit of population to resemble other units that face the same set of environmental conditions'.[25] They argue that professionalization and bureaucratization are not necessarily the product of strategic plans for more rational organizations, but may reflect, or be caused by dependency or closeness to other organizations. They suggest that a general mechanism is at work: 'The greater the dependence

---

[24] Paul J. DiMaggio and Walter W. Powell, 1983, 'The Iron Cage Revisited: Institutional Isomorphism and Collective Rationality in Organizational Fields', *American Sociological Review,* vol. 48, no. 1, April, pp. 147–60.

[25] Ibid., p. 148.

of an organization on another organization, the more similar it will become to that organization in structure, climate, and behavioural focus.'[26] Thus, public enterprises, large or small, began to acquire the characteristics of administrative departments that they were linked to and lost the special character for which they were established. The incentive system, like in bureaucracy, was not related to performance but to the ability to fulfill obligations of hierarchy and the command and control system. Exhortations of national service and work in public interest were relied on to encourage good and efficient performance.

Growth of institutional isomorphism led to even greater difficulties in reforming and professionalizing the public sector. For, unless reforms in civil service were affected, reforms would not follow in the public sector. And, repeated efforts to reform the civil service had ended in failure. The last concerted effort at administrative reform was the establishment of the Administrative Reforms Commission, which submitted its reports in 1969. Despite extensive research that involved a large number of academics, civil servants, and concerned citizens in producing the recommendations, little change that had an impact on the people took place. Under pressure from international funding agencies to downsize government, some more attempts at preparing reports for administrative reforms followed. The Fifth Pay Commission in 1996 included suggestions for reform. The civil service was instrumental in seeing that the recommendations to increase their pay packets were accepted by the government while those that would have led to changes in the structure and working of the government were allowed to languish. The Government of India presented an Action Plan for Effective and Responsive Government to the Conference of Chief Ministers on 24 May 1997. The wait for reform continues.

There is no dearth of policy recommendations for making the government more effective and efficient and most of them were made even before downsizing was the fashion of the day. Public enterprises have been under focus for a long time. It is just that these recommendations rarely get implemented or when implemented fail to get institutionalized. In many cases, the ruling politicians have wrested the authorized initiative from the official hierarchy to stall changes; in other cases, bureaucratic hierarchy has acted as a barrier to any

[26] Ibid., p. 154.

political initiative to bring about reform. What has happened over the years is that bureaucrats have emerged as a powerful component of the decision-making process, largely because the political establishment was only too happy to abdicate its responsibility and to concentrate more on matters that were political. But in providing continuity in civil administration, despite political turbulence and change in governments, the bureaucracy also proved to be an obstacle in the path of prompt action. 'Red-tapism' is as much a product of the rulebook written by the government as its interpretation and application by bureaucrats. The existence of the book has undoubtedly provided crucial checks and balances required to prevent abuse of power by political authority. But it has led to another consequence. A new breed of politicians who have to do things in a hurry has emerged. This breed finds the rulebook an impediment, would like to bend the rules and make them flexible for its own advantage. Bureaucrats are damned if they accept the assertions of such a group of politicians and also damned if they do not. In such an uncertain situation, they have become apprehensive of their future and are therefore prone to stick to their traditional ways. Reforms need bold action and this is not forthcoming.

Lack of institutional and procedural reforms in public enterprises have much to do with what has happened in the governmental sector, particularly because the managers in public enterprises have moved to them after notching up years of experience in traditional government departments and have thus readily accepted the incentive system or the procedures that they have been most familiar with. The difficulties of a private sector executive brought in to manage a public enterprise—Air India—were so indomitable that he had to leave, finding little support for reform either among politicians or bureaucrats or among the managers of the enterprise itself!

In concluding this section, it is important to stress at least a few important features of public enterprises in India. One is that they emerged in order to fill the gaps that could not be met by investment from the private sector. The ideological justifications were added only later. The concerns were more pragmatic and as Nehru declared during his introduction to the Second Plan in Parliament,

May I say here that while I am for the public sector growing, I do not understand or appreciate the condemnation of the private sector. The whole philosophy underlying this Plan is to take advantage of every possible way of growth and not to do something which suits some doctrinaire theory or imagine we have grown because we have satisfied some textbook maxim of hundred years ago.[27]

Second, all enterprises have not performed badly if profit is the only criterion. But it needs to be accepted that they could have done better. Despite an investment of Rs 2,13,610 crores, the net profit was Rs 10,186 crores at the end of 1996–7. Third, the need to reform the public sector has been on the political and administrative agenda literally from the time that enterprises were established, but for various reasons, the reform suggestions have not been implemented in a way that created an impact. It was widely accepted that if the enterprises had to function on a commercial basis, they had to be liberated from government and bureaucratic controls. This wide acceptance could not be operationalized. And, finally, public sector employees have become a political force on their own or as Bardhan points out, a partner in the ruling coalition.[28] They have stalled any move to reform that does not serve their self-interest.

In the face of this situation, the Government of India announced a Statement on Public Sector Policy as part of its industrial policy in the liberalization package of 1991. This policy included recommendations for disinvestments to raise resources and to refer chronically sick public enterprises to the Board of Industrial and Financial Reconstruction for revival or rehabilitation. By 1996, a total of fifty-six central enterprises had been registered with the Board.[29] The sale of equity of these enterprises yielded a very meagre response government of Rs 443 billion, the actual amount of receipts from the sale. Other recommendations included professionalization of the Board of Directors and signing of an MoU.

Three issues emerge from the pace of disinvestments provided by the above data. First, of the 2461 public enterprises (CPEs), only forty CPEs' equity was sold during this period of 1991–6. Second, the quantity of equity that was sold was not significant: in 19 of the CPEs in question, the equity sold added up to less than ten per cent points, in seven,

---

[27] Government of India, 1958, *Jawaharlal Nehru's Speeches*, vol. 3, New Delhi: Ministry of Information and Broadcasting Publications Division.

[28] Bardhan, *The Political Economy of Development in India*, pp. 51–2.

[29] Government of India, 1995–6, *Public Enterprises Survey*, New Delhi: Government of India Publications, pp. 40–2.

between ten and twenty per cent points; in six, between thirty and forty per cent points; and two between forty and fifty per cent points. Finally, the controlling ownership of all the forty CPEs continued to remain with the Government of India. In addition, most of the equity that has been sold so far has been only to public entities in the financial sector like the Unit Trust of India.[30] This was done because, as the Finance Minister put it in the Parliament, it was the government's intention to ensure that the benefits accrued to public sector institutions rather than to private entities in the event of the sales taking place at an underpriced level.[31] No sick public enterprises have been shut down so far.

REFORM EFFORTS AND POSSIBLE REASONS
FOR FAILURE

It is widely believed that public enterprises suffer from what may be called the 'theory of public incompetence'.[32] This incompetence arises from several factors. Centralized planning mechanisms are poor substitutes for people's market demands. Public sector managers lack the personal financial incentives, which profit seekers have. Private employees endanger their jobs if they achieve pay conditions that their employers cannot afford, but there is no such market limit to what organized, hard bargaining, public employees can extract from the tax-payers. And inefficient private enterprises are automatically thrown out of the market, but governments can and do allow inefficient enterprises to continue. While some of these beliefs may be well-founded, the case for privatization rests mostly on the efficient use and allocation of resources. But the efficiency criterion appears to be understood differently in the public sector with its multiple objectives. Even the private sector is hesitant to pursue efficiency single-mindedly. But, what is important is to realize that there is little empirical evidence to show that one is more efficient than the other. According to a recent study by the Reserve bank of India the financial performance of selected private sector corporate firms has decelerated in the last few years.[33] The gross

[30] Gupta, *Beyond Privatization*, p. 110.

[31] Ibid.

[32] Hugh Stretton and Lionel Orchard, 1994, *Public Goods, Public Enterprise, Public Choice: Theoretical Foundations of the Contemporary Attack on Government*, London: St. Martin's Press, p. 80.

[33] Reserve Bank of India, 1997, *RBI Bulletin*, pp. 251–2.

profits declined for a second consecutive year in 1998–9 and growth rates in sales and value of production were also lower. Comparisons are difficult and public and private enterprises rarely produce the same goods under the same conditions with the same purpose.

The quest for efficiency follows a purely economic path, which implies a least cost notion of efficiency. It is achieved when the least amount of resources are used to produce a specific good or service. It does not say how this 'least amount' is achieved. The argument is based on a crude division between productive economic relations and unproductive social relations. The economic motive is given more weight than social motives.[34] Social equity does not feature in this consideration of efficiency. State-owned enterprises all over the world have been burdened with social obligations that the private sector has been generally free from. This is particularly true for the obligations of expanding employment and entering in such sectors or areas of economic activity, which carry a social purpose.

In India, from the very beginning, the public sector was not seen as a profit-making, efficiency machine. It was visualized to fill in the weakness of the private sector which did not have the capability to make large investments in basic and heavy industries and of fulfilling the social responsibilities of the state in developing backward areas, or entering into social sectors where profit was not the goal. Very often, this objective has been achieved by not allowing the prices of their products and services to be raised or to raise capital from the open market to meet the rising costs and inflation.

The second bulwark of privatization is the theory that managers and workers in public enterprises have poorer incentives than their private counterparts. Here again the question of comparison comes up. Incentives in what type of organization? A large enterprise, whether public or private, is managed by salaried employees on behalf of the owners of the enterprise. What matters, then, is the incentives of the owners. Public owners are not profit-seeking but the private owners are, and they use this criterion to induce salaried managers to work for profit. In the public sector, performance incentives are resisted because they run counter to civil service norms. These norms are founded on the presumption that civil servants work for public interest in a spirit

[34] Gupta, *Beyond Privatization*, p. 22.

of benevolence. They are a legacy from the early days of independence when the bureaucracy was considered a protector of the people from the avaricious capitalists, imperialist masters, and the vagaries of the market. It was never considered that people with the same instincts for self-interest might staff the government. Hence, the institutional design was based on the assumed public interest motivations of individuals and allowed for hierarchy and for command and control structures to be dominating concerns in the creation of organizations. Incentives, too, were not related to performance. Institutions were deliberately designed to constrain and influence individuals within public sector management. The issues of incentives and motivations and designing institutions that could mold them to work in consonance with institutional goals has always been considered the most difficult to handle.

Public sector reforms in this area have been difficult to achieve because the civil service has resisted any link between pay and performance. The resistance stems from the belief that public interest traditions will continue to endure. The issue of motivation is complex and there are frequent examples of public-interested bureaucrats, but the point that needs to be accepted, is that the gap between self-interest and public interest as motivators, needs to be narrowed. This can be done only through an appropriate organizational design.

THE DESIRABILITY OF WHOLESALE PRIVATIZATION

It appears that progress on the privatization front has not been very encouraging in India. The question that keeps coming back is whether privatization is the only answer to public sector reforms. The ideological argument for privatization does not seem to have made an impact on policymakers. The image of the private sector has never been one of benevolence in India. Modern capitalists in India have to contend with prejudices and images that portray them as heartless moneylenders, greedy merchants or powerful social exploiters. Profit is perceived as an ill-gotten gain at the expense of the consumer or the labourer or society and not a source of capital accumulation for investment. The celebration of entrepreneurship and that of creating private wealth is a recent phenomenon, mostly associated with the accession of Rajiv Gandhi and the globalization that began with the reform policies of 1991.

Till recently, private capital did not have an influential public political voice. It was able to protect and advance its interests through political channels that were not in the public arena. This further created a public image of a scheming and manipulative private sector that thrived on a relationship with politicians and bureaucrats that could not usually be termed as lawful or honest.

In addition, the political forces that have not allowed public sector reform seem to be in the forefront of opposing privatization. The public sector employs more than two million throughout the country. It has provided opportunities of patronage to both the politicians and the civil servants. It is not an uncommon phenomenon for public sector enterprises to offer jobs as rewards or pacifiers to disgruntled members of the ruling elite. The public enterprises serve so many purposes, and efficiency or profit-making are not among the prominent ones. When a unit suffers losses, closure is not considered an option, and therefore the belief that work performance does not matter has gained in strength. This belief is sought to be justified in terms of the social role of the public sector. It is constantly reiterated in public discourse that the public sector has a social function of providing employment, and its performance cannot be measured by profit alone. Even measuring profit in the public sector is a subject of debate and controversy.[35]

There has been poor mobilization of public opinion in favour of privatization. Policies are neither emerging out of ideological convictions or practical performance of the public sector enterprises. There are mixed experiences and this is what adds complexity to the problem of privatization. What has, however, happened as Rudolph and Rudolph point out, is that the commitment to the public sector has diminished for more pragmatic reasons.[36] Declining confidence in the public sector has been fuelled by a growing perception that an over-directed and over-regulated economy has become an obstacle rather than an agent of economic growth; that the unfavourable

[35] Geeta Gouri, 1996, 'Privatization and Public Sector Enterprises in India: Analysis of Impact of Non-Policy,' *Economic and Political Weekly*, vol. XXXI, no. 48, pp. 63–74.

[36] Rudolph and Rudolph, *In Pursuit of Lakshmi: The Political Economy of the India State*, p. 34.

capital-output ratio of the public as against the private sector, reflects inefficiency, corruption, and poor management; and that the socialist benefits of the public sector have become less apparent and convincing. Public enterprises are being distrusted not because they may prove to be inefficient, but because politicians and bureaucrats can misuse them. Public choice theory embedded in the larger belief of the supremacy of the market has fuelled this expectation.

7

Drought in Parliament
*Representation and Participation**

In India, unlike in the West, the role of legislators in the making of public policy has been a relatively neglected area of political research. It is much more common to find studies on the impact of popular movements or of pressure groups—and sometimes, though rarely, their links with legislators—on policymaking. Indeed, even when research on legislators has gone beyond the studies—whose numbers are legion—of socioeconomic profiles of MPs and MLAs and the social composition of legislatures, they have almost unanimously concluded that MPs play a very limited role in relation to public policy.

The locus of policymaking indeed is, and is widely perceived to be, the administrative apparatus of the state. As such, and being the preserve of the bureaucracy, it is to an unconscionable degree, impervious to popular pressure. However, in a democratic political system—even one as imperfect as ours—there are points at which the formal policy process is, or can be made, receptive, if not responsive, to political or popular pressures. In what follows, we will attempt to identify these points in the specific case of policymaking on drought, and seek to locate parliamentary influence in that context.

* Kuldeep Mathur and Niraja Gopal Jayal, 1993, 'Perspectives on Drought in Parliament', *Drought, Policy, and Politics in India: The Need for a Long Term Perspective*, New Delhi: Sage Publications, pp. 77–91.

We may start by distinguishing between modes of influence, direct and indirect. Direct influence would include popular movements and agitations, which may take the form of pickets, rallies, marches, and demonstrations. These may or may not be affiliated to or sponsored by political parties. Examples of such protest have been recorded in relation to the 1972–3 drought in Maharashtra. There are, however, few parallels in the case of drought at other times and in other places.

At least three different modes of indirect influence are available in relation to drought. The first and most visible of these is the representation, in Parliament, of the demands and needs of the people in drought-affected areas which, it would be logical to suppose, would be most frequently expressed by members from affected constituencies. This is indeed the chief object of our concern, to which we shall presently return.

The second mode of indirectly influencing policy is closely tied to the first: electoral politics. In a case study of Rajasthan Assembly elections of 1990 we investigated the salience of drought as an election issue, and found that it has barely surfaced on the electoral agenda even in one of the most recurrently drought hit districts of the state.[1]

Finally, and in a probably incomparable way, drought relief is conditional upon field visits and surveys by study teams from the Ministry of Agriculture and other ministries, which are supposed to ascertain first-hand the veracity of the state government's claim regarding the extent of drought and the quantum of relief required. A frequent charge against these teams is that they do not meet with the representatives (MPs or MLAs) of the area or with the people directly, but that they make hurried and brief visits, during which they largely stay confined to their hotel rooms and work out their assessments.

Clearly, then, in the absence of collective mobilization for popular action, nationally determined or else cynically expedient electoral agendas, and the inaccessibility of study teams, the channel of influence with the most potential is that of parliamentary intervention in the form of questions and participation in debates.

---

[1] This has been reported in our larger study, *Drought, Policy, and Politics in India: The Need for a Long Term Perspective*, 1993, New Delhi: Sage Publications, pp. 63–6.

In the general area of policy studies, little work has been done to analyse the role of MPs as peoples' representatives. Some research attention has been focused on the socialization processes of the legislators or the influence of their party affiliation in arriving at inferences regarding their political attitudes and behaviour. Others have looked at parliamentary debates to establish the official positions of the Government on various matters, ministerial statements in response to questions or as interventions in the debates being taken as official versions of various policies. What has, however, been neglected is the nature of concerns expressed by MPs.

Several studies of political leadership in Parliament have argued that legislative elites are alienated from the large mass of the people by their social background and therefore cannot represent the interests of the masses in policymaking bodies. The classical elite theory has argued that not only are elites unavoidable and functionally necessary in complex social organizations, but also that they are inherently desirable insofar as they manifest superior intellectual and other attributes. A large number of modern studies of national and local level politics in countries as disparate as the UK, the USA, the erstwhile USSR, and India have repeatedly sought to establish the point that elites are inevitable, even if not desirable, and that their influence on the policymaking process is necessarily such as to bolster elite interests, rather than to secure the common good. Such studies have mostly used the occupation of key positions of authority as the chief criterion for identifying elites in society. Many of them have also tried to establish linkages between control over the economic resources of a community and political influence. For instance, Guttsman's study of the British parliamentary elite over a 100-year period, used indices like occupation and education to show how the political elite, united by their privileged social backgrounds, have an interest in maintaining the social structure which supports these privileges.[2]

Studies of the legislative elite in India have similarly shown that the recruitment of elites is typically from among members of dominant castes or property-owning families.[3] Studies of the role orientation

[2] W. Guttsman, 1964, *The British Political Elite*, London: McGibbon and Kee.
[3] Iqbal Narain, K.C. Pande, and Mohan Lal Sharma, 1976, *The Rural Elite in an Indian State: A Case Study of Rajasthan*, Delhi: Manohar Book Service.

of these elites have suggested that their primary concern is with the preservation and expansion of their support bases and to this end, they pursue personal and factional interests more vigorously than community interests or developmental work. The reason why appropriate policies for the development of the large mass of people are not formulated is that the political representatives are elites within their groups and do not carry concern for those whom they represent. In relation to a variety of policies, it is argued that the choice of the development model and the consequent course of development have encouraged the formation of elites and hence welfare measures or poverty alleviation programmes are devoid of commitment, both in policy formulation as well as in implementation.

Studies of elites and the process of elite formation raise one set of issues regarding representation. The other set of issues that arise relates to the question of whether the elected representatives show any concern for the area from which they have been elected. Certain concerns may cut across population categories. The problems of drought are specific to certain areas and are consequences of their ecological characteristics. Are the MPs conscious of this? How do they express or demonstrate their concern? We would like to search for answers to these questions too. Thus, our interest lies not only in examining the role of the Parliament in putting drought-related issues on the policymaking agenda but also in identifying the concerns of the MPs and assessing how these concerns reflect the long-term interests of drought prone areas.

Some studies of this kind have been done in India. Four such studies may be briefly discussed here to underscore the striking unanimity in their findings. G. Narayana has studied the role of Scheduled Caste MPs in influencing decision-making by analyzing Lok Sabha debates during the period 1962–71 when important issues relating to the Scheduled Castes were being discussed in debates or in the regular question hour. He comes to the conclusion that MPs have a limited role in expanding the policymaking agenda by voicing their concerns in the Lok Sabha. He indicates that even though many of the problems have for long been identified, some of the proposals made were either withdrawn, or not rigorously pursued, or simply inconclusive. The discussion on the Reports of the Commissioner on Scheduled Castes and Tribes was more or less ritualized; some of the Reports were not discussed at all.[4]

In his study on Electronics Policy and the Indian Parliament, R.B. Jain examines the role of Parliament in holding the executive accountable and only briefly analyzes questions and debates.[5] However, his assessment is that the contribution of MPs is limited because a subject like electronics is too technical and complex for common understanding and the questions are reflective of the interests of indigenous industrialists. Concern for the Electronics Policy in a long-term perspective is inadequate.

Rahman and Haritash have also attempted to examine the role of Parliament in influencing policy in a technical area—science and technology.[6] Their study is inspired by the wider concern about the declining role of Parliament and its lack of ability in initiating significant legislation. It has been suggested that neither the procedures nor the organization of legislatures is suited to a world determined by rapidly advancing technology where only 'specialists' can understand it and make 'informed choices'. Basing their study on data from 'question hour' during sessions in 1951, 1961, 1971, and 1978, they come to the conclusion that 'question hour' is used by members more or less as a forum for ventilating their views on specific issues. The influence of Parliament on the functioning of the government in respect of scientific and technological policies and programmes has been meagre through this forum. It does not appear to have been utilized as a means of evolving a perspective on scientific and technological policies.

Finally, Balwant Bhaneja has argued that the lack of scientific knowledge is only one reason for the inability of parliamentarians to influence policy or subject it to critical scrutiny.[7] Even if opposition

[4] G. Narayana, 1980, 'Rule Making for Scheduled Castes; Analysis of Lok Sabha Debates 1962–1971', *Economic and Political Weekly*, vol. XV, no. 8, 23 February.

[5] R.B. Jain, 1985, 'Electronics Policy and Indian Parliament', *Indian Journal of Public Administration*, April–June, pp. 239–74.

[6] A. Rahman and Haritash Nirmal, 1985, *The Role of Parliament in the Formulation of National Science and Technology Policy*, New Delhi: National Institute of Science, Technology and Development Studies.

[7] Balwant Bhaneja, 1979, 'Parliamentary Influence on Science Policy in India', *Minerva*, vol. XVII, no. 1.

MPs could and did concern themselves with the scientific merits of research programmes in the national laboratories, and even if they were supported by the government, they would be faced with the closed ranks of government scientists, and the quality of scientific research could not be assessed. This is why, Bhaneja argues, parliamentary committees on science can do little more than obtain complaints about maladministration and against promotions.[8]

It is interesting that all the four studies mentioned above have explicitly come to the conclusion that Parliament is not very effective in either holding the executive accountable or in giving content and direction to the policy being formulated by the government.

This conclusion does not appear to be incongruent with the findings now available elsewhere too, that in the parliamentary system of government, power seems to be getting concentrated in an increasingly smaller number of functionaries and it may be more appropriate to call such a system of government prime ministerial rather than a cabinet government. These authors have also argued that policy issues are complex and technical and beyond the comprehension of the average MP. This may be true as far as electronics or science and technology policies are concerned.

Unlike science, technology or electronics, however, drought is an area that makes minimal demands in terms of specialized information or knowledge. It is, therefore, not unreasonable to expect greater interest and effectiveness when the issue manifestly belongs to the realm of social welfare. Drought affects large areas, creates conditions of starvation and famine, and demands the provision of vast resources. The consequences of drought for the social and economic system usually have long-term effects. We expect that the concern of the MPs would be well articulated to influence the government to formulate appropriate policies in this area. The framework within which such influence is made possible is clearly that of the theory of democratic representation.

The cornerstone of democratic governance is the accountability of the rulers to those who elect them. Accountability is, however, only one aspect of popular control over government, its natural corollary being responsiveness to the interests and opinions of the public. Democratic

[8] Bhaneja, 'Parliamentary Influence on Science Policy in India'.

representation also provides for leadership and responsibility in decision-making, by encouraging political leaders to pursue long-term national interests, in addition to reacting to pressures of the moment. In a less obvious way, representation confers legitimacy on government; both by mobilizing popular consent for particular policies as well as by providing a safety valve through which citizens can express their dissatisfaction with the government and its policies.

At the operational level, however, this concept presents some difficulties. Among those who have elected a legislator, there may be some vociferous and articulate groups that may make constant demands on him. In his attempts to satisfy these demands, he may ignore the needs of those sections of the electorate who, for a variety of reasons, may not have access to him. The result may be that the legislator's responsiveness may be sectarian and confined to those who may be his vote managers. The needs of the constituency may suffer on account of the clout of the clients.[9] In an open system, poor people generally do not fare well and the larger interests of the constituency suffer because certain groups tend to dominate.

In India, such a situation is typical of those constituencies that fall within the areas where drought is chronic. Even though everyone in the area suffers, the impact of such conditions is particularly severe on the poor. But, unfortunately, the poor have learned to live and adapt themselves to situations of risk, uncertainty, and the indifferent response of the governing institutions to their problems.[10] Consequently, they do not feel the need to make demands for change and they resign themselves to their fate. Articulation here is, therefore, a two-step process: first, creating the awareness that change is possible and that the political and bureaucratic institutions are means to improve the situation; and second, converting these needs into demands on these

[9] Joseph P. Viteritti, 1990, 'Public Organization Environment Constituents, Clients and Governance', *Administration and Society*, vol. XXI, no. 4. Viteritti has made a distinction between client groups and constituencies, and has suggested that the concept of client does not involve the notion of political accountability but that of a constituency does.

[10] For adaptability to risk and uncertainty in drought prone areas and the need to reorient public policies, see Anil K. Gupta, 1983, 'Impoverishment in Drought Regions: A View from Within', (Joint Field Study – SDC/NABARD/ IIM-A) CMA, IIM, Ahmedabad.

institutions. This places on representatives a different set of obligations, in terms of not only satisfying demands but also in helping to create them. The latter role requires some awareness of the ecological problems associated with drought and the ability to make a distinction between the long- and short-term needs of the drought-affected areas.

In examining the question of the political articulation of the needs of drought areas, therefore, there are two issues: one is that of the character of representation and the other of the content of representation. Let us first focus on the members of the Lok Sabha who participated in the major parliamentary debate on the drought of 1987.

A total number of ninety-three members of the Lok Sabha responded to the statement made by the Minister of Agriculture on the drought situation in the country in the House on 10 August 1987. The discussion lasted for six days. Going by the number of members present during the discussion, it did not evoke much interest among them even though the government had characterized the 1987 drought as the 'drought of the century'. The issue of quorum was raised several times and all the members who participated were never present at the same time. A few listened to what the others said and the style was to make a statement and leave. Dinesh Singh commented on this in the Lok Sabha on 11 August:

Today, in the morning, the Honourable Speaker had stated that when the discussion on drought was going on in the House, only 25 members were present. It is very shameful. I think, he should have asked the members of the Cabinet Committee to remain in the House so that they could have known the feelings of the public. Otherwise, the government will not be able to fight drought only depending on the advice of officers.[11]

It was claimed by the government that 260 districts in the country were affected by drought conditions in 1987 (see Table 7.1). This estimate was based on the state memoranda submitted to the central government's request for financial assistance to meet the emergency. Based on the recommendations of the Swaminathan Committee, the government had identified 70 districts where the Drought Prone Area Programme would be implemented and 21 districts (including four cold arid districts) for its Desert Development Programme. Obviously,

[11] Lok Sabha Debates, 1987.

the areas affected by the 1987 drought were far more in number than those that were officially designated as drought prone. Allowing for the exaggerated claims made by the states to procure greater financial support, undoubtedly the scarcity of rainfall had a much wider impact on the country (see Table 7.1).

TABLE 7.1:   Districts Affected by Drought in 1987

States	Districts Affected by Drought		DPAP/ DDP Districts	
	No.	Per cent	No.	Per cent
Andhra Pradesh (23)	18	78	7	30
Bihar	—	—	2	—
Gujarat (19)	17	89	10	53
Haryana (12)	12	100	5	42
Himachal Pradesh (12)	12	100	2	17
Jammu and Kashmir (14)	12	86	4	33
Kerala (14)	14	100	—	—
Karnataka (20)	18	90	10	50
Maharashtra (31)	9	29	10	32
Madhya Pradesh (45)	21	47	6	13
Nagaland (7)	7	100	—	—
Orissa (13)	8	62	4	31
Rajasthan (27)	27	100	15	56
Punjab (12)	11	92	—	—
Tamil Nadu (20)	14	70	3	21
Uttar Pradesh (57)	55	96	10	18
West Bengal (16)	—	—	3	—
Union Territory	12	—	—	—
Total	267	—	91	—

Source: Government of India, 1989, *The Drought of 1987 Response and Management*, Ministry of Agriculture, Delhi.

As can be seen from Table 7.1, the states of Haryana, Himachal Pradesh, Kerala, Nagaland, and Rajasthan claimed that all their districts were affected by drought. Gujarat and Karnataka followed closely in such claims.

The extent of the drought-affected districts was wide and one would expect that with so many districts involved, a large number of MPs would be concerned, especially as parliamentary constituencies are not coterminous with district boundaries. As mentioned earlier, 93 members of the Lok Sabha participated in the debate. The state-wise distribution is listed in Table 7.2.

TABLE 7.2:   State-wise Participation of MPs

State	Total no. of MPs	Participation	
		Debate	Questions
Andhra Pradesh	42	10	17
Bihar	54	4	10
Gujarat	26	4	11
Haryana	10	4	2
Himachal Pradesh	4	1	1
Jammu and Kashmir	6	3	1
Karnataka	28	4	11
Kerala	20	4	12
Madhya Pradesh	40	11	10
Maharashtra	48	6	19
Orissa	21	5	11
Rajasthan	25	8	5
Tamil Nadu	39	3	5
Uttar Pradesh	85	17	10

Source: Author.

The state and constituency identity of six MPs could not be established through 'Who's Who' published by the Lok Sabha Secretariat. As can be seen from the data presented, the MPs from the north-eastern states did not participate at all even though one state, Nagaland, had claimed that all its districts were affected by drought. However, the spread of drought is not reflected in the representational spread of MPs. For example, Rajasthan claimed drought conditions in all its districts but the proportion of MPs that spoke was only 32 per cent of the total number of MPs from that state. Similarly, Gujarat had 90 per cent of its districts affected, but the participation of its MPs was only to the extent of 15 per cent. Such disparity in representation is true for other states too. What is interesting to note is that the constituencies of only 19 MPs who participated in the parliamentary debate were from areas where the DPAP/DDP were being implemented. Most drought-stricken areas, apparently, went unrepresented. It may also be true that the reason why the MPs of well-endowed regions took greater interest in the debate was because their areas suffered more because of drought. The poor and other people living in the drought regions were accustomed to its exigencies and sought less help from the outside. But this does not take away the significance of the fact that of the four Gujarat MPs who participated, three represented the DPAP districts. Half the number of the MPs from Rajasthan also did so.

Exploring further some other characteristics of the MPs who participated in the debate, we found that approximately 50 per cent of them were first entrants to the Lok Sabha and a similar proportion came from the agricultural profession. Not all agriculturists however took interest in the discussion. In the Lok Sabha as a whole, there were 200 of them.

Thus, if participation in the drought discussion is taken as an indicator of legislators' concern for the problems of the poor and the deprived, the Lok Sabha scores poorly. Legislators, also, score low on the representation of their constituencies. Agriculturists do not evince that kind of interest possibly because they are not from the category which is affected most by drought. Whatever be its significance for the backward regions, drought appears to be just another issue for debate and to articulate demands for more funds from the centre.

Another way of expressing concern about the constituency and the method of placing its problems on the policy agenda is the use of parliamentary questions. Members of Parliament can ask written questions. Written questions elicit written answers and the major purpose of such questions is to elicit information about issues of policy or implementation. These questions provide data that parliamentarians can use to continue to probe the government's performance on other occasions. They also serve to direct attention to certain problems and alert the government to issues that people are concerned about. Members can also ask oral questions. The Minister concerned is given notice of the intention of a Member to ask a particular question, which is put to him orally and to which he is expected to respond in the House.

The strength of this type of question is that it allows for supplementaries. The discussion is not only focused on extracting information but used as an occasion to express disagreement with government policy or to demonstrate how it has failed to achieve results. Other members, apart from the questioner, can join in. Thus, an oral question can trigger a debate or a full-fledged discussion of much greater length.

During the five-year period from 1985 to 1989, 372 questions relating to drought were asked in the Lok Sabha. Out of these, 37 were starred or oral questions. Sixty-six questions were jointly asked by more than one Member of Parliament. In all, 141 MPs asked these 372 questions; thus many MPs asked more than one question during this period. Table 7.3 shows that while 61 MPs asked only one question, there were 24 MPs who asked five or more questions. There were six MPs from Karnataka and three each from Andhra Pradesh, Gujarat, Maharashtra, and Orissa who fell in this category. There were only two MPs from Rajasthan who were as active and one of them who represented Barmer, a desert constituency, asked as many as 15 questions—the maximum that an MP asked. Parliament had an overwhelming majority of Members belonging to the Congress (I), and therefore it is not surprising that a little more than 75 per cent of the active Members who raised five or more questions belonged to this Party. Among the remaining, three were from the Telugu Desam, and one each from the Bharatiya Janata Party and the Janata Party. Only a third of these members participated in the debate that took place.

TABLE 7.3:   The Number of Questions Asked in Parliament on Drought, 1985–9

No. of Questions Asked	No. of MPs
1	61
2–4	56
5–7	15
8 and above	9

Source: Author.

Parliamentary questions reflect a sustained interest in the issue of drought while participation in debate may not necessarily do so. A large number of MPs who participated in the debate had not raised any question during the entire five year period. This lack of participation may not be an adequate indicator of the apathy of the MPs. It is a well-known fact that MPs make considerable use of informal channels to influence the Minister concerned or civil servants to get things done on behalf of their constituents. Such influence may be exercised to favour an individual or a group or to attempt to locate a development project in a particular area. By the very nature of the demands, the attempt made by the MP is to attract benefits of a government policy by reorienting the implementation process. Little effort is directed towards changing the policy itself. Thus, one could argue that lack of interest at the parliamentary level reflects lack of interest in policy issues and of concern for long-term developments. Reorienting the implementation process is a method of taking advantage of a policy, not an effort to change it.

It is also significant to note that parliamentarians from drought-affected areas have not been particularly active in representing the conditions of their constituents. Cudgels on their behalf have been taken up by MPs from many other areas. The distribution of parliamentary constituencies, whose representatives questioned the government on drought, does not show any concentration in the drought-affected areas. These states, which claimed to have nearly all their districts suffering from drought conditions, were also not in the forefront of questioning the government.

Among the 24 MPs who were fairly active in asking questions in the Lok Sabha, six were from Karnataka; three each from Andhra Pradesh, Maharashtra, Gujarat, and Orissa; two each from Kerala and Rajasthan; and one each from Himachal Pradesh and Madhya Pradesh. Eight of them had participated in the debate too. The parliamentary constituencies of six of these MPs fell in the drought areas. Apparently, very few MPs have taken the initiative to raise questions relating to drought.

Thus, both in terms of the quantum as well as the spread of concern about drought, it is apparent that very few MPs have taken an active interest in drought-related issues, as evidenced from the extent and character of their participation in the major debate on drought in August 1987.

8

Governance as Networks

Emerging Relationships among the State, Business, and NGOs in India*

Governance is concerned with a network of relationships between three actors—the state, market, and civil society. It is an interactive process wherein the government may like to impose its will, but this acceptance will depend on the compliance and action of others. This chapter explores the concept of networks and shows how the relationship of the state with the corporate sector is based on a transformed view of the role of the state in a neo-liberal economic framework. It questions the possibility of joint decision-making in the socioeconomic context of India wherein adequate efforts have not been made for facilitating state-building activities.

It is fair to say that until the late 1980s, the term 'governance' was not frequently heard within the development community. It became part of public discourse in India only after the economic reforms

* Kuldeep Mathur, 2010, 'Governance as Networks: State, Business, and Politics in India', *Indian Journal of Human Development*, vol. 4, no. 2, pp. 253–79. Thanks are due to the Centre for Democracy and Social Action and to OXFAM for sponsoring this study and to Richa Singh for offering organizational support on their behalf. Thanks are also due to Sunayana for providing research assistance.

were introduced in 1991. Today, it is a buzzword used freely in most publications emanating from donor agencies, academics, and planning and policy documents in India. It is heavily relied upon to explain developmental outcomes. International and multilateral aid-giving agencies have adopted it as a general guiding principle to improve the capability of the recipient countries to handle development assistance better and utilize it more efficiently. However, improving a country's capability to utilize aid better or to work for improved developmental performance does not connote the same meanings for everyone. The meanings range from following liberal economic policies, to strengthening and reforming market institutions, to building capacities of public institutions to perform, to encouraging democratic participation through strengthening civil society institutions, among other things. Some meanings are concerned with reducing the role of the state in economic activities, others with strengthening state institutions to promote the role of the market, and yet others relate to the encouragement of democracy and participation.

In this web of many meanings of governance, there is a baseline agreement that governance refers to the development of governing styles in which the boundaries between and within the public and private sectors are blurred.[1] What were previously indisputably roles of government are now increasingly seen as more common generic, societal problems, which can be resolved not only by political institutions but also by other actors. The main point is that political institutions no longer exercise a monopoly over the orchestration of governance.[2] The concept of governance indicates a shift away from well-established notions of the way in which the government sought to resolve social issues through a top-down approach.

Thus, the core idea of governance lays stress on network relationships among the three actors—the state, the market, and civil society, in steering society. The monopoly of political institutions in providing services is diluted; the private sector and institutions of civil society fill in the space previously occupied by these institutions. New forms of

[1] Gerry Stoker, 1998, 'Governance as Theory: Five Propositions', *International Social Science Journal*, vol. 155, March, p. 18.

[2] Jon Pierre (ed.), 2000, *Debating Governance*, Oxford: Oxford University Press, p. 4.

institutions emerge, which find expression in the blurring of boundaries between the public and the private sectors. A range of participative agencies arise that respond to collective concerns.

The vantage point is not the interest of the organization and its attempt to gain influence on public policy through formal and informal contacts with the central decision-makers.[3] Rather, the focus is on the production of public policy and the contribution of public and private actors to it. As Rhodes points out, 'policy networks are sets of formal institutional and informal linkages between governmental and other actors structured around shared, if endlessly negotiated, beliefs and interests in public policy making and implementation. These actors are interdependent and policy emerges from the interactions between them.[4] Policy networks are also strategic alliances forged around common agendas of mutual advantage through collective action.[5]

At the formal level, policy networks have emerged as public institutions wherein interactions between government, business, and civil society can take place. These interactions lead to policy outputs. In operational terms, governments institute advisory bodies and various kinds of councils wherein representatives of the government and the other two actors—business and civil society—are members. Such policy networks are different from lobby groups, whose role was to influence government to obtain outputs in their favour.

At the informal level, governance implies the opening up of government activities to non-government actors. It is no longer a preserve of hierarchical decision-making, which is often secretive and closed. The three actors, the state, the market, and civil society, interact more frequently in the public domain and attempt to formulate public policies together. This is distinct from an understanding of lobby groups, which tend to influence government to frame or bend policy in their

[3] Eva Sorenson and Jacob Torfing, 2004, 'Making Governance Networks Democratic', Working Paper No. 1, Centre for Democratic Governance, Roskilde, Denmark, available at www.demnetgov.ruc.dk.

[4] R.A.W. Rhodes, 2006, 'Policy Network Analysis', in M. Moran, M. Rein, and R. Goodin (eds), The Oxford Handbook of Public Policy, Oxford: Oxford University Press, p. 426.

[5] Colin Hay and David Richards, 2000, 'The Tangled Web of Westminster and Whitehall: The Discourse Strategy and Practice of Networking within the British Core Executive', Public Administration, vol. 78, no. 1, pp. 1–28.

favour. It is a fundamental change towards a more open government that is willing to listen and become one among three participants in policymaking.

Apart from policy networks, there are operational networks too. These networks are implementation tools which deliver public goods and services, a task that one single actor cannot do. Increasingly, the government has adopted the mode of seeking cooperation of one or the other actor in implementing programmes of public interest. Such cooperation has taken the form of what has come to be popularly known as a public-private partnership (PPP). This type of partnership is being promoted across the world as a strategy of governance in delivering goods and services in many sectors. The partnerships promise to avoid duplication of efforts and are seen to draw on their complementary resources and capabilities to design more effective problem-solving mechanisms. They promise to increase the responsiveness of policies and create accountability by including other actors—the market and civil society—into decision-making processes. They are also presumed to improve compliance with and implementation of political decisions. In addition, the partnerships provide opportunities to the partners to learn from each other.[6] It is widely believed that networks play a significant role in the processes that promote social and economic development. Pingle has argued that shared understandings are vital for the better functioning of economic decision-making.[7] Shared understandings help overcome bureaucratic resistance and prevent the state from falling prey to social and political interests. Industrialists increase their ability to get the necessary infrastructure and collective goods for future growth.

However, this optimism is not shared by many. Critics point out that these partnerships can signify the strategy of the state to evade responsibility. There is considerable belief in the proposition that 'the hierarchical governance of the society by the state is based on substantive rationality. The political values and preferences of the government— supposed to incarnate the will of the people—are translated into

[6] Julia Streets, 2004, 'Developing a Framework: Concepts and Research Priorities for Partnership Accountability', Global Public Policy Institute, Berlin, available at http://globalpublicpolicy.net.

[7] Vibha Pingle, 2000, *Rethinking the Developmental State: India's Industry in Comparative Perspective*, New Delhi: Oxford University Press.

more or less detailed laws and regulations that are implemented and enforced by publicly employed bureaucracies'.[8] These bureaucracies are accountable to the representatives of the people who express these preferences. Thus, networks carry the risk of weakening traditional accountability mechanisms by shifting policy decisions to the realm of partnerships that can circumvent parliamentary control.[9] Further, if partnerships emphasize cost reduction or profit maximization at the price of significant quality compromises, vulnerable populations may not be able to respond appropriately and aggressively. There is always the risk that the poor and the marginalized groups in the population may be excluded due to pricing policies. An impression is growing that networks are cases of privatization by 'stealth' and the bargains have been, in general, more favourable to corporate interests encouraging the corporate sector to embellish their own power and resources.[10]

Despite these concerns, there is optimism about the partnerships, and a complex web of networks is emerging worldwide in which India is not lagging behind. The notion of governance is transforming the organization of the state and its relationships with the private sector and civil society actors. However, little scholarly attention is being devoted to analyzing and debating this transformation of the state and democracy in India. Our aim, in this chapter, is to investigate and unravel the networks that have been created between the state and business in India, and to explore the way they function. We also attempt to map out the way in which the corporate sector has organized itself to participate in these partnerships and networks. A major objective here is to bring out in the public domain the dense relations that are developing among government, business, and some associations of civil society in India, and to raise questions about their impact on democracy and accountability.

[8] Sorenson and Torfing, 'Making Governance Networks Democratic'.

[9] Streets, 'Developing a Framework'.

[10] Amrita Datta, 2009, 'Public-Private Partnerships in India', *Economic and Political Weekly*, vol. XLIV, no. 33, 15 August, pp. 73–8; J.J.A.M. Reijners, 1994, 'Organization of Public-Private Partnership Projects: The Timely Prevention of Pitfalls', *International Journal of Project Management*, vol. 12, no. 3, pp. 137–42; and P.V. Rosenau, 2000, *Public-Private Partnerships*, Cambridge, Mass.: MIT Press; Rhodes, 'Policy Network Analysis', pp. 425–47.

POLICY NETWORKS: GOVERNMENT AND BUSINESS

As is well known, the liberalization of the Indian economy took place in the context of international funding agencies like the World Bank and the IMF insisting on structural adjustment programmes to help India cope up with the financial crisis of 1992. These involved keeping budget deficits within reasonable limits, promoting privatization, and creating space for greater participation of non-state actors in the provision of services. The flow of funds was predicated on India undertaking policy and governance reforms.

In order to promote a much greater role of the private sector in meeting the challenges of development and alleviating poverty, the government envisaged its most important role in provisioning infrastructure—power, transport, roads, et al.—for facilitating private investment. But having taken on the role of providing infrastructure to attract investment, the government found itself in a peculiar bind. It did not have the financial and technical resources to invest in the required sectors of power and transport, but knew that private investment cannot be attracted in the industrial and other sectors without the provision of adequate infrastructure. Public-private partnership appeared to be an attractive proposition to tide over this obstacle of lack of financial resources. The demand of financial resources is formidable if the ambitions of the government have to be realized. It has committed to raise the infrastructure spending to about nine per cent of the GDP at the end of the Eleventh Plan period. This means that around 500 billion USD would be required by the infrastructure sectors over the five-year Plan period.[11]

The Eleventh Plan emphasizes the strategy of public-private partnership for locating these resources and justifies it by saying that 'these partnerships must ensure the supplementing of scarce public resources for investment in infrastructure sectors while improving efficiencies and reducing costs ... Public-private partnerships must aim at bringing private resources into public projects, not public resources into private projects'.[12] In a recent speech, the Prime Minister Dr Manmohan Singh reiterated that 'a synergy between public support and private initiative

[11] Datta, 'Public-Private Partnerships in India', p. 73.
[12] Government of India (GoI), 2006, *Draft Report on the Recommendation of Task Force on Public-Private Partnership for the Eleventh Plan*, New Delhi: Union

can help multiply the productivity of resource utilization'. He went on to say, 'We have been deeply concerned about the efficiency of utilization of public funds, especially in infrastructure development, education, and healthcare. We have been looking for ways of combining our concern for equitable outcomes with our concern for efficient utilization of outlays. PPPs are an effective means of combining these two concerns'.[13]

Attracting private investment for promoting economic development and thus raising the rate of economic growth became the single most important dimension of public policy. A new style of governance was sought to encourage and facilitate the achievement of this aim. For pursuing this aim, a partnership with big business houses was necessary. The economic strategy adopted led to the prioritization of growth as a state goal, supporting large business houses in achieving this goal and keeping labour under control.[14] The changed strategy of economic development had a strong impact on the terms of policy discourse. The state set about searching for market solutions to societal problems. Issues of poverty and inequalities, which were defined as major problems earlier, yielded place to the argument that as the rate of economic growth rises, poverty levels will begin to go down. Inequalities of wealth and incomes were deemed necessary and conducive in providing incentives for wealth creation. The emerging styles of governance underline an 'enabling state', whose role is to create conditions in which private investment can take place. The traditional government forms became problematic and administrative reforms were aimed at relaxing government decision-making processes such that business enterprises could be set up within a minimum time after the application for setting them up had been filed.[15]

Ministry of Health and Family Welfare, available at http://mohfw.nic.in/NRHM/Task_grp/Draft_Report_Task_Group_on_PPP7_9_06.pdf.

[13] Prime Minister Manmohan Singh's address delivered to the McKinsey meet, available at http://pmindia.nic.in/speeches.htm.

[14] Atul Kohli, 2006, 'Politics of Economic Growth in India: 1980–2005', *Economic and Political Weekly*, 1 April, pp. 1251–59, and 8 April, Part II, pp. 1361–70.

[15] In fact, the World Bank conducts a worldwide survey, assessing the business environment and the speed with which a government responds to an application to set up an enterprise. In a survey carried over 183 countries, the

In this broad policy framework, forging partnerships with the other two actors became a measure of good governance and facilitated the increased role of market and civil society in the prime activity of the government. While speaking at a seminar in 2006, the Minister of Company Affairs pointed out that the role of the private enterprise in taking the country to higher and higher growth paths is very important. The government's role is to provide an atmosphere that is conducive for business to flourish. He then went on to emphasize the need for freedom of action and initiative by the enterprises as against the pre-reform mindset of viewing the business and its efforts to achieve growth and expansion, with suspicion. 'We are in the era of PPP', he said.[16] And the search for sectors wherein schemes and projects could be implemented in the PPP mode began.

GOVERNANCE IN THE NEW POLICY FRAMEWORK
The government sought an alliance with big business to pursue this goal of implementing PPP projects. It began by initiating many policies that withdrew the controlling and regulating role of the state and then went on to establish institutional structures that provided a formal forum wherein big business could participate in policymaking. Such a government-business alliance became explicit when the Government of India appointed a three-member Investment Commission in 2004 to enhance and facilitate investment in India. The Commission makes recommendations to the Government of India on policies and procedures to facilitate investment, recommends projects and investment proposals that should be fast-tracked or monitored, and promotes India as an investment destination.[17] Its initial tenure was for three years, but was extended by another three years. The Commission

---

World Bank ranked India at 132 in 2009 with Singapore, New Zealand, United States, Hong Kong, Denmark, and United Kingdom being at the top in that order. See World Bank, 2009, *Doing Business Report*, Washington, D.C., available at www.doingbusiness.org/data/exploreeconomies/India.

[16] Seminar on 'Competition Policy and Law', Indian Institute of Public Administration, 16 November 2006, available at http://www.indlawnews. com/NewsDisplay.aspx?d24e0889-69db-4cdb-b44b-526fd45d1299.

[17] The Commission was set up under Government of India notification F. No. 1/7/2004-FIU. Details are drawn from its website: http://www. investmentcommission.in/.

is chaired by Ratan Tata, with Deepak Parekh (HDFC) and Ashok Ganguly (ICCI) as members. The Report of this Commission is an important policy document not only because its members are major business leaders of the country, but also because the notification of the appointment of the Commission itself laid down the procedure to process the recommendations of the Report. The notification mentioned that it will be located in the Finance Ministry, will enjoy operational autonomy and government support, and that its recommendations will be processed in the Ministry and put up for approval to the Cabinet Committee of Economic Affairs.

The Report, submitted in 2006, formalized the framework policy of pursuing the goal of raising the rate of economic growth and the need for the kind of governance required to respond to this policy.[18] The Commission set the goal of sustained economic growth at eight per cent and proposed that the investment levels in the economy have to rise from 30 per cent of the GDP to 34 per cent over the next five years. Having set this target, the Commission suggested an expansion in foreign direct investment (FDI) of 15 billion USD by the end of 2007–8. It then went on to identify major impediments to investments and then made recommendations to improve the investment climate in the country. A number of recommendations were concerned with reform of the debilitating procedures of decision-making and provided sustenance to the governance reforms being undertaken.[19] As the Commission consisted of leaders of the corporate world, its recommendations further stimulated the pace of forging government-business partnerships that have now become the cornerstone of India's strategy of development.

---

[18] Government of India (GoI), 2006, *Investment Strategy for India: Report of the Investment Commission*, New Delhi: Union Ministry of Finance, available at http://finmin.mc.in/reports/ InvestmentCommissionReport.pdf.

[19] According to a newspaper report, there is a sense of resignation in the Commission on the lack of adequate follow-up by the government on its recommendations and it has asked the government to wind it up instead of extending its term. P. Vaidyanathan Iyer, 2010, 'Want to Call It a Day, So Don't Extend Our Term: Investment Panel to Government', *Indian Express*, 11 January, available at http://www.indianexpress.com/news/want-to-call-it-a-day-so-dont-extend-our-term-investment-panel-to-govt/565842/0.

INSTITUTIONAL ARRANGEMENTS FOR NETWORKS

New formal institutions that reflected this partnership began to emerge and the government began to open itself to advice from, and consultation with, the corporate sector. The economic ministries formed Boards that had leading lights of the corporate sector as members to formalize the collaboration between the government and business in policymaking. The Federation of Indian Chambers of Commerce and Industry (FICCI), the Confederation of Indian Industry (CII), and other such organizations were recognized as legitimate forums for political and bureaucratic leadership to interact with the captains of industry. At the highest level, with the Prime Minister as Chair, a Council on Trade and Industry was created as an institutional framework for partnership between government and business. The Prime Minster emphasized that the partnership flows from the country's overall strategy of economic reforms.

According to the government notification in 1998, a Council on Trade and Industry was appointed with the Prime Minister as Chairperson. This practice was continued with the change of government in 2004 too. The Council provided an opportunity for a policy dialogue between the Prime Minister and members of the Council on important economic issues relevant to trade and industry. The Council ordinarily met once in three months on such dates as decided by its Chairman. The membership of the Council nearly doubled—from 10 to 18 members— between the two years when the government changed, incorporating many more industrialists who were rising on the economic horizon. In addition, special sub-groups were also appointed to interact directly with ministries. Such sub-groups were set up in varied areas like Food and Agro-industries Management Policy, Infrastructure, Capital Markets and Financial Sector Initiatives, Knowledge-based Industries, Service Industries, and Administrative and Legal Simplifications.

The membership of the Board in 1998 and in 2004, when the Government changed, is shown in Table 8.1.

The Council of the Ministry of Commerce and Industry, as shown in Table 8.2, provided avenues of partnership to another dozen corporate giants.

What is significant about the membership of these councils is that trade unions, labour federations, and NGOs were unrepresented. It is presumed that gains in the rate of economic growth or relaxing of

TABLE 8.1:   Council of Trade and Industry, 1998 and 2004

Chairman: Prime Minister	
Members: 1998	Members: 2004
Ratan Tata	Ratan Tata, V. Krishnamurthy
Mukesh Ambani	Keshab Mahindra, R.P. Goenka
R.P. Goenka	Azim Premji, N.R. Narayan Murthy
Kumaramangalam Birla	Rahul Bajaj, Mukesh Ambani
N.R. Krishnamurthy	Kumaramangalam Birla, J. Godrej
Nusli Wadia	Sunil Mittal, Ashok Ganguli
A.C. Muthiah	Deepak Parekh, M.S. Banga
P.K. Mittal	Kiran Mazumdar Shaw, K. Anji Reddy
Parminder Singh	Venu Srinivasan, S.K. Munjal
Suresh Krishna	
Member-Secretary: Principal Secretary to the Prime Minister	

Source: Government of India Notification No. 260/31/C/25/98-E&S1, available at: http://indiaimage. nic.in/pmcouncils/tic/noti1.htm.

TABLE 8.2:   Members of the Board of Trade, Ministry of Commerce and Industry, 2005

Kumaramangalam Birla, Aditya Birla Group	Ishaat Hussain, Tata Sons
Baba Kalyani, Bharat Forge	Malvinder Singh, Ranbaxy
Irfan Allana, Allana Sons	Jagdish Khattar, Maruti Udyog
Ravi Raheja, Shoppers Stop	Prashant Ruia, Essar Group
A.C. Muthiah, SPIC	Harish Neotia, Gujarat Ambuja
Rana Kapoor, Yes Bank	Rama S. Deora, Ampray Labs

Source: 'Kamal Nath Reconstitutes Board of Trade', available at: http://commerce.nic.in/pressrelease/ pressrelease_detail.asp?id=1611.

government norms is a technical problem and can be decided within an expert body and those who can invest. Part of the effort is also to insulate economic decision-making from the political process. In Britain, a three-way partnership was institutionalized in the National Economic Development Council launched in 1962. During the 1980s, the significance of the Council diminished, and its members met infrequently. The Prime Minister, Margaret Thatcher, was of the opinion that trade unions had no legitimate role in policymaking and should, therefore, be excluded. The Council was finally disbanded in 1992.[20]

For networking with the civil society at the policy level, a National Advisory Council had been appointed during the earlier term of the present government but was disbanded after its Chairperson chose to resign. The NAC comprised distinguished professionals drawn from diverse fields of development activity, who served in their individual capacities. Through the NAC, the government had access not only to their expertise and experience, but also to a larger network of research organizations, NGOs, and social action and advocacy groups. The NAC has now been revived with a full complement of members drawn from the groups mentioned, and with Sonia Gandhi as its Chairperson.

Members of the corporate world are also being invited to participate in policy processes in many other areas apart from merely industry and trade. For example, the Ministry of Human Resource Development convened a Round Table to discuss policy issues regarding education. During its first meeting, it was decided that Analjit Singh of Max Healthcare would prepare a concept note on vocational education, Hari Bhartia of Jubilant Organosys would prepare a policy outline on PPP, and Rajendra Pawar of NIIT would recommend measures to ensure that meritorious students get funds for education in private unaided institutions as well as ways to incentivize private investment.[21] To refer to the British experience again, sectoral departments have created their own partnerships with non-governmental actors. These partnerships have been categorized as 'policy communities' that are generally organized around a government department and its network of client groups.[22] These arrangements help the department set its agenda and seek stability in policy. Some of the key policy communities are in the areas of Agriculture, Health, Law and Order, Tobacco, and Transport. Among the primary organized interest groups that form part of this

---

[20] Peter Dorey, 2005, *Policy-Making in Britain: An Introduction*, London: Sage Publications, p. 125.

[21] Akshay Mukul, 2009, 'Corporate Czars for Education Reforms', *The Times of India*, 28 November, available at http://timesofindia.indiatimes.com/india/Corporate-czars-for-education-reforms/articleshow/5277382.cms.

[22] For more details, see Peter Dorey, 2005, *Policy-Making in Britain: An Introduction*, ch. 5.

sub-system are the National Farmers Union, British Medical Association, Association of Chief Police Officers, the Tobacco Advisory Council, and British Roads Federation.

In order to create an improved relationship between the bureaucrats and the private sector, other informal measures are also being attempted. Senior civil servants are being permitted to go on deputation to work in multinational corporations or large corporate houses *in public interest* (emphasis added). Making good use of Section 6(2) of the IAS (Cadre) Rules, 1954, which allows officers to take up assignments outside the government, as many as 115 members of the 5,000-odd IAS cadre are holding assignments outside the government. At last count, 64 IAS officers were working with private firms or NGOs while 51 were on foreign assignments, including those with the India offices of international organizations. The latest officer to head out is a petroleum joint secretary, said to be joining as chief of an oil refinery owned by a corporate major. Meanwhile, to meet the 'shortfall' in the IAS, the government decided to recruit 'more and more' officers—110, 120, and 130, respectively in 2008, 2009, and 2010.[23]

In addition, individuals who have had wide experience of working in senior policy positions with the private sector are being inducted at the policymaking level in government. In 2009, the Planning Commission opened its doors to one such eminent person: Arun Maira, who had worked with Tata Motors and Arthur D. Little and was senior advisor with the Boston Consulting Group in India, was appointed as Member of the Commission.[24] In another recent decision, Nandan Nilekani, Co-Chairman of Infosys Technologies and leading spokesperson for the information technology industry was appointed as Chairman of the Unique Identification Authority of India with the rank of Cabinet Minister. Thus, policy networks are being created and strengthened in various ways.

This growing partnership between the executive and big business is also getting reflected in the membership of Parliament. According

[23] Ashish Sinha, 2007, 'IAS Officers Find Greener Pastures Without Quitting', *The Times of India*, Mumbai Edition, 29 September, available at: http://epaper.timesofindia.com/Repository/ml.

[24] The Planning Commission is the top think-tank of the government and privy to all major policy decisions pertaining to social and economic development.

to a National Election Watch Report, there are around 300 MPs in the Parliament who are millionaires. Out of them, 138 belong to the Congress Party, and Bihar alone accounts for 52 of them.[25] Many of these crorepati MPs have connections with large business houses. For example, Rahul Bajaj is a leading industrialist of the country and is a member of several committees of the government. He has been a member of the Committee on Labour and also of the Consultative Committee for the Ministry of Finance in 2007. Parimal Nathwani, who is closely linked with Reliance Industries, has been a Member of the Committee on Commerce and Consultative Committee for the Ministry of Home Affairs. An MP like Vijay Mallya, who has business interests in the liquor and aviation businesses, is a Member of the Consultative Committee for Ministry of Civil Aviation. These are a few examples wherein avenues of direct influence are accepted in defiance of all issues of conflict of interest.

RESPONSE OF INDUSTRY ASSOCIATIONS TO GOVERNMENT OVERTURES

Associations of industries have also geared themselves to provide platforms for the leaders of government and business to interact and deliberate on public policy. FICCI is the rallying point for free enterprise in India. According to its website, 'it has empowered Indian businesses, in the changing times, to shore up their competitiveness and enhance their global reach.' With a nationwide membership of over 1,500 corporates and over 500 commerce and business associations, FICCI espouses the shared vision of Indian businesses, and speaks directly and indirectly for over 2,50,000 business units. The website further says that 'FICCI maintains the lead as a proactive business solution provider through research, interactions at the highest political level, and global networking.' Thirty-four specialized committees of FICCI on diverse segments of the economy grapple with sectoral issues on a day-to-day basis to provide solutions to business-related problems and suggest pragmatic policies to the government. The government provides its support to the activities of Joint Business Councils formed by FICCI

---

[25] National Election Watch, 2009, 'Analysis of the MPs of the 15th Lok Sabha (2009): High Level Summary', available at http://nationalelectionwatch.org/files/new/pdfs/Lok%20Sabha%20 high%20level%20analysis.pdf.

with India's trading partners. This is what it calls 'track two diplomacy' to open up new business opportunities for Indian businessmen with overseas investors, technology suppliers, and multilateral and bilateral funding agencies. The Annual General Meetings (AGMs) of FICCI have been important national economic events as contemporary developmental issues facing the nation are discussed and debated by the political leadership, business, and the academia during these meetings. These events have helped the Government of India to take stock of the developmental initiatives and to evolve policy corrections based on industry responses.

CII is another significant business association with a direct membership of over 5300 companies from the private as well as public sectors, including small and medium enterprises (SMEs) and multinational corporations (MNCs), and an indirect membership of over 80,000 organizations from 300 national and regional sectoral associations. Its website says that CII catalyzes change by working closely with the government on policy issues, enhancing efficiency, competitiveness, and expanding business opportunities for industry through a range of specialized services and global linkages. With 47 offices in India, 12 overseas and institutional partnerships with 239 counterpart organizations in 101 countries, CII serves as a reference point for industry and the international business community. Paying special attention to its linkages in the US, it set up an office in Washington, D.C. in 1995, and has close working relations with organizations such as the US Chamber of Commerce, the US-India Business Council, The Aspen Institute, and the Brookings Institution. CII has developed strong programmes to brief members of the US Congress and has sponsored a number of delegations of its members to visit India. As a corollary, it also sponsors visits of Indian parliamentarians to the US. The first delegation went in 2003 and consisted of representatives of various parties. It also sponsored a trip of young parliamentarians to Yale University for an orientation programme.

The Prime Ministers and their reform-oriented colleagues have played an important role in seeking support from these associations in initiating policies of liberalization. It must be remembered that Rajiv Gandhi's attempts at deregulation in 1986 faced significant opposition from his own party and bureaucrats, and he needed support from business. Sinha has documented how Rajiv Gandhi played a crucial role in transforming the Confederation of Engineering Industries (CEI) into the CII that was more broad-based and spoke for the entire industry.[26] In 1991, Dr Manmohan Singh, then Finance Minister, faced a similar predicament. He recommended that CII should popularize his ideas of economic reform to the opposition in Parliament. CII began organizing interactive sessions and this practice has since continued. Earlier, Prime Minister Vajpayee had asked CII to invite Benazir Bhutto, Pakistan's former Prime Minister (who was later assassinated in 2007) to India when it was politically difficult for him to do so. Similarly, Finance Minister Chidambaram made a request in 2004, 'I would like CII and FICCI to address some of our friends in the Left parties and convince them to increase the Foreign Direct Investment (FDI) cap'.

The Finance Minister came to address the National Council of CII in August 2009. He elaborated on the measures taken in the last Budget and called for support from the industry to carry out many programmes in the fields of health and education as well. He showed that there were greater opportunities for the private sector because smart cards were being provided to citizens to avail of health services from private hospitals too. Similarly, he underlined the significance of PPPs that were being promoted to tide over difficulties in various sectors like those of infrastructure, health, and education. Lauding the members of CII as leading members of industry, he exhorted them to play a 'stellar role in making the Indian growth story a continuing one'.[27]

The role of CII in influencing public policy is now well recognized and documented.[28] CII has argued for a more open and competitive economy, and promoted greater integration of the Indian economy with the global economy. As quoted by Sinha, Tarun Das, its long time Secretary-General, described 'development as a partnership process

[26] Aseema Sinha, 2005, 'Understanding the Rise and Transformation of Business Collective Action in India', *Business and Politics*, vol. 7, no. 2, available at http://www.bepress.com/bap/vol7/iss2/art2.

[27] Address by Union Minister of Finance, Pranab Mukherjee at CII National Council Meeting, 3 August 2009, available at http://^inmin.nic.in/fmspeech/fmspeech_ciinationalcouncilmeeting030809.pdf.

[28] Stanley Kochanek, 1996, 'Liberalization and Business Lobbying in India', *Pacific Affairs*, vol. 34, no. 3, pp. 155–73; Kohli, 'Politics of Economic Growth in India: 1980–2005'; and Aseema Sinha, 'Understanding the Rise and Transformation of Business Collective Action in India'.

between the government and industry and we (CII) are the junior partner of the government'.[29] It has found representations in delegations to
the WTO and in delegations accompanying the Prime Minister during
the latter's state visits abroad.[30]

The CII, in turn, has established several committees and task forces
that examine issues in specific sectors and raise them in government
interaction. For example, there is a National Committee on Healthcare
(2009–10), which comprises members from hospitals, diagnostics centres,
medical equipment companies, nursing homes, et al. The Committee
is currently being chaired by Dr Prathap C. Reddy, Chairman, Apollo
Hospital Group. The main objective of the Committee is to work on
various issues pertaining to the healthcare sector and to provide inputs
in its interaction with the government.[31]

There is a National Committee on Education chaired by Vijay
K. Thadani, CEO of NIIT. CII's education initiatives are aimed at
promoting both school education and higher education. The CII works
actively in the areas of policy recommendations on PPP in school,
accreditation, the right to education, upgradation of school education and of higher education, PPPs in higher education, et al. The CII
has formed a University Industry Council wherein universities and
the industry come to a single platform to discuss issues and take cor-
rective actions in the area of human resource development (HRD).
The following five task forces exist under the National Committee on
Education:

- Independent Accreditation
- Teacher Empowerment and Development

[29] Sinha, 'Understanding the Rise and Transformation of Business Collective
Action in India', p. 15.

[30] Rajiv Gandhi was the first Prime Minister who invited businessmen to
accompany him on his foreign trips. On hearing of such inclusion in the PM's
entourage, the Indian Ambassador to the USSR is reported to have telegraphed
his displeasure. Rajiv Gandhi told the Foreign Ministry officials to throw the
telegram in the dustbin and proceeded with his plans. Sinha, 'Understanding
the Rise and Transformation of Business Collective Action in India', p. 12.

[31] See http://www.cii.in/CCDetails.aspx?enc=uynmj+oUo63zz/LKp/g+
BD1OhPLKwGOe15ip8+OIYvm2t0vnrVZGzc7y/jThUzAbfeTzcUy+fRmyy
Q05esFM1VtTx6aLR/03fVvGlCJ5YKw0fNERtqC8MAoKNTLHSPYPKARG+
s+V5cg7sEr27a0kGN+I/yogFhdtsTRWFOpjjeulwg6BTt7sFg +oDDiV5vDE.

- Right to Education Bill
- PPP in Schools
- Higher Education Reforms

The CII launched the University Industry Council in May 2007 and since then, it has held three symposiums to establish various linkages between university and the industry, both of which are critical to the economy of the nation, and hence the need to set up collaborative ventures between the two in various areas. CII mentions the following as its achievements:

- Introduction of Open Source philosophy and software in the schools;
- Introduction of web-based teaching-learning in schools; and
- Launch of a free online portal for teachers and students, and a free Training and Empowerment Academy for Teachers.

It has proposed new initiatives in the following areas:

- Commencement of an E-Teaching Certification Programme for school teachers;
- Creation of E-Teaching toolkits for rural schools and teachers; and
- Establishment of a Consortium of B.Ed. Colleges to promote E-Teaching through Open Source and the web.[32]

There are also attempts by the industry associations to reach out to parliamentarians. FICCI, for instance, has a unique mechanism known as the Forum of Parliamentarians, wherein any Member of Parliament interested in joining it can do so on a voluntary basis. According to Amit Mitra who was the Secretary General of FICCI till May 2011, 'about 185 MPs, including those of regional parties, are part of the Forum'. While it is chaired by a member of the ruling party, the co-chair is an MP from the opposition, with the idea of balancing viewpoints. Mitra adds, 'We send briefings to these MPs on various issues. We also put forward our views to all parties involved in policymaking'.[33]

FICCI, in collaboration with the Indo-US Forum of Parliamentarians, launched an India-Yale Parliamentary Leadership Programme in 2007. Since then, young Indian MPs have been sponsored by FICCI to participate in this programme every year. Apart from attending the

---

[32] See http://cii.in/Sectors.aspx?enc=prvePUj2bdMtgTmvPwvisYH+5En GjyGXO9hLECvTuNsJ Kom60HRHReZ5/udUByhH.

[33] See P.T. Sebastian, 2008, 'Small but Strong', *Outlook Business*, 27 December, available at http:// business.outlookindia.com/article.aspx?101794.

programme at Yale University, the parliamentarians are also provided an opportunity to meet US business leaders.

Thus, the CII and FICCI are relating themselves to the government not only in terms of demands for an improved enabling environment for doing business, but have gradually taken steps to organize themselves to sustain their influence on other sectors too and to forge partnerships in them. The emerging networks span many areas concerning the roles and responsibilities of the government that were exclusive to it before the advent of economic liberalization.

PARTNERSHIPS AS IMPLEMENTING AGENCIES

Infrastructure

Flowing from policy networks, the concept of partnership is also applied at the level of providing goods and services that were earlier the responsibility of the state alone. PPPs now constitute a popular strategy of implementing development programmes primarily due to the limitations of government resources and the capacity to cope with the rising demands of infrastructure and social sector needs.

The Investment Commission calculated that in infrastructure alone, the demand for the next five years would touch around 246 billion USD.[34] This demand for resources does not include the estimated demand for social sectors like education and health, which are important components of the Millennium Development Goals (MDGs). It is argued that this massive investment is possible only through the support of the private sector. In addition, it is frequently reiterated that the private sector brings in new technology and greater efficiency in delivering goods and services. In a presentation to a Chief Secretaries Conference in 2007, the Finance Secretary, Government of India, underlined the role of PPPs in bringing private sector efficiencies to the public sector and reducing the costs of delivery. It is due to these reasons—resource deficiency with the government and delivery efficiency with the private sector—that the government stresses that the PPPs have to be successfully implemented. Bovaird provocatively suggests, 'Of course, this gives rise to the possibility that these partnerships have not been

---

[34] GoI, *Investment Strategy for India: Report of the Investment Commission.*

marriages based on love, or even on respect for the qualities each could bring to the relationship, but rather marriages for money'.[35]

Promoting PPPs

The Government of India, quoting a World Bank study, expressed disappointment in the fact that, by 2005, only 85 PPP projects had been awarded by some 13 states and select central agencies (including power and telecom). The total project cost was Rs 339.5 billion when the requirement of investment was far greater. The government decided to take urgent measures to promote PPPs. The private sector, including international financing agencies, were responding favourably to the immense business opportunities in India by demanding greater flexibility in procedures for approvals and other facilities.[36]

According to data available on the Government of India website, as in February 2009, 136 PPP projects had been approved.[37] The total investment on these projects was estimated to be more than Rs 1,40,000 crores. There are another 333 projects assigned to the states that are in various stages of implementation. Most of the projects are in the road sector, a sprinkling in the ports and tourism sectors, while around 67 are in the area of urban development.

The government has taken several steps to accelerate the process of investment and remove impediments. As a sign of the importance attached to this strategy, a Committee on Infrastructure was established in 2004 under the chairmanship of the Prime Minister, as infrastructure demands the highest volume of investment. In 2009, this Committee was converted into a Cabinet Committee for Infrastructure Projects chaired by the Prime Minister.

A PPP cell was established in the Ministry of Finance to support a coherent policy framework. Simultaneously, nodal officers of the rank of Joint Secretaries were appointed in the relevant ministries to expedite approvals. The states were also encouraged to appoint such nodal officers.

---

[35] T. Bovaird, 2004, 'Public Private Partnerships: From Contested Concepts to Prevalent Practice', *International Review of Administrative Sciences*, vol. 70, no. 2, p. 201.

[36] See GoI, *Investment Strategy for India: Report of the Investment Commission*.

[37] For details, see http://www.pppinindia.com/database.asp.

A key initiative of the government to promote PPPs is the Viability Gap Funding Scheme. This is meant to provide financial support to those infrastructure projects that are economically justifiable but are not commercially viable. The eligible list of projects contains projects in the urban and tourism sectors apart from those pertaining to roads and airports, among others. Such projects would be eligible for a grant of 20 per cent of the total cost of the project. The India Infrastructure Finance Company (IIFC) was set up with the specific mandate to play a catalytic role in the infrastructure sector by covering long-term debt for financing infrastructure projects. IIFC raises funds from the domestic and international markets on the strength of government guarantees.[38] In addition, the government announced in the Budget for 2007–8 that a revolving fund of Rs 100 crore was being set up in the Department of Economic Affairs, Ministry of Finance, to support the development of credible and bankable PPP projects that could be offered to the private sector.[39]

In order to help the sponsoring authorities of PPPs at the central and state levels, the government has pre-qualified a panel of firms which can provide commercial/financial and legal services to them to facilitate smoother and more efficient implementation of PPP projects. The Panel is intended to: (a) streamline the tendering process for the engagement of Transaction Advisors; (b) enable fast access to firms that have been pre-qualified against relevant criteria; and (c) ensure transparency and accountability through a clear definition of the process and the roles and responsibilities of the agencies and the private sector.[40] The panel consists of firms that also have multinational partners and probably it is for this reason that guidelines for choosing a panel member specify that the member must confirm that there is no conflict of interest in taking up the job. A panel member selected by a sponsoring authority would be responsible for all transaction services till the approval of the

[38] Government of India (GoI), 2008, *Public-Private Partnerships: Creating an Enabling Environment for State Projects*, New Delhi: Department of Economic Affairs, Union Ministry of Finance.

[39] The full text of the speech is available at http://indiabudget.nic.in/ub2007-08/bs/speecha.htm, Accessed on: 23 December 2009.

[40] Government of India (GoI), 2008, *Panel of Transaction Advisers for PPP Projects: A Guide for the Use of the Panel*, New Delhi: Department of Economic Affairs, Union Ministry of Finance, p. 1.

project. As can be seen from the list of Transaction Advisors, not only are interlocking members present in the consortium, but they may also have conflicts of interest in bidding for projects. The government recognizes this but has left the responsibility of resolving the conflict to the states which are launching the projects.[41]

Apart from providing technical assistance to the states and the central government to expedite projects in the PPP mode, efforts are also being made to provide training to the functionaries at the state and local levels. Through the support of the World Bank and the Asian Development Bank (ADB), a curriculum of training is being developed at the State Administrative Institutes.

The Comptroller and Auditor General of India (CAG) has undertaken the task of issuing guidelines for auditing the infrastructure projects in the PPP mode. The guidelines emphasize that:

Public auditors of PPP projects must note that in respect of PPP projects, the important principle is to bring out in their reports, what has been achieved rather than how it was achieved by the private partner responsible for constructing and managing the project. There is no doubt that good governance is a *sine-qua-non* in PPP projects as well, but since the objective of the audit is not to audit the private partner as such, but to verify primarily the value for public money, the focus of the audit reports will be the review of end results rather than the how of achieving them.[42]

It stresses the need for an assessment of the 'value for money' concern. Audit reports have not yet been commissioned on this basis.

However, PPP projects have come in for adverse comments when taken up by legislatures for discussion. The Joint House Committee

[41] The relevant clauses are: (1) There may be potential conflict of interest in the case of Panel members such as if IL&FS and IDFC Limited are selected as the Transaction Advisers for a project for which they could be potential bidders. It is, therefore, recommended that the state governments/local governments appointing the Transaction Advisers should take an undertaking from the selected consortia that they/their affiliates will not bid for the same projects. (2) There may be potential conflict of interest in case the agencies with CRISIL consortia are selected as the Transaction Advisers.

[42] Government of India (GoI), 2009, *Public-Private Partnerships (PPPs) in Infrastructure Projects: Public Auditing Guidelines*, New Delhi: Comptroller and Auditor General, available at: http://infrastructure.gov.in/pdf/PPP-PROJECT.pdf.

of Karnataka, probing the construction of the Bengaluru International Airport, has indicted several public functionaries and officials for the faulty design and construction of the Airport. It has recommended blacklisting of the firms responsible for building the Airport for the 'poor quality of workmanship'.[43] The Committee on Public Undertakings of the Parliament has 'flayed' the National Highways Authority of India for irregularities in the execution of the traffic-intensive Delhi-Gurgaon highway, claiming that it made certain exceptions to the usual approach to projects in order to benefit the private concessionaire. For the first time, the Committee raised the question as to what should be the reasonable profit for the private investors, which operate and collect toll for periods extending to 20 years in such stretches. The private partner saw profit in light of the balance of risk and award, and anticipating considerable risk in this case, pitched in with a higher rate of profit.[44] There is, therefore, a need for evaluation of such large projects in the PPP mode when they are being questioned in terms of both the criteria of the quality of work and the level of profit. There appears to be room for benefiting the private partner on both the counts and this necessitates constant vigilance.

Without careful evaluation of partnerships in the projects, there appears to be a sense of urgency in accelerating the pace of PPP-ization in India as demonstrated by the rapid publication of enabling conditions and establishment of approval mechanisms at the highest levels. There is a push by international development agencies as PPP is central to their development strategy. A large part of the FDI and loans being made available by the World Bank or the ADB are premised on the assumption that the projects would be implemented in the PPP mode irrespective of whether they are in the infrastructure or social sector. For the private sector, PPPs in infrastructure represent opportunities for heavy investment, windows for entering a market that is very large, and market space to stay for a long period of time. The government finds that this partnership helps bring in finances and world-class technology,

[43] The Times of India, 2009, 'TNN House Panel Indicts Murthy for faulty Airport Design', Times of India, 22 December.

[44] Economic Bureau, 2009, 'Panel Says NHAI Swerved Procedure for Benefit of Private Player', Indian Express, 18 December, available at http://www.indianexpress.com/news/panel-says-nhai-swerved-procedure-for-benefit-of-private-player/555652/2.

and so partnerships seem to have worked in the infrastructure sector. However, projects have yet to be evaluated for efficiency, costs, and adoption of the latest technology.

PPPs in Health Services

While the challenge that policymakers face in the infrastructure sector is that of creating a more favourable 'enabling state' to attract greater private sector investment, PPP projects in the social sector face an additional challenge. This is concerned with not only creating the physical infrastructure that can provide health and education services, but also of providing them equitably. PPPs in the health and education sectors appear to face problems that those in the transport, roads or energy sectors do not face. These are in terms of reaching the poor and those who are deprived of these health and education services.

It is now widely accepted that India's performance in the social sector has been dismal over the years. There has been low government investment with the quality of health services provided by the implementing machinery to the poor and to the marginalized being of a very low quality. A situation has arisen wherein super-specialty hospitals, financed by the private sector, are growing to serve the rich and the urban elite while healthcare services for the large mass of people continue to be inadequate and of poor standards. A Concept Note issued by the Ministry of Health and Family Welfare has underlined the fact that the present healthcare system is pro-rich as a majority of the expenditure on healthcare by the government ends up subsidizing the healthcare of the rich more than the poor, as a result of which the poor end up spending proportionately more from their pocket than the rich. The dilemma is that the poor cannot get adequate health services from the public sector, but when they seek these services from the private sector, they face further impoverishment due to the high expenditures.[45] As a way out, the government has begun to explore the possibility of PPPs in the health sector wherein the private sector can provide the massive investment needed to create the requisite infrastructure (hospitals, beds,

[45] Government of India (GoI), 2006, *Draft Report on the Recommendation of Task Force on Public-Private Partnership for the Eleventh Plan*, New Delhi: Union Ministry of Health and Family Welfare, available at: http://mohfw.nic.in/NRHM/Task_grp/Draft_Report_Task_Group_on_PPP7_9_06.pdf.

equipment, doctors, nurses, and para-medical staff), while the government itself provides for other infrastructure facilities like land or buildings to enable provision of healthcare facilities for the poor.[46]

The state governments in India, within whose jurisdiction lies the health sector, are experimenting with partnerships with the private sector to reach the poor and underserved sections of the population.[47] Currently, several PPP initiatives are under implementation in various states. However, there is no uniform pattern of the emergence of these PPPs.[48] One reason for this is that there are multiple providers of health services in India. What is referred to as the non-government sector comprises several types of medical traditions that range from allopathy to indigenous therapies such as *ayurveda*, *unani*, and *siddha*, and from individual doctors and practitioners of medicine, private clinics, and nursing homes, to large super-specialty hospitals. NGOs are also involved in providing health services in an organized fashion. In this complex space, the government has sought partnerships with the 'for profit' private sector that usually runs large hospitals and technical services, and with NGOs, who are willing to provide health services in an equitable cost-effective way.

Baru and Nundy have identified three types of partnerships: contracting of services, franchising, and social marketing.[49] The largest numbers of projects in the PPP mode fall in the first category of contracts, which are with the 'for profit' private sector, NGOs, and private practitioners. In addition, there are cases wherein the government has provided land at subsidized rates or reduced import duties on technical equipment

[46] Government of India (GoI), 2006, 'Concept Note on Public-Private Partnerships', Union Ministry of Health and Family Welfare, New Delhi, available at http://mohfw.nic.in/PPP%20concept%20note-final.htm.

[47] See discussion on this issue in the study by Venkatraman and Bjorkman in A. Venkat Raman and J.W. Bjorkman, 2006, *Public–Private Partnership in the Provision of Health Care Services to the Poor*. Indo-Dutch Programmes for Alternatives in Development, Research Report. Delhi: Faculty of Management Studies, University of Delhi.

[48] For the forms that PPP has taken in the health sector, see Rama Baru and Madhurima Nundy, 2008, 'Blurring of Boundaries: Public-Private Partnerships in Health Services in India', *Economic and Political Weekly*, vol. 43, no. 4, 26 January, pp. 70–1.

[49] Ibid.

to corporate hospitals as a partnership venture. It also appears that partnerships with NGOs are favoured for primary healthcare services and with corporate hospitals for advanced technical services in the tertiary sector.

In most cases, an important purpose of the partnership is to provide free services to the poor and to the deprived. However, monitoring this part of the partnership remains the biggest challenge. In most cases, the identification of BPL (below poverty line) persons poses the greatest source of harassment to the patients and gets a whimsical response from the administrators. There is no accountability mechanism that places responsibility for particular decisions. A study by Venkatraman and Bjorkman cites this difficulty in the case of a Jaipur hospital wherein X-Ray services were contracted out.[50] On the other hand, in Delhi, the High Court issued a notice to Apollo Hospital for allegedly charging money from patients belonging to the economically weaker sections of society. 'It is completely unfair on the part of Apollo that they are not abiding by orders of giving free treatment to poor,' observed a division bench of the Delhi High Court.[51] The Delhi government, for example, has only recently made some of the provisions of the partnership transparent. In a meeting with medical superintendents of private hospitals, which had acquired land at concessional rates by promising free treatment to BPL patients, the state officials instructed them to update details on the bed vacancy at the end of each working day on the website of the Directorate of Health Services. The state government also appointed a nodal officer exclusively for Indraprastha Apollo hospitals, which had gone to court against paying for consumables to treat poor patients. A doctor was posted there for three months to ensure that 200 beds were kept aside for BPL patients.[52]

[50] Venkat Raman and Bjorkman, *Public–Private Partnership in the Provision of Health Care Services to the Poor*.

[51] IANS, 2009, 'Notice to Apollo Hospital for Charging the Poor', CNN-IBN, available at http://ibnlive.in.com/news/notice-to-apollo-hospital-for-charging-the-poor/106155-3.html.

[52] Vidya Krishnan, 2009, 'Private Hospitals Told to Update Bed Vacancy Status on Internet', *Indian Express*, 3 November, available at: http://www.indianexpress.com/news/Private-hospitals-told-to-update-bed-vacancy-status-on-internet/536395/.

In a recent interview, Delhi's Health Minister also expressed some misgivings in this regard. She was asked, 'When you assumed office, you expressed enthusiasm about PPPs. Has there been any change in emotion?' Her answer was, 'Yes there has [been a change]. We have felt cheated [at] the hands of big corporates like Apollo and Fortis. After that, we decided that our Dwarka hospital will be a wholly government project.'[53]

Among the many problems that PPPs in the area of health services face is that the managers in the government sector are ill-prepared to properly design the partnership, monitor the performance, and provide an enabling environment for the execution of the project. Indeed, the system of evaluation of performance is not adequate. Another major problem has been that of accountability. The government is responsible for providing health services and if there are any deficiencies, it is held accountable. But at the operational level, one stakeholder tends to blame the other. How then can the partnership be held accountable? As Baru and Nundy point out, the experience of PPPs in health services shows that these partnerships have been built without the requisite organizational and administrative preparedness, which raises questions about their role, accountability, and effectiveness.[54]

A comment in the Report of a Working Group constituted by the Planning Commission on PPPs to improve healthcare delivery for the Eleventh Five-Year Plan (2007–12) under the Chairmanship of the Secretary, Department of Health and Family Welfare, Government of India, sounds an alert. It says significantly, 'However, it may be reiterated that private partnerships are not sufficient to resolve the dilemma of inadequate healthcare for the people. The focus of public policy in the context of the Eleventh Five-Year Plan should be the flagship march for strengthening the public health sector.'[55] Despite the realization that PPPs may not adequately fulfill the goals of the health

---

[53] Kiran Walia, 2010, 'Bhalla Jaya Shroff Delhi's Health has Long Been Ignored Health Minister Kiran Walia Promises More Hospitals Facelifts and Medical Insurance for the Poor', interview, *Hindutan Times*, 12 February.

[54] Baru and Nundy, 'Blurring of Boundaries: Public-Private Partnerships in Health Services in India', p. 69.

[55] GoI, *Draft Report on the Recommendation of Task Force on Public-Private Partnership for the Eleventh Plan.*

policy in India, the process of using them for this purpose continues unabated.

PPPs in Education

The Ministry of Human Resource Development has also brought out a Concept Note on PPPs in Education, which suggests that it is an approach used by the government to deliver quality services to its population by using the expertise of the private sector. It goes on to point out that this approach has been used in India for a long time. The most common form that it has undertaken is that of the government-aided schools system in the country. In 2006–7, 30.05 per cent of higher secondary schools and junior colleges, 27.15 per cent of high schools, 6.75 per cent of upper primary schools, 3.19 per cent of primary schools, and 5.15 per cent of pre-primary schools were run by private institutions with substantial financial assistance from the respective state governments.[56]

However, the government is moving towards different forms of PPPs and also establishing more schools only in this mode. In 2009, the HRD Minister announced that the PPP would be the basis of educational expansion in the country over the next two years. He added that the schools would be set up in PPP mode as part of the government's efforts to strengthen the human resource base and then went on to urge the corporate houses to invest in a big way in the education sector, emphasizing that developing human resources is the key to the success of any nation.[57] This commitment to PPP in the education sector had been articulated earlier in a session on the knowledge economy at the Pravasi Bharatiya Divas meeting. Admitting that it was not capable of meeting the challenges of the education sector on its own, the government invited the participation of overseas Indians in the field.[58] FICCI has been holding summits in higher education from 2004

[56] Government of India (GoI), 2009, *Public-Private Partnership in School Education*, New Delhi: Union Ministry of Human Resource Development.

[57] Express News Service, 2009, '2500 Model Schools to Come up in 2 Years: Sibal', *Indian Express*, 29 August, available at: http://www.indianexpress.com/news/2-500-model-schools-to-come-up-in-2-yrs-sib/508769/.

[58] ENS Economic Bureau, 2009, 'NHAI Swerved Procedure to Benefit of Private Player', *Indian Express*, 17 December.

onwards.[59] It has been organizing them as annual international events
with the support of the Ministry of Human Resources Development
and the Planning Commission. In 2008, Ernst and Young joined FICCI
to prepare the background paper for these meetings. In the paper
prepared for the 2008 summit, titled 'Leveraging Partnerships in India
in Education Sector', the need for PPPs in the higher education sector
was underlined. While arguing that it is necessary to meet the financial
constraints of the government and to meet the demand for skilled
persons for industry, the paper identified various types of partnerships
and recommended collaboration with foreign universities for research
and student exchanges.[60] Other institutions and researchers have also
joined in stressing the need for introducing PPPs in the education
sector for similar reasons and also for fulfilling the commitment of
raising literacy levels. In a World Bank study, Jagannathan explored
the working of six NGOs that extended primary education to rural
children in India.[61] She argued that these NGOs had demonstrated
effective grassroots action to enhance the quality of basic education
and had also influenced mainstream education through the replication
of their models and through policy dialogue with the government.
While suggesting that NGOs are best suited for small projects and
micro-level interventions, she strongly advocated a sustainable and
enduring partnership with the voluntary sector that would strengthen
the government's efforts to actualize the goal of universal elementary
education. In their official documents, both the World Bank as well as
the ADB have advocated the policy of 'PPP-ization'.[62]

The Centre for Civil Society launched a School Choice Campaign
in 2007, arguing that what the poor need today 'is not just the Right to
Education, but the Right to Education of Choice'. It advocated PPPs

[59] See http://www.ficci-hes2009.com/htm/e&y-executive-summery.pdf.

[60] FICCI and Ernst and Young, 2008, 'Leveraging Partnerships in India's Education Sector', *Report of FICCI Higher Education Summit 2008*, New Delhi, available at http://www.tru.ca/_shared/assets/FICCI14822.pdf.

[61] Shanti Jagannathan, 2001, 'The Role of Non-Governmental Organizations in Primary Education: A Study of Six NGOs in India', *Policy Research Working Paper 3530*, Washington, D.C.: The World Bank Institute.

[62] Government of India and Asian Development Bank, 2006, *Facilitating Public-Private Partnership for Accelerated Infrastructure Development in India*, New Delhi: Department of Economic Affairs, Union Ministry of Finance.

through the use of a voucher system. At a conference in 2009, the speakers included representatives of the World Bank and the private sector, and stressed the need for quality education by providing choices to the poor. This scheme was meant for funding the students and not the schools, and giving choice to the students through a voucher system.[63]

Thus, international donor agencies and some civil society organizations have demanded greater PPP in the education sector. Having articulated its commitment to provide education for all through the enactment of the Right to Education Act, the government has also become receptive to these ideas as it continues to face a resource crunch and lack of capacity to run a responsive and efficient educational system.

However, even after having articulated its commitment to PPPs in education, the government is still at the experimentation stage. For one thing, the forms that partnerships can take at the primary and secondary levels of education are diverse. There are also few takers for schools in rural areas and for education facilities for poorer people. At the higher education level, the forms it can take are in terms of establishing research collaboration between the government and industry, giving space to private entrepreneurs to enter the field, and opening up of partnerships with foreign universities. For quite some time, large business houses were big players in the field of higher education like engineering and medical education. These institutions were primarily colleges affiliated to universities, which exercised control over their academic norms. By the mid-1990s, the promoters of private colleges perceived the regulatory control of the affiliating university and state governments as cumbersome, impeding the full utilization of the market potential of colleges. Thus, they wanted to wriggle out of the control of state governments and the affiliating universities. This resulted in a proliferation of private universities and private deemed universities. While in the field of higher education, it is resource deficiency that is driving the government to seek partnerships with the private sector, at the primary school level this is not the only reason. Another reason is inefficiencies in the delivery system. Thus, in both the health and education sectors, the government is seeking

---

[63] The speeches are available on its website: http://schoolchoice.in/scnc2009/index.php.

partnerships—with NGOs at the local and grassroots levels, and with the 'for profit' private sector at a higher level.

ISSUES AND CHALLENGES

In conclusion, it needs to be re-emphasized that the advent of governance in government is taking place within the broad framework of neo-liberalism in which the role of the state is being recast. The preeminent place that it occupied in steering society is now yielding to a more shared space with market and civil society. In this sharing, many responsibilities that were exclusively undertaken by the state are now being given to the other two actors while some are being undertaken in a partnership mode. But the neo-liberal framework demands increasing privatization of the provisioning of goods and services, leaving what are called the 'core' functions with the state. The clear demarcation of 'core' functions is still fuzzy because, many of them, up to now considered as 'core', are either being privatized or being undertaken in a shared mode. Education and healthcare have emerged as clear examples of this duality.

In this process of transformation, the state is being seen as a problem and the consistent demand of the liberalizers is that it should become an enabling state, a facilitator and not a hindrance to the promotion of the market. The creation of policy networks and the emergence of PPPs are efforts in that direction. These are also new institutions of governance that have the government, the market, and civil society as partners. They promise to prevent the duplication of efforts and are seen to draw on their complementary resources and capabilities for designing more effective problem-solving mechanisms.

As discussed, the government and the corporate sector are developing close links with each other in determining public policies. There are formal institutions in which they participate to take policy decisions and there are also informal ways in which the government bureaucracy and its related institutions are encouraged to empathize with the interests of the corporate sector. Currently, the policy perspective is to pursue the goal of raising the rate of economic growth and the expectation is that the networks will strengthen the dedication and commitment of the government to achieve this goal. The corporate sector, in turn, is creating forums wherein the representatives of the two partners can debate issues in the public domain—the government is interested in learning what the needs of the corporate sector are. The exchange of ideas is important in the negotiations that take place in the formal networks. The industry associations have devised several instruments for this purpose.

Network governance is assumed to contribute to the production of public purpose within a certain area. This public purpose is an expression of social vision and the direction that the policies should take to achieve this vision. However, network governance relies on political and social processes at work in society, which may not necessarily be conducive to the production of public purpose on all occasions. Even the Prime Minister, while speaking at a public function, expressed doubts about the way things are going and alerted the country to the growing symptoms of 'crony capitalism'. The reason for this is that in the Indian context, it is possible for big business houses to influence decisions in their favour and get away with it. The data on the Indian economy is a testimony to this view. Quoting Jessop,[64] Sorenson and Torfing have also argued that governance networks can fail. They suggest that, 'There has been much talk about state failure and market failure, but we should also analyse the conditions for governance network failure. Network governance relies on precarious social and political processes and there are many things that can go wrong and prevent the production of public purpose.'[65]

This brings up the issue of the capacity of the state to negotiate and bargain in these networks. There is ample evidence to show that both political as well as bureaucratic leadership has been comfortable in taking personal advantages and benefits that the liberalization policies have offered. Consequently, their capacity to negotiate is weakened. In addition, with the blurring of boundaries between public and private interests, public servants may not feel the urge to carry the burden of pursuing public interest alone. Thus, the partnerships are not equal and can allow certain private interests to dominate.

However, the state's capacity is not only a function of legitimacy. It is also a function of the performance of institutions and their ability to rise

---

[64] B. Jessop, 1998, 'The Rise of Governance and the Risks of Failure: The Case of Economic Development', *International Social Science Journal*, vol. 50, no. 155, pp. 29–45.

[65] Sorenson and Torfing, 'Making Governance Networks Democratic'.

up to the tasks allocated to them. Bureaucracy is the most important instrument of implementation of public policies. It has not yet adjusted to the new paradigm of governance and continues to act in a mode that is reminiscent of an era gone by. Innumerable committees and commissions have been set up to reform it but the elephant has moved very slowly. This is one of the foremost challenges of good governance in India today. Unless the government institutions themselves have the capacity and capability to deliver high performance, their ability to negotiate in forums of partnerships and networks with other actors will be weakened considerably.

Over the years, after independence, there has been a gradual decline in the effectiveness of institutions of accountability. It is now being increasingly left to civil society to raise issues connected with financial probity and administrative responsibility. The Right to Information has attempted to fill in the accountability gap and the tool of Public Interest Litigation (PIL) has also helped aggrieved groups to fight the arbitrariness of the state. However, getting redressal under PIL is not easy and continues to be a struggle against state mechanisms. Even the process of decentralization after the Constitutional Amendments has been an uphill task. In the face of weaknesses in other institutions of accountability, the Right to Information is proving to be a strong instrument of curbing corruption and holding public officials accountable for their public functions. Perhaps, it is now the most important advance in the quest for good governance.

The central point is that as the web of institutions of governance becomes more and more dense, and the new institutions of partnerships with the corporate and voluntary sectors multiply, the state's capacity to negotiate and bargain for pursuing public interest has to be strengthened. In addition, if the new partnership institutions are being kept out of the ambit of the government's hierarchy, the challenge of making them accountable becomes even more acute. What the country is facing today is the consequence of its faltering efforts at bureaucratic or institutional reform. Even though the issue of corruption is high on the public agenda, the instruments to control it have weakened over the years. Little attention is paid to the reports of the Comptroller and Auditor-General, which are themselves based on events that took place years ago. The findings of the Central Vigilance Commission (CVC) and also of the Central Bureau of Investigation (CBI) are ignored. The challenges that PPPs face as vehicles of implementing public policies are embedded in this broad perspective of state capacity and accountability. As has been mentioned here, PPPs are being celebrated as constituting a key strategy for delivering services in India. From infrastructure projects entailing the building of roads, ports, and airports to providing healthcare and educational services, the government is entering into a partnership mode. International financial institutions, the private sector, and NGOs are being mobilized to support this effort. The government is also attempting to marshal private financial and technical resources to provide goods and services to society.

It has also been pointed out that partnerships are being forged not only because the government is seeking private resources for public causes but also because of bureaucratic deficiencies. Thus, the one important reason for entering into partnerships with the private sector is that the government is unable to single-handedly implement complex projects that are critical to the development of the country. The government is too weak or too corrupt to operate a public service. However, it is a mystery as to how the government believes that the same bureaucracy, which is so weak and corrupt, can be any better at working in a partnership or regulating partnerships involving large multinational companies. Thus, we also need to know why the private sector is interested in partnerships. What is its motivation?

An important dimension of partnership projects is that the private investment is assured of returns irrespective of the outcome of the project. There is a provision of viability gap funding as also that of user fees. Whatever be the nature of the services provided—roads or airports, primary healthcare facilities or specialty health services, or drinking water supply or primary education or highly skilled education, users have to pay a fee. This goes to refund the private investor. Both the World Bank and the ADB have been promoting cost recovery through 100 per cent rational user charges because 'without improved cost recovery, the quality of utility services will not improve and opportunities for engaging the private sector in these utilities will be limited'.[66] Thus, the stipulation that the private sector bears the burden of risk in a partnership is not entirely correct.

[66] Vinay Baindur and Lalitha Kamath, 2009, *Re-engineering Urban Infrastructure: How the World Bank and Asian Development Bank Shape Urban Infrastructure*

Partnerships in the social sector face an additional challenge. Health services for primary healthcare may have been established but the health of the beneficiaries does not improve. Or schools are provided but the quality of education is poor. Or the benefits of delivering services do not reach the poor. The government, therefore seeks partnerships to deliver services in a more effective and equitable fashion. If this does not happen, then the purpose of setting up a partnership gets defeated. To meet this challenge, regulatory agencies and accountability mechanisms are required. It has been suggested that partnerships seem to work well in the United States because there is strong regulation, transparency, and tenacious NGOs with resources.[67]

Finally, the most important challenge is of delineating accountability procedures of PPPs. In the government documents that were surveyed, there is near silence on this very important dimension. A widely accepted view is that the partnership approach to public issues fragments government structures and processes, and weakens accountability. In a government hierarchical system, there is a clear line of individual accountability while the institution's responsibility is to the Parliament. The question in a partnership is: Who is accountable to whom and for what? There are multiple partners who have different ways of holding their agents accountable, but that may not satisfy partnership accountability. And the MoU should be in the public domain so that partnerships are transparent and accountable.

The new governance structures that have emerged in the era of the liberalized economy are making the collaboration between the government and business more open and transparent. However, network governance obscures the process and accountability for public policy formulation, decision-making, and execution. Yet, conversely, it opens the door to involvement by a wider range of actors and in

---

Finance and Governance in India, New Delhi: Bank Information Centre, South Asia, p. 15.

[67] *The Hindustan Times* (21 February 2010) reports that civil society organizations in Delhi have won a year-long struggle and made the National Highways Authority of India (NHAI) agree to place an agreement with the construction firm responsible for the Gurgaon Expressway on its website. With this, the agreement will now be under public scrutiny. The residents have continued with their struggle. See 'Gurgaon Residents Up in Arms against NHAI', *The Hindustan Times*, 9 March 2010.

ways that are less constrained than those applying to institutions of political authority.[68] However, sometimes partnerships can be used as a form of back door entry by the private sector in the provisioning of services and goods. A partnership necessitates a clear understanding of the roles of the partners, their mode of financing, the agreed design of the project, the goals of partnership, and how it is going to work. It is this understanding that needs to be placed in the public domain for the benefit of those people who will be affected by it. In most cases, this does not happen. The interests of the beneficiaries suffer.

In conclusion, it may be said that partnerships have come to stay. Since they constitute an integral part of not only the governance framework but also of the neo-liberal paradigm, they cannot be completely rejected, yet they cannot be completely accepted either. There are significant challenges in their functioning, which must be attended to. Their functioning needs to be brought increasingly into the public domain for ensuring transparency and accountability. This demands a more rigorous examination of their role and functioning. As Miraftab points out, one must ask: Under what political, social, and economic conditions and institutional environments, and with what processes, can PPPs succeed or fail as synergistic relationships that benefit all partners, including poor populations and their allied organizations?[69] Policymakers and practitioners, who formulate a partnership programme focused on the nuts and bolts of the scheme, must also give profound consideration to its socio-political environment and the pitfalls that may lie in wait there. Otherwise, they risk having the state fade away after project formulation, with the result that the power-sharing scenario intended to serve the interests of all partners dwindles into a familiar charade. Like the Trojan horse, these partnerships might arrive with the promise of a gift but only to further dispossess the poor from their local resources.

[68] Navdeep Mathur and Chris Skelcher, 2007, 'Evaluating Democratic Performance: Methodologies for Assessing the Relationships between Network Governance and Citizens', *Public Administration Review*, vol. 67, no. 2, March–April, p. 235.

[69] Faranak Miraftab, 2004, 'Public-Private Partnerships: The Trojan Horse of Neo-liberal Development?', *Journal of Planning Education and Research*, vol. 24, pp. 89–101.

9

Strengthening Bureaucracy
State and Development in India*

I deas are the moving force of history. When supported by organization and finance, they have considerable impact on the way academic
agendas are formed and reproduced. One such idea has been that of
development which captured the imagination of people all over the
world in the years after the Second World War. It was Truman who,
for the first time, used the term 'underdeveloped', signifying the division of the world into those who were developed and those who were
not. He also placed on those who were developed the responsibility
to help develop those who were not. This was the end of the Second
World War and a programme of reconstruction was being initiated in
Europe through massive American aid that came to be known as the
Marshall Plan. Its success inspired a model of development that was
also perceived to be appropriate for those countries that were emerging from colonial rule. For these countries, which together with some
others came to be known as the Third World, the prospect provided
hope. It was now possible for them to aspire to be like the West and
also to be optimistic about fulfilling this aspiration. The West emerged

* Kuldeep Mathur, 1999, 'Strengthening Bureaucracy: State and Develop-
ment in India', *Indian Social Science Review*, vol. 1, no. 1, pp. 7–28. Also in,
Bidyut Chakravarty and Mohit Bhattacharya (eds), 2003, *Public Administration:
A Reader*, New Delhi: Oxford University Press, pp. 359–81.

as a role model both as an end and as a process by which this goal could be achieved.

The world has not remained static since then. International agencies came up to promote development and public policies in countries rich and poor, which reoriented themselves to respond to the demands of developmental goals and process. Also, the academic world gave birth to two new concerns—development economics and development administration. Although they do not match each other in either rigour of analysis or content, these two concerns are most popularly associated with the issue of development. For a long time in the post-1950 world, these two concerns attracted the best intellectual talent and by far the largest financial support for their aims. One focused on devising economic policies, the other on strengthening state capabilities to implement them. To that extent, one supported the other in its endeavours.

When international assistance for development began on a large scale in the 1950s, it was realized that many of the recipient states did not have the capability to utilize the aid that was being given. Strengthening state capability through improvement of administration became high on the agenda, and a new field of endeavour known as 'development administration' took shape, overwhelming the traditional discipline of public administration. But the 'development' decades of the 1960s and 1970s proved frustrating and disappointing for most countries of the world and academic attention began to wane. By the 1980s, a new challenge had appeared on the horizon. Even though most countries of the world failed to respond to Western developmental efforts, some East Asian countries like Japan, Korea, Taiwan, and Singapore attained heights similar to those of the developed nations. The major South Asian nations (India, Pakistan) in very sharp contrast remained mired in poverty. Answers were sought for this contrast. It was argued that the East Asian countries relied on the free market and got rich very quickly, while the South Asian nations fell prey to the temptation of state intervention and got bogged down by economic stagnation. Consequently, for a large number of policy planners and international donor agencies, a free market became the key determinant of development. However, on closer examination, the success of the East Asian economies also began to be attributed to their strong and autonomous states.[1] A new scholarly tradition emphasizing state power in promoting development emerged.

Development administration as a way to improve state capability had faded by the 1980s. A new approach—governance—to strengthen state capability emerged and promised to take its place. The purpose of this chapter is to examine the scope and content of these two conceptualizations and examine the potential of success of this new concept where the old one had failed.

In the early 1950s, development administration demarcated itself as a field of study and practice. One of the earliest users of the term argued that the aim of the term was to specify the focus of administration on the support and management of development as distinguished from law and order. He went on to claim that 'the function of development administration is to assure that an appropriately congenial environment and effective administrative support is provided for delivery of capital, materials and services where needed in the productive process—whether in public, private or mixed economies'.[2] While the term seems to have been coined in the early 1950s, the prime mover in conceptualizing the field was the Comparative Administration Group (CAG) led by Fred W. Riggs. Financially supported by the Ford Foundation, CAG sponsored research, conducted seminars, and published books and monographs. Much of this history has been documented extensively by Riggs himself when reviewing the work of CAG.[3] The point is that during the decades of the 1960s and 1970s, which were also known as the development decades, development administration had an unprecedented influence in shaping the academic agendas of universities and in influencing the policies of international donor agencies like the UNDP and the Ford Foundation.

[1] A.H. Amsden, 1989, *Asia's Next Giant: South Korea and Industrialization*, New York: Oxford University Press; Chalmers Johnson, 1982, *MITI and the Japanese Miracle: The Growth of Industrial Policy*, Stanford: Stanford University Press; and, R. Wade, 1990, *Governing the Market: Economic Theory and Role of Government in East Asian Industrialization*, Princeton: Princeton University Press.

[2] George Gant, 1979, *Development Administration: Concepts, Goals, and Methods*, Madison: University of Wisconsin Press, p. 20.

[3] F.W. Riggs, 1976, 'The Group and the Movement: Notes on Comparative and Development Administration', *Public Administration Review*, vol. 36, no. 6, pp. 648–54.

Relying on the belief that the administrators in Third World countries were agents of change and nation-builders, the development administration movement directed its energies at improving their capacities. The major thrusts were to strengthen bureaucracy by professionalizing it and giving it a management orientation. An additional thrust was to change the attitudes and behaviour of the bureaucrats to make them development-oriented. It was assumed that a broad agreement existed about the goals of nation-building and socioeconomic development in the country and all that was needed was an effective administration to translate them into reality. The broad perspective was that of a technically-oriented, professionally competent, politically and ideologically neutral bureaucracy. Such a bureaucracy was seen to be a mirror image of the bureaucracies in the Western world. Thus, a related perception was that institutional imitation was bound to produce results similar to those obtained in the developed world: efficiency, increased rationality, and the like, at a very general level. The more developed (that is, bureaucratic and Westernized) an administrative system became, the greater the likelihood that it would have developmental effects.[4]

The strategy proposed to bring about this kind of reform was to impart extensive training to civil servants. While structural and procedural changes were not ruled out, it was expected that training would create awareness among the bureaucrats so that they themselves would design these changes without external suggestions. In a United Nations document[5] that succinctly summarized the direction its programme on public administration was taking, training found an important place. It argued that a formal training programme often speeds up the learning process and thus brings civil servants, including new recruits, to a satisfactory standard of performance, in a relatively short period of time. The economy of this method is one of the reasons why formal training is important in development administration and should be one of its key features.

After nearly two decades, disillusionment set in about the whole concept of development administration and its intended focus on

[4] O.P. Dwivedi and Keith M. Henderson, 1990, *Public Administration in World Perspective*, Ames: Iowa State University Press, p. 13.

[5] United Nations, 1975, *Development Administration: Current Approaches and Trends in Public Administration for National Development*, New York: Department of Economic and Social Affairs, p. 87.

bringing about reform in the developing countries. The proliferation of scholarly contributions was not sufficient to get ideas of reform implemented. Increased knowledge did not lead to improved practice. Then, the nature of this knowledge began to be questioned, as well as the framework used to generate it. The influence of CAG, which had shone as a star on the academic firmament, began to wane in the 1970s and it lost its financial support from the Ford Foundation. In addition, more important questions began to be raised about the intellectual components of development administration and the reasons why the developing countries neither accepted nor adapted to its message.

It became increasingly evident that the task of nation-building and the goals of development were issues of keen contestation in the countries concerned. There were social groups that mobilized power to design development programmes and strategies in such a way that they stood to benefit from them. The actual design of development then emerged from political compromises and bargains. While there was a possibility that these bargains could be in the larger public interest, it was not always so. The way political power was exercised determined whether or not a programme or policy was in the interest of the larger society. Administration could not merely play a neutral role among contending groups and design policies that would benefit all. Neglecting politics deprived an understanding of its important link with administration, which was seen as a stand-alone solution. Paradoxically, this happened in spite of cautious contributions about the relationship of bureaucracy to political development. Riggs and many of his colleagues attempted to point out the imbalance in the power equations of political and administrative systems in developing countries and to argue that for democratic development the political systems needed to be strengthened.[6] In many cases, without effective political control, strengthening bureaucracy opened vistas for misuse of its role, particularly where other weak social groups provided little or no countervailing force. In most colonial countries, civil or military bureaucracy was the most powerful instrument of imperial rule and it was naive to believe that pious intentions would change

---

[6] See in particular, F.W. Riggs, 1965, 'Bureaucrats and Political Development: A Paradoxical View', in J. La Palombara (ed.), *Bureaucracy and Political Development*, Princeton: Princeton University Press, pp. 120–67.

their behaviour, especially if such change would dislodge them from a position of power.

In such a situation, attempts at strengthening bureaucracy created administrative situations that were imitative, ritualistic, and symbolic rather than conducive to real change. The Western myth of a rational bureaucracy, neutral in its decisions, was held as an ideal for which to aspire. With little empirical support for this formulation of leaving value-laden decisions to the politicians and for keeping administrators out of this domain, the emphasis on professionalizing bureaucracy, and making extensive use of training to do so induced public administration to be inward looking and out of touch with social reality. Insulation made it unresponsive to democratic demands and arrogant in offering technical solutions to social problems.

The seriousness of such evaluation of the movement can be gauged from the 1998 introspection by Fred Riggs himself. He says:

The experts returned from the developing countries confused and frustrated. They felt that the advice based on the prescriptions was often unwelcome or unproductive and sometime inappropriate.... We assumed that all bureaucracies could be essentially non-political instruments of public policy, subservient to the basic political choices made by some kind of representative government. Our myth of a dichotomy between politics and administration permitted us to ignore the growing prevalence in the Third World of bureaucratic politics-regimes in which appointed officials, led by military officers, were politically dominant. We tended to overlook the political role of public bureaucracies....We assumed that bad practices were due to ignorance and that knowledge of better practice would lead folks anywhere to adopt them... We did not question whether what worked in America would also work in other countries; nor did we suppose that people in other countries may have good reasons for doing what they did or that there were people with vested interests in the status quo who would resist changes that might infringe on their privileges.[7]

The purpose of quoting so extensively from Riggs is to emphasize that we need to learn from experience and to realize that reform and change are not value-neutral terms. Changes in society are driven by social and political forces, which are history-specific.

[7] F.W. Riggs, 1998, 'Public Administration in America: Why Our Uniqueness is Exceptional and Important', *Public Administration Review*, vol. 58, no. 1, pp. 22–9.

Externally induced reform has not been easy anywhere. The ecological aspect of public administration was recognized very early and Riggs himself wrote extensively on the subject. Paradoxically, his concern did not weave itself into the mainstream thinking of development administration. Thus, a grand project that involved many intellectuals, spawned donor agencies, created training institutions, and gave a different slant to studies in public administration came to grief. The waning of enthusiasm coincided with despair about development experiences and with the perceived failure of the state when aspiring to be an engine of growth. Development economists of those years had also believed in the key role that the state had to play in promoting economic development. As Bhagwati notes, even India's highly statist strategy was well-received by prominent Western economists who were extremely optimistic and well disposed towards India's planning efforts and methods.[8]

Even though there was frustration with Western development efforts, it began to be noticed in the 1980s that some of the Southeast Asian countries which had been on the margins of development in the 1950s had done remarkably well in the following decades. It came to be widely believed that this happened because these countries, in contrast to others, had worked to release market forces and to limit the role of the state in the economic sphere. The invisible hand of the market had worked the magic. Liberal neoclassical economics rose in influence. But another scholarly tradition also emerged which saw the developmental achievements of these countries as a result of the existence of a strong state. There was not only a call for bringing the state back,[9] but explanations began to be sought for the transformation of these Asian countries into 'Asian tigers', in terms of the role of the state.

It was argued that while emphasis on loosening up of market forces was important, strong states were still necessary to promote industrialization projects. In this formulation, strong states provided good governance, and good governance was the key to the transformation

[8] J.N. Bhagwati, 1993, *India in Transition: Freeing the Economy*, Oxford: Clarendon Press, p. 7.

[9] Peter B. Evans, T. Skocpol, and D. Ruschmeyer (eds), 1985, *Bringing the State Back In*, Cambridge: Cambridge University Press.

of a predatory state into a developmental one. Good governance in this sense is related to the reduction of the role of the state and the entire case is built on how state intervention creates monopoly rents through regulation and control over the economy. Political pressures dominate economic policymaking and there is widespread corruption in bureaucratic allocations of investment licenses and award of contracts. A consequence of this system is that the state machinery gets used increasingly for private purposes. When this happens, a predatory state is born. The issue is how contradictions can be created to move such states into becoming developmental ones, so that resources are invested for the good of the society as a whole.

The profile of developmental states is based on the experiences of the Asian tigers. Sorenson contends that the reflection on the possible features of a developmental state have from the very beginning been plagued by the fact that they commenced not with deliberations concerning state theory and the proper definition or content of states in general and developmental states in particular, but with empirical assessment that some East Asian countries are remarkably more successful than other Third World countries in terms of certain economic indicators.[10] Drawing from these experiences, many scholars have suggested that the role of the state should be confined to the creation and support of institutions that help the markets to perform most effectively. The state can perform this task successfully when the bureaucratic and technical elites in charge of policymaking are insulated from the pulls and pressures of everyday politics. Among the enabling conditions for this insulation are the Weberian characteristics of bureaucracy.[11] Based on Johnson's account of the golden years of MITI in Japan,[12]1Evans argues that Japan's startling post-war economic growth occurred in the presence of a powerful, talented, and prestigious economic bureaucracy, which also had the capacity to network with other social instructions, plus sufficient flexibility to deal with changing technical and market conditions. He describes this networked insulation of the

[10] George Sorenson, 1993, 'Democracy, Authoritarianism, and State Strength', *European Journal of Development Research*, vol. 5, no. 1, pp. 6–34.

[11] Peter B. Evans, 1989, 'Predatory, Developmental, and other Apparatuses: A Comparative Political Economy Perspective on the Third World State', *Sociological Forum*, vol. 4, no. 4, pp. 561–87.

[12] Johnson, *MITI and the Japanese Miracle: The Growth of Industrial Policy*.

top bureaucracy as the embedded autonomy of the state and regards it as the key to the success of Japan. The idea of embedded autonomy or networking bureaucracy is different from autonomy of decision-making by itself. Bureaucratic autonomy was located in an unusual degree of cooperation from the private sector in furthering developmental goals. It forged a unity among elites that was reflected in the success of MITI and similar institutions in Korea and Taiwan.

Most contributors to the discussion of the processes of transformation to a developmental state drew inspiration from this so-called state-centric model of development. The question of autonomy, that is, freedom of elected and bureaucratic officials in economic decision-making, was seen as a primary characteristic in pursuing the goals of development. The capacity of state structures to arrive at this autonomy emerged from a rationalized bureaucratic system. Emphasis on creating conditions of autonomy and rationality have become an integral part of the agenda of good governance and are now part of the advice being offered by multilateral aid-giving agencies. As a matter of fact, there is little doubt that development assistance is increasingly suffused with the discourse on governance.[13]

However, doubts about implicating these features of governance in other countries have begun to be raised. It has been pointed out, for example, that Zaire's elite was strikingly unconstrained by any set of organized social interests. In this sense, it was relatively autonomous but it did not work for societal growth and development.[14] Taiwan began as an oppressive regime but changed into a developmental state in a short time. The puzzle that Sorenson highlights is: why some states, enjoying a high degree of autonomy, do not exploit it in the service of development and why some states do not choose to promote development in a consistent and efficient manner.[15] Autonomy can be used by the elite for any purpose. By itself, it does not work for development alone.

[13] Niraja Gopal Jayal, 1997, 'The Governance Agenda: Making Democratic Development Dispensable', *Economic and Political Weekly*, vol. 36, no. 8, pp. 407–12.

[14] Paul B. Evans, 'Predatory, Developmental, and other Apparatus: A Comparative Political Economy Perspective on the Third World State', p. 571.

[15] Sorenson, 1993, 'Democracy, Authoritarianism, and State Strength'.

A more significant criticism of this model of governance entails denial of political processes in development. Too much is made of the development impact of bureaucratic and technocratic decision-making while other characteristics are ignored. Leftwich points out that all development states have been *de facto* or *de jure* one-party states for much of the last 30 years.[16] The effect has been to concentrate very considerable and unchallenged political power at the top in these states, thus enhancing political stability and continuity in public policy. Japan, South Korea, Taiwan, and Singapore, all leading examples of developmental states, are also marked by a strong degree of cultural homogeneity as well as tendencies towards an authoritarian state. Many scholars view authoritarian rule as an essential part of East Asian development,[17] but the point still needs to be made that such governments can resist pressure from both business and labour. Growing democratization in many of these states will show whether they will continue to be able to resist such pressures in the future.

Keeping democratic politics out also means that somehow the state is perceived as being outside society and that development goals emerge out of its own predilections without reference to those of society. The state is seen as an actor, a force independent of social dynamics. In a book arguing for bringing the state back in, Skocpol says that, 'states may formulate and pursue goals that are simply not reflective of the demands of interests of social groups, classes or society'.[18] If so, can we conclude that the interests of the state, different from those of society, will always be pro-development?

The immediate question that arises is the lesson to be drawn from the East Asian developmental state model experiences. Is the developmental state model transferable? The concepts of development administration and of governance seem to have grown from the experience of specific countries. In one case, the West is the model; in the other it is East Asia. The efforts in both were directed towards increasing state capability

---

[16] A. Leftwich, 1994, 'Governance, the State, and the Politics of Development, *Development and Change*, vol. 25, pp. 263–85.

[17] E.C. Deyo, 1989, *Beneath the Miracle: Labour Subordination in the New Asian Industrialism*, Berkeley: University of California Press.

[18] T. Skocpol, 1985, 'Bringing the State Back In: Strategies of Analysis in Current Research', in Peter B. Evans, T. Skocpol, and D. Ruschmeyer (eds), *Bringing the State Back In*, Cambridge: Cambridge University Press, pp. 20–1.

to implement developmental projects. Strengthening the state in both versions has also meant focusing attention on the role of the bureaucracy and accepting the assumption that bureaucrats work for developmental goals. In both cases, there are powerful institutions that project them. The Ford Foundation, USAID, and UNDP are some of the organizations that provide intellectual as well as financial support to the spread of the idea of development administration. The World Bank and other financial agencies have done the same for the concept of good governance.

Perhaps one should not exaggerate this similarity between governance and the role of the bureaucracy in transforming a predatory state into a developmental one, nor equate it with the much wider issues of what development administration did. In the discussion of the processes of transformation of a predatory state into a developmental one, the issue of autonomy has to be seen within the circumstances of unity among the elite in the policy perspectives that provided support to the bureaucracy in taking hard decisions. There was a great degree of cooperation between the public and the private sector. The single-minded pursuit of growth and productivity could be undertaken because problems of distribution were largely ignored. East Asian countries had undergone a radical land reform process while the depredations of war had equalized the level of deprivation among industrialists. In most developing countries, such a situation does not exist. Distributional goals are very much part of their developmental agenda and severe inequalities exist. In the Indian context of a plurality of contending heterogeneous groups, a close liaison and harmony of interests between the state and private business would raise an outcry of foul play and strong political resentment among other groups, particularly organized labour and farmers which, unlike East Asian politicians, India's politicians cannot ignore.[19] The tightly integrated relationship of government with private business, which is the concept of embedded autonomy identified by Evans, is very difficult to envisage in the Indian case.

Clearly, the effectiveness of bureaucracy is linked with other features of society and politics in these countries. To that extent, any attempt to implement the model extracted from the experience of East

[19] P.K. Bardhan, undated, 'The Nature of Institutional Impediments to Economic Development', mimeo.

Asian countries will prove counterproductive. As Onis emphasizes, the transfer of specific policies and strategies to new environments will be self-defeating in the absence of the political and institutional conditions required for their effective implementation.[20] What emerges from these experiences is that any one-dimensional view of development must be replaced by the understanding that there are multiple linkages and interactions in society and that bureaucracy is not a 'stand-alone' solution. The gain from the experiences of the journey of the concept of development administration should be to investigate these multiple linkages in order to understand the role of the bureaucracy, its strength, and its autonomy in the act of governance.

Indian experience provides an interesting case of passing through the stage of development administration and now becoming the recipient of the various ideas assumed to have moved a predatory state into a developmental one. India sought to shape a developmental state through an ambitious strategy of economic planning, wherein the state was assigned a central role. An effort was made to give a certain amount of autonomy to economic decision-making by establishing the prestigious Planning Commission. The problem of development came to be evaluated in technical terms and was largely seen as a problem of correct policy formulation and design. The Nehru-Mahalanobis strategy that became the hallmark of the 1950s and 1960s was dominated by the discussion of prioritization of investment allocations, trade, and industrial strategies, etc. As noted by many commentators, this was the time when development economics was coming into its own and the Indian experience had much to offer. It is not too much to say that the Indian development strategy was remarkable in its use of planning models, the sophisticated development which planning engendered, and the extensive utilization of such models with respect to formulation.[21]

The successive five-year plans took it for granted that their rationale would be accepted and that people would behave accordingly. If difficulties arose, they would be merely difficulties of implementation. The development policy design was regarded as technically correct, while

---

[20] Z. Onis, 1991, The Logic of the Developmental State', *Comparative Politics*, vol. 24, no. 1, pp. 109–21.

[21] T.J. Byres, *State, Development Planning, and Liberalization in India*, p. 14.

failures were seen to be the result of social and political constraints and implementation. Till 1991, it was being argued that the 'primary failure in several developing countries, including India, has been in implementation'.[22] The technical argument was extended to implementation and the professional thrust of development administration immediately attracted the attention of Indian planners and policymakers. But more of this later.

The technical aura perceived around planning became possible by creating the Planning Commission as a unique institution away from the normal functioning of the government. It was a tribute to this uniqueness when critics called it a 'super cabinet'. The power of the Planning Commission flowed from Nehru's own patronage, a dependence that ironically also made it vulnerable and institutionally insecure. Economic development was entrusted by Nehru to a small group: over a decade, the membership of the Planning Commission was drawn from a pool of about 20 men.[23] Most were civil servants and some represented private interests too. Professional economists and technocrats very quickly came to dominate public discussion about India's economic development. The Planning Commission became the exclusive theatre where economic policy was formulated. The subject was taken away from the cabinet and Parliament, which were merely informed of decisions taken by the small cohort of experts. Khilnani cites the Second Plan as an instance where political decisions were camouflaged in technical terms needed to insulate it from public deliberations.[24] Since this Plan entitled decisive re-channeling of investment towards heavy industry, there was a choice about consumption (less now for the promise of more later) that was undoubtedly a matter for public debate.

But even though the activities of the Planning Commission have left a lasting impression on India's development performance, its period of ascendancy was brief and did not last long after Nehru left the scene. The erosion of the role and status of the Planning Commission occurred soon after. Economic decision-making began to shift towards the

[22] B. Jalan, 1991, *The Indian Economy: Problems and Prospects*, New Delhi: Viking Press, p. 87.

[23] Khilnani, *The Idea of India*, p. 81.

[24] Ibid., p. 86.

Finance Ministry and subsequent prime ministers did not raise its status or insulate it from governmental politics. As a matter of fact, it lost its preeminent position when the rupee was devalued in 1966 because the decision for doing so received severe criticism from both professionals and the political leadership. Institutionally, several steps were taken to redefine the position. Members of the Planning Commission were now to have fixed terms, unlike under Nehru when they enjoyed unlimited tenure. The Cabinet Secretary, who is the top civil servant of the country and had served as the Secretary of the Commission, was detached from it. In addition, a prime minister's secretariat was created as an alternative adviser to the Prime Minister. This new office was headed by a senior civil servant who was a trained economist and more inclined towards the market mechanism. This was the beginning of the period when economic policymaking became the arena of political battles that in the past had always been overwhelmed by Nehru's ideological certitude and political stature.[25]

This was also the period when the potential of being a strong state was seen in terms of the state's dominance in the economic sphere and its 'ideological advantage as the presumed defender of collective interests and socialist purposes and as the enemy of private and partial gains'.[26] The Rudolphs pointed out that the Indian state had sought, over the decades of the 1960s and 1970s, to insulate itself from the exigent pressure of a mobilized society and suggested that the Nehruvian state of the 1950s provided a credible if partial embodiment of relative autonomy. On the other hand, Myrdal explained the feeble development record of the Indian state by drawing a distinction between soft and strong states.[27] He argued that if Indian poverty was to be overcome, a strong state was needed which could divest itself of the influence of special interests and enforce social discipline. The failure of effective structural changes in the Indian economy in the heyday of the Nehruvian state has been well-documented. This has been described as the fundamental paradox of the Indian political economy: 'a commitment to radical

[25] Ashutosh Varshney, 1995, *Democracy, Development, and the Countryside: Urban-Rural Struggles in India*, Cambridge: Cambridge University Press, pp. 51–2.

[26] Rudolph and Rudolph, *In Pursuit of Lakshmi: The Political Economy of the Indian State*, p. 13.

[27] Gunnar Myrdal, 1968, *The Asian Drama: An Inquiry into the Poverty of Nations*, New York: Pantheon Books.

social change and yet an equal determination to avoid a direct attack on existing structures'.[28]

The 'paradox' does not remain a paradox when state capability is seen as determined by pulls and pressures of various groups in society. State action does not emerge as a rational response to an economic situation by a unified, omni-competent political institution. Rather, different groups of officials and/or parts of state compete over policy; in many instances their goals and interests can only be understood by reference to or interaction with non-state actors.[29] Conflict and contradictions among these actors will impinge on state policy. States have to be situated in their social setting and the reasons why individuals and groups respond differently to market signals and policy incentives have to be analyzed and understood.

India inherited a colonial land settlement, which assigned ownership to renter zamindars or cultivators (*ryots*) in return for the rent paid to the Raj. Economic power was widely dispersed and also entrenched in these propertied classes. Industry was at a nascent stage but powerful regionally based and family-centred business houses had begun to emerge. In both the agricultural as well as the industrial sectors, there were powerful individuals or groups who commanded significant economic power. This economic power relationship was defended by a powerful social order based on caste, family, and region. The development strategy that was hammered out during the early years was one that kept these economic power equations in mind. Dominant caste groups and their relationships were also kept under consideration while framing policies. The major problems were those of very unequal distribution of land ownership and very low levels of productivity. The power equations severely constrained and strictly circumscribed the capability of the state and its scope of action. In a much later explanation for the lack of investment in long-term growth, Bardhan suggested that politicians presided over a dominant coalition with three main elements: the industrial bourgeoisie, rich farmers, and public sector employees.[30] Each strived to maximize benefits from the development

[28] Francine Frankel, 1978, *India's Political Economy, 1947–77*, Princeton: Princeton University Press, pp. 1–78.

[29] Cal Clark and K.C. Roy, 1997, *Comparing Development Patterns in Asia*, London: Lynne Reinner, p. 6.

[30] Bardhan, *Political Economy of Development in India*.

policies and the state was unable to rise above their interests or work for the society as a whole. Radical postures may have been taken but they could not be translated into action. What happened then was that the state was strong on regulatory law and weak on enforcement.

If these were the political conflicts which fractured the necessary support for industrialization and planned development, then Nehru had to look elsewhere to have his ideas translated into action. This task began to be increasingly entrusted to the civil service, even though Nehru had demanded a radical transformation of the ICS during the independence movement, and it had been left to Patel to argue for its place in the Constitution. The ICS was seen to represent state interests and to be relatively autonomous of local pulls and pressures. The doctrine of neutrality and impartiality was seen as its predominant behavioural trait, and it was assumed that its successor, moulded in the same tradition, would withstand the parochial pressures on the state. Together with Nehru, civil servants were the vanguard of the lobby for an industrial strategy, which sought to create and expand the public sector to run basic and heavy industry under the Second and Third Five-Year Plans. However, the national orientation and professional ethos soon lost their gloss because public sector undertakings could not be managed efficiently and profitably.

While the Indian bureaucracy is often cited as having Weberian characteristics, it is not known for creating sufficient state autonomy to pursue developmental interests. It has turned out to be a weak instrument of the state and the networks that it has created have usually been of a rent making variety. There is increasing evidence that the alliance between politicians and bureaucrats has been in the pursuit of mutual gain. The demands of career advancement are of paramount significance for a civil servant and an obliging politician is ready to do anything for a civil servant who bends rules to favour his political master. The close linkage of civil servants with caste or communal groups, business houses, and the large farmer community has to be seen in this perspective of mutuality of interests.[31] It is also not possible for the bureaucracy in the Indian situation to harmonize its interests with those of the private sector for an additional reason. For one thing,

[31] C.P. Bhambri, 1998, 'Of a Partisan, Self-Serving Bureaucracy' *The Pioneer*, 23 September.

the private sector itself does not have identical interests and for another, the bureaucracy has grown on the belief that it is the only group that works in the public interest. It has not been easy for it to give up its self-perception of being the 'guardians' in the old British colonial sense. This has considerably restricted its initiative in mobilizing support for public policies and their implementation.

The Indian design of state intervention was usually engulfed by the characteristics of its larger administrative system, but a few successes in innovative institutional experiments occurred because they could move away from its stifling stranglehold. When India became independent, it was among the very few countries of the world that had a strong and effective bureaucratic machinery in place. As a matter of fact, the strength and coherence of its civil service was so striking that it was known as a steel frame. The Indian Administrative Service (IAS), created in the image of the ICS, was moulded as a monolithic instrument and an image of elitism was deliberately built in to provide a sense of separation from the common society. This was supported by frequent movement of officials from one position to another and a few people, whirled about by rapid transfers, were propelled by automatic promotions into higher positions exclusively reserved for them at all levels of government. On the way, they commanded handsome salaries and social status forever denied to others.[32] The District Collector was the head of the district and all other local offices were subservient to him. A direct line of command was established with central/state authorities and the district officer was recognized as the kingpin of the system. Vesting so much power in an individual also meant that higher levels of the government came to depend on him for all information and advice in matters pertaining to his local area. In the social context, he could be above local politics because of the prestige and status that came to him by being in the government hierarchy. Conversely, he could align himself with an individual or a group at the local level and wield considerable power himself or in conjunction with his ally.

The structure of the Indian administrative and civil service system has not changed much since colonial days. On the contrary, the political system has sustained it. A powerful bureaucracy and the

---

[32] Potter, *India's Political Administrators*, p. 33.

structure existing prior to independence have influenced the design of state intervention. However, faith in it has been so great that no new organization or institutional design could be put on the ground which did not take these factors into consideration. This pervasive influence was felt in institutions that sought autonomy from day-to-day government operations, but were gradually pushed into being semi-autonomous and then, operationally, came under the purview of politicians and administrators in the 'public interest. Public sector manufacturing and service units were among the initial victims, but as the state expanded its role, institutions in education or health or rural development followed suit. The expectation that a bureaucracy would work in the public interest on its own has been belied. Just as it is necessary to analyse the concept of public interest, the instrument of fulfilling them also needs to be reexamined.[33]

It was not as if there was no concern expressed for poor administrative performance or for the inability of administration to respond adequately to the challenges of implementing development plans.

The First Five-Year Plan (1951–6) had set the tasks very clearly: 'From the maintenance of law and order and collection of revenue, the major emphasis now shifts to development of human and material resources and the elimination of poverty and want... There is also a need for structural changes to raise the level of administration.' Administration came under scrutiny by many committees and the government demonstrated its commitment to administrative changes by accepting the offer of the Ford Foundation to bring in an American consultant, Paul Appleby. The thrust of development administration—of professionalism and behavioural change—was also accepted. Universities reoriented their teaching programmes, training institutions were strengthened, and their number multiplied.[34] International assistance in sending civil servants abroad for training and reorientation was also accepted as part of the aid given for development projects. The Ford Foundation alone spent USD 360,000 in grants and USD 76,000 in providing funds to

[33] J.W. Bjorkman, 1995, 'Ethics and the Public Interest: Towards Understanding Public Choice in Developing Countries', *Indian Journal of Public Administration*, vol. XLI, no. 3, pp. 275–95.

[34] Kuldeep Mathur, 1996, 'Introduction', in K. Mathur (ed.), *Development Policy and Administration*, New Delhi: Sage Publications, pp. 13–23.

specialists and consultants to improve public administration in India during 1951–62.[35]

The efforts at administrative reform were accompanied by reliance on the administrative system to bring about a change in rural society. Programmes to involve the people in making collective efforts for development usually resulted in domination by the administrative system, which suffocated people's participation. It had been hoped that the Community Development Programme would become a people's movement, but it faded away leaving a legacy more of administration than of participation. Efforts at decentralization also suffered from a similar malaise and the ineffectiveness of panchayati raj institutions is well documented.[36] The three levels of panchayats from the district downwards were closely associated with local level administrators and government reports themselves reveal how this association led to obstacles in democratization and decentralization.[37] Bureaucrats were hesitant to part with power and colluded with local ruling groups in taking decisions. This picture was common to other institutions as well, such as those established to implement poverty alleviation programmes. The experience of panchayats in West Bengal is frequently cited as a contrast to this prevailing picture. It must be emphasized that this success stems from the political commitment of the state leadership, in making this level of government work effectively. The 73rd and 74th Amendments to the Constitution seek to advance the concept of self-governance by providing for regular elections, minimal suppression of PR bodies through an administrative fiat, and regular finances through statutory distribution by state finance commissions. The aim is to reduce the margin of political and administrative discretion and to allow the decentralized institutions to gather strength on the basis of people's involvement. The success of these amendments making decentralized structures part of the Constitution has yet to be seen—not only because they were only instituted in 1993, but also because

[35] Ralph Braibanti, 1966, 'Transnational Inducement of Administrative Reform', in J.D. Montgomery and W.J. Siffin (eds), *Approaches to Development: Politics, Administration, and Change*, New York: McGraw-Hill, p. 148.

[36] Government of India (GoI), 1978, *Report of the Committee on Panchayati Raj Institutions*, New Delhi: Ministry of Agriculture and Irrigation.

[37] Ibid.

the states have shown little evidence of implementing the requirement through their own statutes.

Another pillar of the earlier development strategy was the establishment of cooperative societies which were meant to serve the smaller asset holders in rural areas. Meant to be self-governing institutions where people came together to fulfill their economic needs, they have actually served the ambitions of local politicians and administrators. The legal framework envisaged in the Cooperative Societies Act throttled the growth of a movement and the government department of cooperative societies became an instrument for perpetuating the hegemony of the government and the bureaucracy.[38] Rather than protecting cooperatives from petty sectional interests, the law in numerous instances has been unabashedly used by politicians and petty bureaucrats to stifle their growth by superseding elections to their boards for decades. There has been a strident demand for abolishing the very government department that was set up as the promotional agency.[39]

If little thought was given to structure state intervention to support panchayats or cooperative institutions, even less effort was made to ensure that the government's own institutional innovations in the rural development sector were embedded in a supportive environment. These institutions—like the Small Farmers Development Agency established in 1970, which was transformed into the District Rural Development Agency in 1979—were established with the aim of keeping them outside the normal bureaucratic framework so that the implementation of poverty alleviation programmes would be more effective. Government documents provided their rationale through phrases that would have one believe that it was ardently committed to decentralization, semi-autonomous local organizations, and local-level planning for locally prioritized schemes of assistance to remove poverty. What happened? Effective decentralization did not take place, local accountability of these programmes was absent, and the government

[38] Tushaar Shah, 1996, 'Agriculture and Rural Development in the 1990s: Beyond Redesigning Relations between the State and Institutions of Development', in K. Mathur (ed.), *Development Policy and Administration*, pp. 85–125.

[39] L.C. Jain and Karen Coelho, 1996, *In the Wake of Freedom: India's Tryst with Cooperatives*, New Delhi: Concept Publishers.

stifled the operating agencies through its administrative policies.[40] These weaknesses were identified not only by academic researchers, but also by committees appointed by the government itself. Yet little was done. The urge for change to help rural communities and to create economic opportunities remained more in government documents than in reality. This account supports the view that there is greater effort in India to give an appearance of a developmental state than a commitment to create one. When institutions fail to perform, blame is laid at the door of rural society. Apparently, formal establishment of a public institution demonstrates state commitment to development and failure in its performance demonstrates weaknesses in society— illiteracy, backwardness, social conflicts, etc.

Clearly, state intervention was not designed in a way that development organizations could grow. The systems for economic planning and those for mobilizing financial resources tended to reinforce central tendencies of the entrenched administrative system. In a situation where a strong bureaucracy had sought to curb local initiative in order to gain social power and create a strong control and command system, the vastly expanded state intervention merely entangled individuals in increased socioeconomic obligations towards the state. Autonomy without concomitant accountability meant bureaucratic license, and bureaucratic networks increasingly became opportunities for colluding for personal aggrandizement. A kind of dependency syndrome inhibited individuals and communities from taking social and economic initiatives; wherever such initiatives received state support but were left relatively alone, they have shown success. Dairy cooperatives in Gujarat and sugar cooperatives in Maharashtra come immediately to mind.

The perception that the state has the capability to provide a supportive environment to sustain and nurture local institutions does not emerge only from the experience of cooperatives in Gujarat and Maharashtra. Innovative institutions also appear in common property resource management. Evidence from fields as diverse as irrigation and forestry shows that user groups, when allowed to manage such

[40] Kuldeep Mathur, 1995, 'Politics and Implementation of Integrated Rural Development Programmes', *Economic and Political Weekly*, vols 41 and 42, pp. 2703–8.

resources, can exclude free riders, monitor the behaviour of their members, and enforce rules to sustain and maintain resources.[41] In order to reduce conflicts between state agencies and user groups, Joint Forest Management committees are being facilitated to respond to national needs and local management requirements. The national guideline to support such committees envisages people's involvement in the development and protection of forests. It states that one of the essential features of forest management is that the forest communities 'should be motivated to identify themselves with development and protection of forest from which they derive benefits'.[42] West Bengal has taken a lead in the matter and has formulated an official programme providing legitimacy to grassroots resource management. Encouraged by the extensive and generally successful experiences of Joint Forest Management in West Bengal, NGOs are attempting to spread the experiment elsewhere in the country. Through increasing dialogue between participating communities, NGOs, and governmental agencies, new ideas are emerging and local groups are being encouraged to work for themselves and in the process help develop and manage local resources. These are hopeful signs, and greater support must be elicited from voluntary groups to accelerate this process.

The purpose of relating the Indian experience of development during the last 60 years was to focus on the issue of governance being articulated today. The 'success' of the early years of planning can be attributed to some extent to the consensus that had emerged during the national movement about the role of the state in development; it had therefore been possible to see the state as a powerful 'third actor'. But other powerful actors in society circumscribed its power. The inability to take them along led to a crisis and to the dismantling of the regime

[41] R. Chambers, N.C. Saxena, and T. Shah, 1989, *To the Hands of the Poor: Waters and Trees*, New Delhi: Oxford and IBH Publishers; E. Ostrom, 1991, *Governing the Commons: Evolution of Institutions for Collective Action*, Cambridge: Cambridge University Press; and M. Poffenberger and Betsy McGean (eds), 1996, *Village Voices, Forest Choices: Joint Forest Management in India*, New Delhi: Oxford University Press.

[42] M. Poffenberger and Chatrapati Singh, 1996, 'Communities and the State: Reestablishing the Balance in Indian Forest Policy', in M. Poffenberger and Betsy McGean (eds), *Village Voices, Forest Choices: Joint Forest Management in India*, p. 62.

of planning. The introduction of economic reforms in a limited fashion shows the inability of the state to face the powerful social groups that influence public policy.[43] While reform is in the air, precious little has been done to change or reform bureaucracy. It was the distortions produced by bureaucratic interventions that economic reforms sought to correct; yet it is precisely here that the state has not succeeded. Political action is needed to make the bureaucracy more accountable to the political system and to curb its dominance in the sphere that clearly should be democratic.

The thrust of development administration failed to energize Indian bureaucracy and one should be cautious about transplanting the experience of the East Asian tigers. The issue of distribution is a very important political issue in India and cannot be brushed aside in any discussion of development. When the East Asian countries started on their path of development, many of their equity concerns had already been resolved. Effective land reforms had taken place, there had been leavening in the assets of the private sector, and literacy levels were much higher than what India has now reached after sixty years of independence. If there is lack of compatibility in the historical and socioeconomic context, the nature and character of the bureaucracy is also different for the same reasons. The bureaucracy in India carried the heritage of colonial power and its concern was to maintain its role in the political system. It resisted any reforms that tended to whittle down its power and prestige. Without effective political control and social accountability, the bureaucracy used its autonomy to support the predatory forces in society.

In order to deepen democracy and create countervailing institutions that can strengthen civil society and counter bureaucratic influence as well, institutional pluralism needs to be promoted. We need to search for institutional alternatives and accept the idea that an array of diverse institutional managements are possible to respond to available opportunities. Cooperatives and joint committees between users and government and user associations are examples that provide opportunities for improved collective decision-making. We must build

---

[43] James Manor, 1995, 'The Political Sustainability of Economic Liberalization in India', in R. Cassen and Vijay Joshi (eds), *India: Future of Economic Reform*, New Delhi: Oxford University Press pp. 341–63.

upon the common understanding and the shared experience of people in their particular circumstances. These may require changes in legal and contractual arrangements, explicit codification of rights, as well as attendant obligations. Yet, tasks should be high on the agenda of governance.

The main insight that emerges from this discussion is that the meaning of the notion of a strong state should not be limited to the institution of a strong bureaucracy alone. A high degree of bureaucratic autonomy and capacity may not necessarily lead to a developmental state because the bureaucracy may not be able to rise above its own interests. What is required is consent for policies pursued and legitimacy for mobilizing resources needed for future investments. This can come only through the strengthening of the democratic processes where there is negotiation and debate. Agreements arrived at in this way strengthen the capacity of the state to take strong decisions. Even within the neo-liberal agenda, the state needs to intervene to facilitate development, but the instruments of this intervention need not be the bureaucracy alone. A multiple institutional framework is needed and it must be recognized that there have been a host of other factors that have led the developmental states to fulfill their national goals.

10

Administrative Reform in India

*Policy Prescriptions and Outcomes**

Concern about reforming public administration in India is not new. What is new is the context in which it is being talked about today. The period beginning from 1991 was marked by the emergence of a liberal economic regime that is attempting to dismantle the centrally directed framework of economic development. It was also the initiation of the period when international multilateral agencies began to attach conditionalities while giving aid. These conditionalities, initially, were limited to prescriptions on how the aid would be administered, but have now gradually broadened their scope by suggesting reforms in the overall framework of governance itself. This is happening the world over. Reform is in the air and no country is left out of this global discourse. Changes in the intellectual climate that provided a new understanding of the role and scope of public administration propelled this discourse, while David Osborne and Ted Gaebler's landmark publication *Reinventing Government* summarizes and celebrates this new understanding.

* Kuldeep Mathur, 2004, 'Administrative Reform in India: Policy Prescriptions and Outcomes', in Surendra Munshi and Biju Paul Abraham (eds), *Good Governance, Democratic Societies, and Globalization*, New Delhi: Sage Publications. Also in Chakravarty and Bhattacharya, 2005, *Administrative Change and Innovation*, New Delhi: Oxford University Press, pp. 278–94.

When talking about the failure of the planned strategy of development, particularly with respect to the various five-year plans, the discussion usually veers around the impediments created by the inherited
bureaucratic and administrative system of the British colonial days.
The planners were quite conscious of the need for a different system
to implement the planned objectives of development and wrote so
in chapters of several plan documents. The government responded
to this concern by appointing many committees to suggest changes
in the system. In this expression of concern for administrative reform,
public administration emerged as an academic discipline in India
and provided the intellectual background for suggestions to improve
public administration in practice. Intellectual analysis of the problems
of public administration and the nature of efforts at administrative
reform are closely linked. The purpose of this chapter is to examine
the efforts at administrative reform in India and to analyse the context
in which they were made. It is debatable whether these efforts made
any substantive impact on the practice of public administration in India.
The second part of the chapter will discuss some reasons why these
efforts merely chanted same litany of complaints against an ineffective
administration without making any headway on the ground. Finally, it
will focus on the challenges facing the government in the post-economic
reform period to see whether the experience will be different from the
earlier one.

THE COLONIAL LEGACY

The building blocks for the study of public administration in India were
provided by the contribution of many British administrators, mainly
belonging to the Indian Civil Service. Many of these contributions were
in the nature memoirs and apart from being descriptive of the customs
and manners of Indian society were rich in detail of the working of
the British Indian administration. One of the major outcomes of these
writings was the creation of what has come to be known as the 'ICS
mythology' and a romantic view of field administration. One of the premier representatives of the most romanticized version of the role of the
ICS is 'The Guardians', the second volume of Philip Woodruff's well-
known study 'The Men Who Ruled India'.[1] Even though Woodruff

---

[1] Philip Woodruff, 1954, *The Men Who Ruled India*, London: Jonathan Cape.

asserted that the term guardians was his own, several writers (ex-civil servants) joined him in perpetuating the myth of the altruistic characteristics of the ICS in which a platonic guardianship and men being of superior virtue dominated. The love of outdoor life, commitment to the district and the welfare of its population, courage and a daring streak in decision-making, independence and integrity, were among the many other virtues that the ICS seemed to possess. The Indian members of the ICS helped in perpetuating these myths through their own writings in the post-independence era.[2]

A number of scholars, particularly the British, also joined in this chorus. A rhetorical question such as the following was asked: 'How is it that 760 British members of the ruling Indian Civil Service could, as late as 1939, in the face of the massive force of India's national movement led by Gandhi, hold down 378 million Indians?'[3] The question implied that the British had the skills to govern India. This assertion was based on three essential myths: the myth of the popularity of the civil service as a profession that attracted the best minds; the myth of efficiency in administering India; and the myth of sacrificial esprit de corps of the ICS which ostensibly infused the government with the primary concern of working for the welfare of the people.

For the British, the perpetuation of this myth served many functions. It came as a defence of British imperialism in the court of world public opinion. Teddy Roosevelt, at the end of his second term as President in 1909, cited British administration in India as a prime example of overwhelming advancement achieved as a result of white or European rule among the 'peoples who dwell in the darker corners of the earth.'[4] It also helped to assuage internal opinion in England, reassuring the British elite classes that British rule was beneficial to India.

This myth not only survived but also prospered many years after independence. The basic framework of administration continued as if the colonial administrators had not departed at all. As an Indian journalist later remarked, 'this would be unbelievable were it not true',

---

[2] See S.K. Chettur, 1964, *The Steel Frame and I*, Bombay: Asia Publishing House; K.L. Panjabi (ed.), 1965, *The Civil Servant in India*, Bombay: Bharatiya Vidya Bhawan.

[3] Quoted in Bradford Spangenberg, 1976, *British Bureaucracy in India: Status, Policy, and the ICS in the late 19th Century*, Delhi: Manohar Book Service, p. 4.

[4] Ibid., p. 7.

but Nehru and his colleagues sought to build 'a new India, a more egalitarian society....through the agency of those who had been the trained servants of imperialism—it is as if Lenin, on arrival in Russia, had promptly mustered the support of White Russians he could find.'[5] What is paradoxical is that this myth has persisted well into the 1980s and has resulted in the general posture adopted by the civil servants and professionals in dealing with politicians and development processes.

The inability of the national leadership to bring about change in the early 1950s set the old system of administration in firm saddle. Nehru, writing much before independence, had said,

I am quite sure that no new order can be built up in India so long as the spirit of the ICS pervades our administration and our public services. That spirit of authoritarianism...cannot exist with freedom.... Therefore, it seems essential that the ICS and similar services must disappear completely as such before we can start real work on a new order.[6]

In the spring of 1964, Nehru was asked at a private meeting with some friends what he considered to be his greatest failure as India's first Prime Minister. He reportedly replied, 'I could not change the administration, it is still a colonial administration.'[7]

The essential point is that the British administration, upheld by its many myths, survived and entrenched itself well into the post-colonial period. However, the introduction of the Community Development Programme first raised the demand for a new type of administrator who would be unrelated to the colonial prototype. The administrators began to be told that a programme of social change like that of community development could not be implemented successfully through colonial administrative structures and procedures. The administrators were exhorted to identify with rural life.

THE REFORM EFFORT

The emphasis on the schism between the old and the new gained scholarly attention after Paul Appleby, a Professor at Syracuse

---

[5] Quoted in David C. Potter, 1986, *India's Political Administrators 1919–1983*, Oxford: Clarendon Press, p. 2.

[6] Jawaharlal Nehru, 1953, p. 445, quoted in Potter, 1986, *India's Political Administrators 1919–1983*, p. 2.

[7] Potter, *India's Political Administrators*, p. 2.

University, USA, was invited by the Government of India to report on Indian administration. He expressed the view that there was a dichotomy between bureaucratic dispositions and development needs in India.[8] Some Ford Foundation experts reinforced this view when they recalled their work in community development programmes, and commented that '…the inadequacies of the Indian bureaucracy are not due to the fact that it is bureaucracy but due to considerable fact that it carries too much baggage from the past.'[9] This view gained further support when scholars like La Palombara wrote, 'public administration steeped in the tradition of the Indian Civil Service may be less useful as developmental administrators than those who are not so rigidly tied to the notions of bureaucratic status, hierarchy, and impartiality.'[10]

Simultaneously, the development administration movement was gaining momentum within the discipline of public administration. This thrust had several dimensions among whom at least two dominated. One was of professionalization of the administration through the acceptance of a management orientation. It was argued that management techniques and tools could be used successfully to improve the implementation of development programmes, and administrators must spend significant time and effort in learning these techniques and applying them. Improved education and training became the core efforts at professionalization.

Another dimension of this movement had to do with changes in the behavioural orientation of public administrators. This focus was aptly summed up by a leading contributor when he suggested that only by becoming less oligarchic, less technocratic, less stratified, closer to the administered and the managed, and more deeply rooted in the aspirations and needs of the ordinary people, can the public service

---

[8] Paul Appleby, 1953, *Public Administration in India: Report of a Survey*, Delhi: Government of India.

[9] Carl Taylor, Douglas Ensminger, Helen W. Johnson, and Jean Joyce, 1966, *India's Roots of Democracy: A Sociological Analysis of Rural India's Experience in Planned Development since Independence*, New York: Praeger, p. 579.

[10] Joseph La Palombara (ed.), 1963, *Bureaucracy and Political Development*, Princeton: Princeton University Press, p. 1.

become a force with which the people of a developing country may identify and in whom they repose justified confidence.[11]

It was this message that the academics and consultants from the West, particularly the United States, brought to India and through financial and technical aid influenced the theory and practice of public administration in the country. The Ford Foundation alone spent USD 360,400 in grants to institutions and USD 76,000 in providing consultants and specialists to improve public administration in India during between 1951 and 1962.[12] An important consequence of this financial and technical aid as well as the intellectual thrust of development administration was that it began to be believed that change in the colonial administrative system lies in changing the behaviour and the professional capacity of the individual bureaucrat. This was possible through education and training programmes. Training institutions proliferated and studies that supported this broad argument multiplied. Large numbers of scholars were attracted to the field of development administration, motivated not only by scholarly reasons but also by the belief that administration was the instrument of change and administrative behaviour could be transformed without structural changes in the colonial administrative structure and procedure.

During the period 1952–66, policies of administrative reform were heavily influenced by developments in disciplinary understanding of public administration in the United States and the perceptions of these academics and consultants of the problems of administration in developing countries like India. It was at the request of the Government of India that the Ford Foundation readily made available Prof. Paul Appleby to suggest changes in the administrative system of the country. He presented a Report in 1953 that set the tone of much of what was done later. What is important to note is that till 1966, no other committee was appointed to have a broad look at administration. As a consequence of the Appleby Report on Organization and Methods, divisions were established in each government department to take care of the everyday issues of procedural efficiency. Another recommendation

[11] P.M. Gross, 1974, 'The Limits of Development Administration in the United Nations', Proceedings of the Inter-Regional Seminar on Organization and Administration of Development and Planning Agencies, New York: United Nations, pp. 84–97.

[12] Braibanti, 'Transnational Inducement of Administrative Reform', p. 148.

of Appleby to establish an Indian Institute of Public Administration was also accepted. This Institute was supposed to take up reform measures on a continuous basis but based on research studies.

In operational terms, the effort at administrative reform during this period was based on education and training programmes for civil servants. International aid was extensively utilized for this purpose. A large number of training institutions were established at both the central and state levels. The pattern of recruitment to the higher civil services was changed and the training system was also reformed.

A comprehensive examination of the Indian administrative system was undertaken with the appointment of the Administrative Reforms Commission in 1966. It was patterned after the Hoover Commission of the US, having a political and civil servant membership with experts coming in to write reports after study and research. The Commission worked over a period of four years making a total of 581 recommendations.[13] Little impact of the Commission was felt for no recommendations of consequence were accepted. The politicians who became members did not command prestige and influence with the government of the day. As a matter of fact, the government itself was in a flux. Lal Bahadur Shastri, the Prime Minister, who had appointed the Commission in 1965, suddenly died and Indira Gandhi took over. For the years up to 1971, she was fighting for her political survival, attending to crises and did not find time to reflect on administrative change. When the Commission finished its tasks, the country was facing a war for the liberation of Bangladesh and subsequently was caught in the turmoil of national emergency. The ruling party was comfortable working with the existing administrative system and reforming it was not on the agenda of the political parties in opposition. The Administrative Reforms Commission just faded away, leaving behind a pile of reports and frustration at the national inability to reform a colonial administrative system.

If during the early period of India's independence, administration was seen as an instrument of change, in the period after the Third Plan of 1961–6, it began to be seen as an impediment to development. Plan performance had been poor and policymakers saw lack of effective

---

[13] S.R. Maheshwari, 1993, *Administrative Reform in India*, Delhi: Jawahar Publishers, p. 116.

administration as a major contributing factor. As a matter of fact, in 1969, the Congress party itself raised the issue of the inability of a neutral civil service to implement the goals of development. It pleaded for a committed civil service. The question, 'committed to what' was left open. A fierce debate followed in which retired and serving bureaucrats participated freely.[14] No formal change took place, but the practice of shifting bureaucrats on the demands of the political leadership began a characteristic that is spread widely across the system, even today. The period of the emergency when loyalty became an important criterion for holding a pivotal position in government was replicated when the Janata Party came to power defeating the Congress and Mrs Gandhi. The return of the Congress and defeat of the Janata Party in 1980 signalled the beginning of the process again. The practice has spawned what is colloquially known as the 'transfer industry' and the central government began to reflect what was confined to the states only.[15] Formal acceptance of this idea would have transformed the role of the civil service, but this did not happen. What could not be formalized was openly accepted in practice.

FAILURE OF THE REFORM EFFORT

One possible reason that administrative reform failed to make a dent in the inherited administrative system was the weakness on the conceptual front. No alternative was offered. What was offered were ways to improve the existing system, and these were too inconsequential. Intellectually, adherence to the Weberian model and Taylorian norms of work considerably constrained the generation of alternatives. Overwhelming academic response to administrative problems was through analyses of structural attributes that caused bottlenecks in coordination or communication, or of the behavioural irritants that led to friction either in a team of bureaucrats only or one of bureaucrats and politicians. The prescription was already decided and not questioned,

[14] See P.R. Dubhashi, 1971, 'Committed Bureaucracy', *Indian Journal of Public Administration*, vol. xvii, no. 1, pp. 33–9; M.K. Chaturvedi, 1971, 'Commitment in Civil Service', *Indian Journal of Public Administration*, vol. xvii, no. 1, pp. 40–6; and Chaturvedi and Dubashi, 1973, 'Committed Civil Service: A Symposium', *Seminar*, vol. 168, August.

[15] Dan Banik, 2001, 'The Transfer Raj: Indian Civil Servants on the Move', *The European Journal of Development Research*, vol. 13, no. 1, June, pp. 106–34.

and therefore when the problems persisted, the solution was to increase the dosage of further division of labour, specialization or tighten controls through improved lines of communications and authority.

The problem was that the empirical insights did not reflect the dominant concerns in the intellectual study of public administration where Weberian influences held the attention of most scholars who explained variations in administrative performance by examining issues of neutrality, training and professionalism, structure of hierarchies and processes of work, and behavioural orientations. Another source of explanation was the emphasis on the abilities and qualities of an individual and the belief that it was an individual who made the difference, whatever be the structural constraints. A development-oriented bureaucrat implemented programmes well in spite of the prevailing administrative system. The memoirs of the civil servants are replete with illustrations that show how they as individuals dealt with new political issues.[16]

Little concern for administrative reform was expressed in the 1970s and later. Severe indictment of the civil service was made by the Shah Commission of Inquiry, which reported that they carried out instructions from politicians and administrative heads on personal and political considerations. There were many cases where officers curried favour with politicians by doing what they thought the people in authority desired. In short, the evidence showed, as a journalist remarked, '(the Emergency was) the high water-mark of the politicians' victory in the long drawn out struggle against the civil service.'[17]

Since the 1980s, the story of administration as an impediment to development has taken a drastic turn. If the beginning of the Plan period saw an effort to strengthen state intervention as a recipe for triggering development, the 1980s ended with disastrous accounts of failures of regulatory and interventionist states and with strong pleas to dismantle state machinery and its roles. Neo-liberal economic theory tended to build its case on how rulers extract resources and invest them. It argued that rulers in interventionist states tend to use resources for their own benefit to the detriment of the development of their

---

[16] See, for example, R.K. Dar (ed.), 1999, *Governance and the IAS: In Search of Resilience*, New Delhi: Tata McGraw-Hill.

[17] Quoted in Potter, *India's Political Administrators 1919–1983*, p. 157.

societies. The argument of state failure was based on how monopoly rents are created through the imposition of regulation and control of the economy. Political pressures dominate economic policy formulation and execution. A consequence of this system is that government machinery is used for personal interests. The policy recommendation that follows from this diagnosis is to minimize state intervention and to rely increasingly on markets for resource use and allocation.

RENEWED EFFORTS

The above diagnosis of the failure of government in development led to a rethink about the structure and role of public administration. A kind of revolution occurred and the foci shifted from control of bureaucracy and delivery of goods and services to efforts to privatize government and shape its role as an entrepreneur competing with other social groups and institutions to provide goods and services to the citizens. Osborne and Gaebler's book *Reinventing Government: How the Entrepreneurial Spirit is Transforming the Public Sector* was a landmark in the growth of ideas that have sought to build a new public administration. Public administration was admonished to 'steer rather than row' for 'those who steer the boat have far more power than those who row it.'[18] Since then, these ideas have swept across the world and international and multilateral agencies have used them to influence public management of their economic aid programmes. The common theme in the myriad applications of these ideas has been the use of market mechanisms and terminology, in which the relationship of public agencies and their customers is understood as based on self-interest, involving transactions similar to those occurring in the market place. Public managers are urged to steer not row their organizations and they are challenged to find new and innovative ways to achieve results or to privatize functions previously provided by government.[19] In this new world, the primary role of government is not merely to direct the actions of the public through regulation and decree, nor is it to merely establish a set of rules and incentives through which people will be guided in the proper direction.

[18] David Osborne and Ted Gaebler, 1992, *Reinventing Government: How the Entrepreneurial Spirit is Transforming the Public Sector,* USA: PLUME, p. 32.

[19] Robert B. Denhardt and Janet V. Denhardt, 2000, 'The New Public Service: Serving Rather Than Steering', *Public Administration Review,* vol. 60, no. 6, November/December, p. 550.

Rather, government becomes another player in the process of moving society in one direction or another. Where traditionally government has responded to needs by saying 'yes, we can provide service' or 'no, we cannot,' the new public service suggests that elected officials and public managers should respond to the requests of citizens by saying 'let us work together to figure out what we are going to do, and then make it happen.'[20]

Operationally, these ideas have advocated:

- managerially oriented administration;
- reducing public budgets;
- downsizing the government;
- selective privatization of public enterprises;
- contracting out of services;
- decentralization;
- transparency and accountability; and
- emphasis on civil society institutions and NGOs to deliver goods and services.

When India embarked upon an ambitious programme of economic reform in 1991, the ideas about public administration reform had already entered the package of aid that was promised by the World Bank and the IMF. It will be fair to say that they were reflecting a change in the disciplinary thrusts of public administration too. Country after country was deciding to change and reform their governments. There is little doubt that this change was being triggered by the wave of policies of structural adjustment and liberalization prompted by a new globalization that set in after the collapse of the Soviet Union. So, while administrative reforms are profoundly domestic issues, the fact that they are being seen as part of a package of the 'new deal' makes them open to external pressures and influences. Reform is stylish today, and for more than one reason. Technological changes are calling for managerial changes. The information technology with its computer base has caught the imagination of both administrators and politicians. Demands for greater decentralization are being met because of changes in the political scenario. People's groups are becoming more aware of their rights and demanding improved government services that are transparent and accountable to them. This is apart from the influence

[20] Denhardt and Denhardt, 'The New Public Service: Serving Rather Than Steering', p. 554.

that the international financial agencies are exercising on government to reform in order to be eligible for more loans and aid, and directly funding NGOs to implement development programmes.

Efforts at reducing the size of government began with successive budgets presented by the Union Finance Minister from 1992. The imperative need was to reduce the fiscal deficit and cut down on unproductive expenditure. In a bid to bring about fiscal prudence and austerity, the centre imposed a 10 per cent cut across the board in the number of sanctioned posts as on January 1 1992. The Fifth Pay Commission that submitted its report contained a recommendation for a whopping one-third cut in government size in 10 years. The downsizing exercise was later taken up by the Expenditure Commission, which further recommended a cut in the number of sanctioned posts as on January 1 2000. As a matter of fact, instructions for cutting sanctioned posts were renewed in 2000, directing a 10 per cent reduction in the posts created between 1992 and 1999.[21] Statistics maintained by the Ministry of Finance show that the pay and allowances bill of the central government was Rs 33,977.79 crore for the year 1999–2000, showing a hike of Rs 31,560.19 crore over the previous year. The number of central government civilian regular employees was 38.55 lakh on 1 March 2000, down from 39.07 lakh on 31 March 1999. There had been a decrease of 51,605 posts, which constituted a mere 1.32 per cent reduction.[22] As one can see, the impact of these efforts has been minimal.

In 1996, a Chief Secretaries Conference reiterated the popular policy prescriptions for a responsive and effective administration. The Conference recognized that the public image of the bureaucracy was one of inaccessibility, indifference, procedure orientation, poor quality and sluggishness, corruption proneness, and non-accountability for result.[23] The Fifth Pay Commission took on board the concerns of the Chief Secretaries and listed among many of its recommendations

[21] Jay Raina, 2002, 'Downsizing Maybe Uphill Task', *The Hindustan Times*, New Delhi, 8 February.

[22] D. Mishra, 2002, 'Quality Government for Sound Economy', *The Hindustan Times*, New Delhi, 8 February.

[23] Government of India, 1996, 'Action Plan for Effective and Responsive Administration', Statement Adopted at the Conference of Chief Ministers, New Delhi.

the need to downsize the government and to bring about greater transparency and openness.[24]

Two developments of significance took place. A Chief Minister's Conference endorsed the issue of transparency through the citizens' right to information in 1997. In addition, the concept of a Citizen's Charter took shape. Both were a follow-up to the recommendations of the Pay Commission, which in turn was in a way responding to grassroots' demands in the villages of Rajasthan.

A people's organization in Rajasthan, known as the Mazdoor Kisan Shakti Sangathan (MKSS) had been in the vanguard of this struggle and forced the government to respond to the demands of information and accountability. As documented in Roy et al.,[25] the people began to understand that their livelihood, wages, and employment depended a great deal on the investments made by the government as a development agency. If these benefits were not coming, then they had the right to know where the investment occurred and how much of it was actually spent. The right to economic wellbeing got translated into the right to information. As Roy et al., point out, the struggle became one for *hamara paisa, hamara hisab*.[26] In other words, accountability became a critical issue in the public hearings organized in the five blocks of four districts. Four demands were made: transparency in development spending, accountability, sanctity of social audit, and redressal. This campaign began in 1994 and gradually gained momentum spreading to most parts of the state. It reached to the level where assurances had to be provided by the Chief Minister.

The essence of the campaign that steamrollered into a movement for the right to information was the *jan sunwai* (public hearing) where villagers assembled to testify whether the public works that had been met out of the expenditures certified by the government actually existed or not. The first *jan sunwai* was held in a village of Kot Kirana in 1994. Since then, they have caught the imagination of the MKSS that has held them at several places. Beawar was the scene of a major event in April 1996. It was followed by a 40-day *dharna* in which activists were

[24] Government of India, 1997, *Report of the Working Group on Right to Information and Promotion of Open and Transparent Government*, New Delhi.

[25] Aruna Roy, Nikhil Dey, and Shanker Singh, 2001, 'Demanding Accountability', *Seminar*, vol. 500, April.

[26] Ibid., pp. 91–7.

fed and sheltered by the public. Another 53-day *dharna* was organized at Jaipur.[27] The Rajasthan government responded reluctantly, but the Chief Minister ultimately announced that the people had the right to demand and receive details of expenditure on development works in their villages.

Three months after the event in Beawar, politicians, jurists, former bureaucrats, academics, and others joined in demanding a right to information legislation at a conference in New Delhi. A committee under the chairmanship of Justice P.B. Sawant was authorized to draft a model bill. The central government too came under pressure to introduce legislation in the Parliament that could be followed by the states.

The Government of India set up a Working Group on the Right to Information and Promotion of Open and Transparent Government in 1997. The terms of reference of the Group included the examination of feasibility and need to introduce a full-fledged Right to Information Act so as to meet the needs of open and responsive government. The Working Group placed its tasks within the broad framework of democracy and accountability and emphasized, 'democracy means choice and a sound and informed choice is possible only on the basis of knowledge.'[28] It also argued that transparency and openness in functioning have a cleansing effect on the operations of public agencies and approvingly quoted the saying that 'sunlight is the best disinfectant'.

The Working Group accepted the following broad principles to the formulation of the legislation:

- Disclosure of information should be the rule and secrecy the exception;
- the exceptions should be clearly defined; and
- there should be an independent mechanism for adjudication of disputes between the citizens and public authorities.

Transparency in government also became an issue on the agenda of the Conference of Chief Ministers held on 24 May 1997. The Conference issued a statement that provided an Action Plan for Effective and Responsive Government at the Central and State levels. In this statement, the Chief Ministers recognized that secrecy and lack

[27] See Bunker Roy, 2001, *The Village Voice*, *The Asian Age*, 30 May.

[28] Government of India, 1997, *Report of the Working Group on Right to Information and Promotion of Open and Transparent Government*, New Delhi, p. 3.

of openness in transactions were largely responsible for corruption in official dealings. The government set for itself a time limit of three months to ensure easy access of the people to all information relating to government activities and decisions, except to the extent required to be excluded on specific grounds like national security. The statement also gave an assurance that the Report of the Working Group on Right to Information would be quickly examined and legislation introduced before the end of 1997. Political events have taken over and the Act has yet to come into existence.

It is clear from the above that this dimension of administrative reform that stresses transparency and right to information is an issue that has been spearheaded by the people. It is not a change attempted by a well meaning and benign government. However, the struggle has not yet been enough to get legislation passed by the Parliament or the state legislatures. There has been resistance not only from the political leaders who swear by the name of democracy but also from the bureaucrats whose norms of work had been dictated by secrecy and confidentiality. The Rajasthan experience has shown that even the local level administrators have found ways to thwart attempts at opening the administration closest to the people for scrutiny.

The reason of resistance is not far to seek. Much of the corruption that occurs in official dealings takes place under the cover of state sanctioned secrecy. The norm has been to keep information away from the people on the pretext of guarding public interest. A large number of national scams occur because no one knows what is happening in closets of government. At the local level, even the information on muster rolls is deemed to be confidential. So the movement for information has as its genesis in the fight against corruption and the demand for accountability. The muster rolls in Rajasthan's villages, in fact, carried false names and this could be identified only by the local people and not by the audit parties sent by the government. Who advises what will not be told. The recent incident, widely reported in the press, when the Urban Development Minister's order for placing a particular file on land deals for public scrutiny was reversed by the bureaucrats shows the fear of open decision-making.[29]

[29] See, *The Statesman*, 1998, 'Bureaucrats Misled Cabinet on CVC Draft, Charges Jethmalani', *The Statesman*, New Delhi, 13 September, p. 1.

Information, then, is also associated with the power that the government exercises. By restricting information, people in government become more powerful than those who are outside it. Thus, the demand for transparency and information is also about the sharing of power. It is possible to misuse power when it is concentrated rather than when it is shared among a broader stream of people. As information grows, the arbitrariness of government tends to reduce. But the resistance from the local level functionaries is growing in response to the *jan sunwais* held by MKSS is Rajasthan. For instance, a 2002 newspaper report mentioned how over 240 *sarpanchas* organized themselves and waited on the Chief Minister to resist further *sunwais*.[30]

It is this kind of resistance that has delayed the actual passage of the bill. It is necessary for the parliament to take early steps to pass the law on the right to information. Godbole rightfully fears that the longer the delay in the passage of the Bill, the weaker and more anemic it is likely to be.[31] Each successive draft bill on the subject prepared by the central government is a watered down version of the earlier bill and is a bundle of compromises affected to accommodate the stiff opposition to the proposed measures at the political and bureaucratic levels.[32]

The citizen's right to information has been coupled with the idea of a Citizen's Charter. The aim of the Charter is to make available to the citizen the information to demand accountability, transparency, quality, and choice of services by the government departments. It was first introduced in Britain in 1991 to streamline administration and make it citizen friendly. A core group was set up under the Chairmanship of the Secretary (Personnel) for monitoring the progress of initiatives taken by those Ministries and Departments that have a substantial public interface. So far, 61 Charters have been formulated which include 27

[30] Special Correspondent, 2002, 'Rajasthan Public Hearings Hit Sarpanchs Hard', *The Hindu*, 13 March.

[31] Madhav Godbole, 2000, 'Right to Information: Write the Law Right', *Economic and Political Weekly*, vol. 35, no. 17, April 22, p. 1423–8.

[32] The Right to Information was passed in 2005 and already its weak provisions were being highlighted. See *Indian Express*, 2005, 'RTI Being Subverted, One RTI Custodian Writes to PM', *Indian Express*, 9 December.

for public sector banks and four for hospitals.[33] For lack of effective monitoring, this has remained an exercise on paper.

* * *

Some lessons can be drawn from the experience of administrative reforms in India. Those who resisted change have derived great inspiration from the support that Sardar Patel, India's first Home Minister, gave in saving the ICS and the steel frame. At the time of India's partition, he warned that chaos would result if the civil service were removed from the scene. Nehru agreed and civil service reform was not a high priority at the time when riots and uprisings had to be handled to maintain the integrity of the country. Since then, one crisis or the other has taken precedence and administrative reform commanded little attention. When it did, it was an administrative matter to be handled by the administrators themselves. The committees and commissions that came to review administration had administrators themselves as members. The administrators, for purposes of feasibility of implementation, processed even the recommendations of the Administrative Reforms Commission, 1966–70, that had a wide range of consultations with people from various professions. One reason could be that the understanding of public administration was heavily influenced by a paradigm that was inward looking and perceived bureaucracy as a more-or-less autonomous instrument for implementing development policies and programmes.

Another could be that the political leadership saw advantage in maintaining the status quo while continuing to articulate the need for radical reforms for public rhetoric. Mrs Gandhi and her group quickly saw that the civil service could be 'committed' while continuing the public posture of neutrality. The Emergency period and the subsequent years of 'transfer industry' are ample evidence of keeping to form, rather than to substance. Even in questions of downsizing the government, a mantra from 1992, the same evidence is forthcoming. The A-level positions continue to remain largely untouched while all reforms—reduction of positions or contracting out principles—are

[33] Vivek K. Agnihotri, 2000, 'Government of India's Measures for Administrative Reforms', in Vinod Mehta (ed.), *Reforming Administration in India*, New Delhi: Indian Council of Social Science Research and Har Anand Publications, p. 126.

targeted at lower levels. The IAS or the IPS that have held critical positions in government have never been under scrutiny for reforms in spite of the public outcry against their role and behaviour. The only time that a serious attempt was made was when the Administrative Reforms Commission made the recommendation of delimiting areas of specialization in the secretariat and manning these areas from personnel drawn from all sources through a mid-career competitive process to include more specialists in the senior positions. This recommendation was scuttled and not accepted by the government when the IAS itself sought specialization through trainings and postings.

In the ultimate analysis, civil service reform in India has neither enhanced efficiency nor the accountability of the civil service in any meaningful manner. As far as the common citizen is concerned, it has not been effective. If Maheshwari commented that India's effort at reform has amounted to correction slips to the inherited system,[34] Das, himself an IAS officer, has gone a step further to indict the reform effort, around a quarter of a century later, by saying that they were not even correction slips—they were more in the nature of endorsement slips.[35] Probably, the present time of structural adjustment, liberalization, technological imperatives, and grassroots pressures may provide the best confluence of forces that could break bureaucratic resistance and generate the political will to make the administrative system more open to reform and change.

The impact of such a confluence of forces is not without risks, however. The global advocates of reform have assumed that one-size-fits-all and any government could be improved by the magic of market, privatization, participation, and efficiency. But the expectations of people of their governments are different in different societies and they are critical in redesigning reform activities. Reinventing government in the US is based on different assumptions and these may not even hold true for the UK. As Peters points out, 'the central problem for implementing public management reforms in developing countries is that their success to some extent depends on the existence of public

---

[34] Shriram Maheshwari, 1972, *The Administrative Reforms Commission*, Agra: Laxmi Narain Agarwal, p. 55.

[35] S.K. Das, 1998, *Civil Service Reform & Structural Adjustment*, New Delhi: Oxford University Press, p. 213.

service values and practices that support accountability and effective management.'[36] Deregulation and granting autonomy may mean that the empowered decision-makers may use the new found freedom to serve themselves rather than the public.

India faces the major challenge of redesigning an administrative system that can sustain itself in an environment of globalization and economic reform. The earlier efforts were partly failures because they assumed an image of the administrative system that was divorced from reality. It was rigid for most people, but very flexible for the privileged among them. Rules were flouted with impunity, privatization of public office was common, and procedures were discarded at many personal pretexts. The classic Riggsian formalism was at work. It is the common citizen that lost confidence in administration and this has to be restored first. This cannot come about only through tinkering with administrative design, but what is needed is a challenge to the basic issues of governance itself.

[36] B. Guy Peters, 2001, *The Future of Governing*, Lawrence: University Press of Kansas, p. 167.

Index

About the Author

Kuldeep Mathur is Retired Professor, Jawaharlal Nehru University (JNU), New Delhi. He has also taught at the Indian Institute of Public Administration (IIPA), New Delhi. He is former Director, National Institute of Education Planning and Administration (NIEPA), and former Rector of JNU. A recipient of awards for his academic contributions from University Grants Commission (UGC), Indian Council of Social Science Research (ICSSR), and IIPA, he has been a member of the United Nations Committee of Experts on Public Administration (UNCEPA). He has published widely on subjects such as public policy processes, bureaucracy, decentralization, and state–society relations. His recent publications include *From Government to Governance: A Brief Survey of the Indian Experience* (National Book Trust, India, 2008), and *Policy-Making in India: Who Speaks? Who Listens?* (co-authored with James Warner Björkman) (Har Anand Publications Pvt Ltd, 2009).